CONTENTS

South-East France

South-West France

LIST OF ILLUSTRATIONS

PUBLISHER'S PREFACE

A critic of Georges Pillement's previous travelogues has ventured to hint that any motorist who followed his itineraries in detail would have some difficulty in reaching his destination in time to enjoy his holiday at the other end.

Despite this, however, we have not hesitated to christen the present volume "The Roads to Spain". May be, if you have a day or two to spare, you will prefer anyway to travel by the quieter and safer roads, rather than entrust yourself to the murderous traffic of the Routes Nationales. On the other hand, even if you are in a hurry you will have to stop somewhere! If you are travelling along the N.9, why not relax for a few moments amongst the narrow streets of the sleeping city of Pézenas, the town of Molière, and see the architectural glories of a former age, or nearer the Spanish border turn aside the few hundred yards from the highway to see the 12th century frescoes of Saint-Martin-de-Fenouillar; or, alternatively, on the south-west side pause a moment as you speed along the N.10 to see the fortified churches of the Landes?

If you do so, you will quickly find that in this book you have a treasure house of information that will provide you with interest and relaxation for your holidays throughout the years.

You will perhaps, for instance, in due course be enticed into a study of the curious Romanesque art of Roussillon— that happy, fertile plain bordering the Mediterranean just north of the Pyrenees—which has undergone so many vicissitudes through the years. First Roman, then Visigothic, later belonging to Aragon and, for a time, Majorca,

Roussillon did not pass to the French Crown until the Treaty of the Pyrenees in 1659; this checkered history forms the background to several of the itineraries of this book.

In South-West France you are reminded of the pages of our English history as you travel through Acquitaine, Guienne and Gascony.

Once again it can be mentioned that all the showplaces described by the author are open to visitors, even if sometimes in return for a small entry fee: and there are frequently guides. Though it is as well to remember that the French lunch hour tends to last from 12 noon until 2.30 p.m. and that, during that time, most activities cease.

We have pleasure once more in paying tribute to our translator, Mr. Arnold Rosin, for his enthusiasm and his interest in these works. We must also thank the author and Messrs. Bernard Grasset for their continued help.

DONALD MCI. JOHNSON

JOHNSON PUBLICATIONS,
LONDON, S.W.7.

SOUTH-EAST FRANCE

〜

ITINERARIES I–VI

From AVIGNON to PERPIGNAN

From FOIX and from CARCASSONNE to
PERPIGNAN

Three routes from PERPIGNAN to THE SPANISH
BORDER

FRANCE—South East

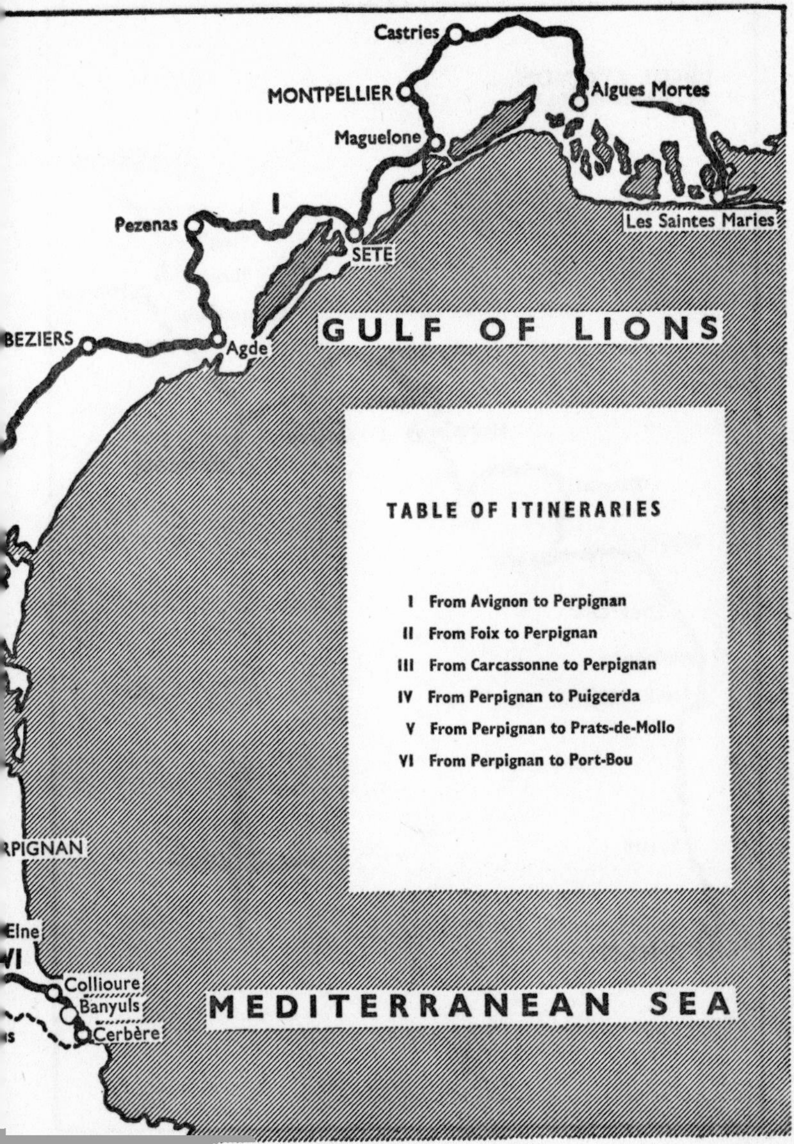

Castries

MONTPELLIER

Aigues Mortes

Maguelone

Les Saintes Maries

Pezenas

I

SETÉ

BEZIERS

Agde

GULF OF LIONS

TABLE OF ITINERARIES

RPIGNAN

Elne

VI

Collioure
Banyuls
Cerbère

MEDITERRANEAN SEA

FROM AVIGNON
TO PERPIGNAN

AVIGNON
Barbentane
Boulbon
Tarascon
St Gabriel
Montmajour
Arles
Castries
Montpellier
Maguelone
Aigues-
Mortes
Stes Maries
Pezenas
Sète
Béziers
Aqde
Ensérune
Narbonne
Fontfroide
Salses
PERPIGNAN

n

ITINERARY I

FROM AVIGNON TO PERPIGNAN

Barbentane — Boulbon — Tarascon — Saint Gabriel — Abbaye de Montmajour — Les Saintes-Maries — Aigues-Mortes — Castries — Montpellier — Château d'Eau — Château de la Piscine — Celleneuve — Château de la Mosson — Château de l'Engarran — Abbaye de Vignognoul — Maguelone — Vic-la-Gardiole — Sète — Loupian — Abbaye de Valmagne — Pézenas — Agde — Béziers — Ensérune — Narbonne — Fontfroide — Salces.

IN *Défence et Illustration d'Avignon* I have listed the beauties of this art city which were destroyed throughout the whole of the last century; and this is a destruction which unfortunately continues during the present one. If there are plans to demolish the Quartier de la Balance, to bring disgrace upon its ramparts, and to tear down a section of them for the opening of a new road, at least the military for the most part have left the old Convent of the Célestins, and the chevet of the church in the Rue Saint-Michel has fortunately been cleared. On the other hand, the buildings which overlook the Gothic cloister and which themselves date from the 15th century have not had the respect which they deserve. The kitchens for a military canteen have been installed in what is probably the old chapter-house with complete lack of conscience. Would it not be possible to have these kitchens somewhere other than in an ogival vaulted room which deserves better treatment?

But rather than lingering to deplore the misfortunes of Avignon, we will take the N. 570 which crosses the Durance over the Pont de Rognonas. We will leave it to take the D. 34 which leads to BARBENTANE. We will visit the church which is a mixture of Romanesque and Gothic architecture with, opposite, a delightful gallery construction and a 16th-century turret. The castle, which was built towards the middle of the 18th century by the Marquis de Barbentane who was the French Ambassador to Florence, is very plain and has little character. Of the ancient town walls which were constructed in the 14th century, two gates and some curtain wall sections remain. Overlooking the town is the beautiful Tour Anglica, which is the keep of the old episcopal castle. It was constructed in 1365 by Anglicus Grimoard, brother of Urban V, on a rock which is accessible from one side only. The architect took his inspiration from the Tower of Philip the Fair at Villeneuve-lès-Avignon. It was restored in the 17th century. In 1760 Cassini used it as an observatory.

The road approaches the Rhône, passes opposite Aramon where, if the bridge had been rebuilt, we could have visited a 17th-century castle built within the mediaeval fortifications, and a Provençal Romanesque church with a single nave, to which a side-aisle and lateral chapels were added in the 15th or 16th century.

We reach the entrance to BOULBON where in the cemetery we can see the Chapel of Saint-Marcellin which is Romanesque. (The key to this can be obtained from the presbytery in Boulbon.) It is a little edifice of charming proportions with two chapels having transversal vaulting which act as transepts. The one on the left contains a very fine 14th-century tomb with its recumbent effigy and mourning figures. The door is quite plain with its twin mouldings without any decoration. In the cemetery there can be seen a tomb which dates from the 14th or 15th century.

The inhabitants of Boulbon are very strange. They possess a beautiful 15th-century Gothic church with a square apse and a single nave whose vaulting rests on consoles, yet they have preferred to let it fall into ruin and to construct a modern church which is horrible.

The same is true of the magnificent castle built on a steep rock overlooking the town and which is separated from a nearby hill by a ravine of unusual beauty. They have used the ravine as a rubbish dump. As for the castle itself, it is practically inaccessible, so also are the superimposed terraces which were arranged in the 16th or 17th century and which are shaded by some wonderful pine trees. All this is extremely regrettable, for the Château de Boulbon, which was constructed about 1400 by the Count of Provence around a much older heavy square tower, is of much interest and deserves careful restoration.

This castle belonged to Geoffroy le Meingre, known as Boucicaut, son and brother of Marshals of France, who laid siege to Pope Benedict XIII at Avignon in 1398. Resorting to treachery, he seized two of the cardinals who were faithful to the Pope, Martin de Salva and Bonifaccio Degli Ammanati, and imprisoned them for five months in a dreary dungeon in the Château de Boulbon.

The D. 35 leads to TARASCON, which is described in Itinerary III of Volume One of *Unknown France*, and we take the D. 570 which joins the D. 33 at the beginning of which we find the beautiful Romanesque CHAPEL OF SAINT-GABRIEL, which dates from the first half of the 12th century. It is one of those edifices that best show how much the Romanesque school of Provence was influenced by Roman monuments which were then more numerous throughout the entire area than they are now, especially at Arles and Nîmes which are quite near.

The arrangement of the façade is purely Roman, with its large semicircular arcade containing the portal flanked by two columns with Corinthian capitals, surmounted by an entablature which supports a semicircular archivolt. Two columns, much larger, flank the two small ones and support a triangular pediment. All the decorative elements have been taken from Roman architecture; but the tympanum, which represents Daniel in the Lions' Den and Adam and Eve, a bas-relief in the pediment which shows us *The Annunciation* and *The Visitation* beneath three arcades, are

B

strictly in the Romanesque style and of an archaic quality which some scholars had originally wanted to date from the 11th century.

The key to the chapel may be obtained from a nearby farm. The nave with three bays terminates in a barrel-vaulted apse. It is a very plain little edifice but quite characteristic of Provençal architecture. In the 13th century it was surmounted by a square, uncrowned tower built in a fine, embossed masonry. Originally, without doubt, it was a watch-tower which subsequently was completed by a castle whose remains have survived.

We then reach Fontvieille where we can visit Alphonse Daudet's mill in which a small museum has been installed devoted to the author of *Les Lettres de Mon Moulin*.

Then, taking the D. 17, we proceed to the ABBAYE DE MONTMAJOUR which is built on a rocky height once surrounded by marshes which the monks drained. Traces of prehistoric, Celtic and Roman occupation have been found on this mound. In the 10th century the Cathedral chapter of Arles made it a Christian necropolis and it was guarded by a community of hermits. At the end of the 10th century, it became constituted into a chief abbey, observing the Benedictine rule. A "pardon", founded in 1030, was celebrated there on 3rd May, the day of the finding of the Holy Cross, and it attracted huge crowds. The multitude of pilgrims numbered as many as 150,000. Yet access to Montmajour was difficult, for the abbey was still surrounded by swamps which had to be crossed in boats. The abbey swarmed with numerous priories throughout Provence. Then came the decline; fallen *in commendum* in the 16th century, it was reformed by the Benedictines of Saint-Maur in the 17th century, and suppressed in 1786.

The constructions date from every period. Let us begin with the oldest. Alongside of the building in ruins, at the foot of the keep and the chevet of the church, we will find a Gothic door and, near it, a 14th-century bas-relief representing Saint Peter treated in a rather clumsy manner. We will descend a staircase hewn out of the steep sides of the rock and below we will find the Chapel of Saint-Pierre which is partly subterranean and which dates from the abbey's foundation. It consists of a rectangular barrel-vaulted vestibule with two rock tombs, a nave with crude vaulting terminating in a small apse and flanked, on the left, by a side-aisle hewn out of the rock. The side-aisle leads to a room with paving stone and is fronted by a small vaulted sanctuary known as "The Confessional of St. Trophime". A seat whose back seems to have been rebuilt in the 13th or 14th century is hewn out of the rock. The capitals are rather archaic, those with interlacing design could be Merovingian, while others in the Corinthian style seem to be of a later date, not earlier than 950. However, it is a very touching little edifice which should not be missed, the key being obtainable from the guardian. The exterior decoration of the window and the cornice dates from the 12th century.

Another chapel, the Chapelle Sainte-Croix, merely dates from the end of the 12th century. It is enclosed by tombs which have been hewn out of the rock and consists of a square bay with cloister vaulting and flanked by four apsidioles. It is fronted by a porch. It is a little building of rare elegance. The church, which is Romanesque, was built during the middle of the 12th century. It consists of a large, unfinished single nave which has only two semicircular bays on cross ribs, followed by a transept whose crossing was given ogival ribbed vaulting about the year 1200 and whose arms, less elevated, have transversal pointed vaulting. There opens out of each one an oven-shaped apsidiole flanking a large apse also oven-shaped, decorated with five flat plain mouldings and preceded by a short choir bay with pointed barrel-vaulting.

In the 14th century a chapel was added in the extension of the north transept arm for the Gothic tombs, now mutilated, of the Abbot Bertrand de Maisand, who died in 1310, and his brother. A sacristy and a room for the treasure and the archives were built on the north side of the nave in the 15th century.

A staircase descends to a gallery with barrel-vaulting and leads to the crypt, which is really a lower church built about

1150 to compensate for the declivity of the ground. It consists of a gallery which corresponds to the transept with two apsidioles and, beneath the apse, of a circular chapel with cupola-vaulting enclosed by an annular ambulatory with barrel-vaulting opening on to five radiating chapels, which obtain their light through the enormous foundations of the upper apse. We must admire the beauty of the stereotomy of constructions of such wonderful nobility.

The cloister, which dates from the close of the 12th century, is, after Saint-Trophime, the most beautiful Romanesque cloister in Provence. Each bay, which consists of three or four arcades supported by twin slender columns and held by a single relieving arch, is shouldered, as at Arles, by a fluted buttress. The galleries have semicircular vaulting, the cross ribs resting on consoles adorned with masks or fantastic figures. The capitals of the south gallery date from 1375, they resemble those of Aix and many are historiated. We can recognise *The Meal in the House of Simon*, *The Annunciation*, *Pentecost* and *The Coronation of the Virgin*. Those of the east gallery are Romanesque, while those of the north gallery were rebuilt in the 19th century. The west gallery was remodelled in 1717.

The east gallery leads to the chapter-house with its three barrel-vaulted bays on cross ribs. The dormitory above is in ruins; it was remodelled about 1300, as is witnessed by the Gothic windows which can still be seen. The refectory, whose four bays have barrel-vaulting on cross ribs, leads to the south gallery. The door is flanked by disfigured Romanesque statues representing Solomon and the Queen of Sheba, imitated from Provençal Roman statuary.

The keep, which rises isolated on the south apse, is a very beautiful rectangular tower measuring 90 feet in height with a projecting staircase on the west façade. It was erected by the Abbé Pons de l'Orme in 1369 with square dressed stones, the surface being left rough. It is crowned with machicolation and crenels with round watch-towers at each angle. The ground floor has barrel-vaulting, the next two have marquetry and the last has ogival vaulting.

The buildings, which were constructed in the 18th century by Pierre Mignard d'Avignon, are also worthy of interest. Let us appreciate the perfect construction, the dignity and nobility of the design, especially that of the large monumental staircase.

We return to the N. 570 which passes through Arles and plunges into the Camargue between the swamps of Palunlongue and those of la Grand Mar.

We may stop at the *Auberge du Pont de Gau* to see the birds of the marshland gathered in a sanctuary, and to have lunch in a very pleasant rustic setting. Four kilometres farther on we reach LES SAINTES-MARIES-DE-LA-MER, which is famous for the pilgrimage of the gipsies.

Here according to tradition arrived the three Marys— Mary of Bethany; Mary, the mother of the Apostles; and Mary Magdalene—accompanied by Sainte Marthe, who slew the monster of Tarascon; Sarah, their black servant; Lazarus risen from the dead; and Saint Maximus. They were fleeing the persecutions in Judea and disembarked on a little island which lay at this spot and which has since been connected to the mainland by the alluvial deposits of the Rhône. The island, which had already been occupied by the Romans, enjoyed great prosperity as early as the 13th century and the Counts of Provence granted important privileges to *il Santo*, later confirmed by the Kings of France.

In the reign of King René the remains of Mary of Bethany, of Mary, the mother of the Apostles, and of Sarah were discovered. The remains of Sarah are interned in the crypt of the church and those of the two other Saints in the upper chapel. Those of Sarah are an object of great veneration both to the French and many foreign gipsies whose patron saint she is; while the remains of the first two Marys are kept suspended from the tower in a chest which, on the annual pilgrimage on 24th and 25th May, is ceremonially borne forth into the waves amidst the admiring gipsies. Every three or four years a queen is elected. Another pilgrimage is made on 22nd and 23rd October in honour of the other two Saints. The festivities include horse races, bullfights, bull branding and farandoles.

Les Saintes-Maries must have presented a wonderful sight when the small town still preserved its fortifications which faced the sea and the swamps. They enclosed the fortified church which acted as a keep. The ramparts were destroyed at the Revolution, but happily the church still exists and it is probably the most beautiful fortified church in France.

It was built from 1140 to 1180 to replace an oratory which had been built by the Saintes Maries on the remains of a pagan temple. When the nave proved too small for the pilgrims who came here, attracted by the relics which had been discovered in 1448, it was enlarged at the end of the 15th century with two bays.

It consists of a vast single nave in the Provençal style, of great nobility, and terminates in an apse which is decorated with an ornamental arcade whose capitals are remarkable. They represent *The Annunciation, The Visitation, The Sacrifice of Abraham* and *The Apparition of the Angel to Joseph*. There is a well which provided water for the defenders of the church in a time of siege.

The rather plain crypt, which had been built beneath the choir by King René, contains the shrine with the bones of Sarah. There can be seen a *taurobolium*, a pagan altar of Mithras, and a fragment of a 3rd-century pagan sarcophagus embedded in the altar.

The apse is surmounted by a watch-tower dating from the beginning of the 13th century, flanked by a spiral staircase. In 1394 the tower was vaulted and raised. It supports a handsome 15th-century steeple-arcade and houses the Chapel of Saint-Martin in which the celebrated relics have been placed. It is adorned with 18th-century wood-panelling.

The entire church is surrounded by machicolation, which was added in the 14th and 15th centuries, held between narrow buttresses and surmounted by crenels. The handsome Romanesque façade should be fronted by a porch whose columns were supported by marble lions. But these have been placed in the side-walls of the bay added in the 15th century.

We should not miss visiting the *plage* of Les Saintes-Maries which has inspired many talented painters such as Yves

Brayer and François Salvat. We then return along the N. 570 as far as Maguelone-le-Sauvage where we take the D. 85. We cross the Petit Rhône by a ferry, the Bac du Sauvage, then ascend through the Petite-Camargue between the Petit Rhône and Etang des Fourneaux. The D. 58 which crosses a grandiose, but stark landscape between swamps, spans the canal of the Rhône and we join the N. 579 which we will follow to the left.

When St. Louis planned the Seventh Crusade he lacked a Mediterranean seaport, and that is why he bought from the Abbey of Psalmodi the land bordering the sea from where he embarked in 1248. Work was begun on the port, but it was not until the reign of Philip the Bold that the work was actively pursued.

To defend it, St. Louis had undertaken the construction of the Tour de Constance, but it was not until 1272 that work on the ramparts of AIGUES-MORTES (*aquae mortuae*, dead waters) was begun after a contract drawn up with the Genoese, Guillaume Boccanegra. But two years later he died and work was suspended; then in 1289 Philip the Fair engaged another Genoese, Nicholas Cominelli, to continue work on the ramparts and to put the port in order. The Tour Carbonière, which is but two kilometres from the town, also dates from this period and we will see it as we leave.

The walls of Aigues-Mortes, which are probably the most perfect and most homogenous military *ensemble* of the second half of the 13th century remaining to us, are for this reason absolutely unique in France.

The Tour de Constance built by St. Louis derives its name from another tower whose site it occupies and which itself owes its name to Constance, daughter of Louis VI and wife of Count Raymond V of Toulouse.

St. Louis considered that the tower was sufficient for the defenders of Aigues-Mortes. Later on, because it was 90 feet in height, it acted as a lighthouse and was surmounted by a turret where fires were lit. The crowning was rebuilt in the 16th century for artillery use.

It consists of a circular keep with a slight enlargement at

the base, with no other apertures except a rectangular window on the ground floor, another one, smaller, on the first floor and a few loopholes. Each floor has a vaulted room connected by a spiral staircase. Access is by a vaulted corridor which begins at two entrance doors which are separated by a portcullis and defended moreover by inner machicolation.

The room on the ground floor is a large rotunda vaulted by twelve ogival ribs, which are joined to a central crown and rest either on corbels or on slender columns surmounted by capitals. A circular excavation leads to a basement. Lighting is provided by four very narrow archery windows and heating by a huge canopy fireplace. At the top of the vault, a narrow gallery arranged in the wall thickness overlooks the room with eleven pointed bays, which made it possible to overcome any assailants who had forced their way into the tower.

The spiral staircase leads to a narrow corridor covered by heavy ogival ribs and defended by machicolation, and then to the room on the first floor and terminates on the other side in a kind of oratory with keystone and sculptured capitals. The room known as the "Knights' Room" is arranged similar to the one below. It was in this room that Marie Durand, who was imprisoned for 37 years and is venerated by the Protestants of southern France, engraved the word "Resist" on the edge of the central opening, for the Tour de Constance served mainly as a prison. Abraham Mazel, head of the Camisards (the Protestant insurgents of the Cévennes), succeeded in escaping with 16 of his companions.

The ramparts, which were constructed by Boccanegra with thick carefully-set embossed stones, are 21 feet in height and flanked by 20 towers with a heavy round tower at each angle. There remain two full towers, five rectangular ones which are pierced by small gates and six others which enclose the five principal gates. They are surmounted by crenellated platforms and by projecting or inner machicolation commanding the gates. The curtain walls are surmounted by rather spaced crenels whose merlons are split in the centre by a loophole. Rooms for archers are arranged in the interior, at the foot of the ramparts.

As Aigues-Mortes was built in the midst of swamps, the only road which leads to it, and which is the one we will take to leave, is closed two kilometres away by the Tour Carbonnière beneath which the causeway passes. It was defended by two portcullis, two fall traps and archery windows. In the 16th century it was flanked by watch-towers.

We then pass through Marsillargues whose Renaissance *château* was partially destroyed by fire in 1936 and at Lunel we rejoin the N. 113 which we will follow as far as Baillargues where we will take the D. 26 which leads us to Castries.

The CHATEAU DE CASTRIES, constructed from 1560 to 1570 by Jacques de la Croix de Castries, was partially destroyed by fire in 1662 by the Protestants of the Duke of Rohan and was restored in 1656 by René-Gaspard de la Croix de Castries, who built a monumental stone balustraded staircase and arranged a salon measuring 95 feet in length in which the Etats du Languedoc met. In 1666 Le Nôtre was summoned to design the gardens. He raised the wing, which had been burnt by the Calvinists, to the first storey and had it fronted by three terraces. To feed the fountains, the engineer Riquet constructed an aqueduct in 1670 which extended almost seven kilometres and which is carried over arches for a distance of 1,300 yards. It is still in use.

It was the Marquis de Castries, Intendant of the Bas-Languedoc, who supported Riquet's project for the famous Languedoc Canal.

At the Revolution the *château* was pillaged and sold as national property, but it was repurchased in 1828 by the Marquis de Castries who restored the central building in the taste of the time, razed the keep, but preserved the Renaissance wing.

The *cour d'honneur* is rather severe with, on one side, the Renaissance wing and, in the centre, the principal building decorated with balustrades and corner stones. In the interior there can be seen some fine furniture *ensembles* and decorative paintings. The terraces and gardens have been restored.

From the *château* there is a fine view towards the Pyrenees, and as far as the Cévennes and the Alps.

Taking the N. 113 we reach MONTPELLIER. From the point of view of tourism, this university city is scarcely visited which is quite regrettable.

The Wars of Religion in these parts were extremely violent and after the three revolts of 1615, of 1621, which was followed by a siege which lasted eight months and was led by Louis XIII, and of 1628, the town was utterly ruined.

Consequently, there remains nothing prior to the 17th century except the cathedral which we will shortly visit, a fine pointed portal at No. 10 Rue de l'Argenterie, a façade with Gothic bays at No. 3 Place Saint-Ravy, and a few Gothic rooms on the Plan Pastourel or Rue de l'Ancien-Courrier.

But in the reign of Louis XIII Montpellier became a city of parliamentarians who in the 17th and 18th centuries built an entire *ensemble* of *hôtels* which for the most part still exist and rival those of the same period in Paris, Versailles, Aix and Bordeaux.

The first of these *hôtels*, built by unknown architects, felt the double influence of Parisian and of Italian architects, perhaps because they were as close to their Genoese models as their Parisian ones, and also because these first structures were better suited to the climate of Languedoc than those of the Ile-de-France.

Moreover, for lack of architects, Italian stucco workers and artisans were certainly active at Montpellier at the same time as local painters, like Antoine Ranc and his pupil, Jean de Troy.

The Hôtel des Trésoriers de France, at No. 5 of the street of the same name, was constructed on the site of the Hôtel Jacques-Coeur and was almost entirely reconstructed by the Trésoriers de France. It lacks an exterior façade, but there is an impressive façade on the central courtyard consisting of two superimposed colonnades, like the Hôtel Lambert, but with twin columns. Behind it, the large staircase, which was built in 1675, has a ceiling decoration by Jean de Troy representing the Discovery of Truth by Justice. A second floor is adorned with suns and pilasters.

The Hôtel de Manse at No. 4, Rue Embouque-d'Or, also has, facing the courtyard, a façade of superimposed colonnades with Ionic capitals on the ground storey and Corinthian ones on the first storey which are separated by a flowery garland decoration and by balustrades. Above the cornice of the first storey with its consoles, there is an attic with five sculptured panels, whose subjects have been borrowed from Greek classical history, and coats-of-arms.

The Hôtel de Castries at No. 31, Rue Saint-Guilhem, built around 1650 by the Cardinal de Bonzi, President of the Etats du Languedoc, for his sister the Marquise de Castries, presents, facing the street, a façade decorated with pilasters of composite capitals, between which, on the storey above, are some elegant dormers. The courtyard offers four identical façades in the Louis XIII style whose doors and windows are framed by ornamentation. The interior decoration, which still partly exists, is quite wonderful and contrasts with the utter simplicity of the façades. Originally from Florence, the Bonzi no doubt summoned Italian decorators, especially for the grand salon which recalls the Salle des Géants in the Palais Doria at Genoa, with its walls covered with panels of gypsum adorned with medallions of Roman Emperors and surmounted by an important sculptured cornice with consoles. A monumental fireplace is adorned with garlands of fruit, rams' heads and a medallion of a Roman Emperor framed by trophies.

The Hôtel de Salas at No. 1, Rue Fournarie, is also in the Louis XIII style. It has a splendid portal with broken pediment in which a dormer has been set. The door consists of three folding sections, the compartments adorned with metal cabochons.

Other *hôtels* dating from this period are the Hôtel Lazare Rivière at No. 3, Rue du Cannau; the Hôtel de Ginestous at No. 15, Rue du Trésorier-de-la-Bourse; the Hôtel Grilhe at No. 1, Rue du Canneau; and the Hôtel de la Vieille-Intendance at No. 9, Rue de la Vieille-Intendance.

The Maison Antoine Armand, at No. 20, Rue de Candolle, characteristic of the beginning of the reign of Louis XIV, is of great simplicity. Two pilasters, which terminate in an animal figure and an acanthus leaf, support an entablature from which a sculptured head emerges at the centre of the lintel. A similar design is found in the house of the Counsellor Fizes at No. 6, Rue Puits-du-Temple.

A second group of *hôtels* built in the 18th century is no less remarkable. Its architects were d'Aviler, initiator of the Montpellier school of architecture, and the Girals, assisted by excellent carpenters and cabinet makers.

Although the Hôtel de Beaulac at No. 6, Rue du Cannau, is not by d'Aviler, nevertheless his influence can be felt. The inner courtyard is decorated with elliptical-arch porticoes and sculptured keystones, which are surmounted by four columns and two half-columns with composite capitals separated by balustrades. A large curved pediment, with coats-of-arms framed by foliage, rests on an entablature which is decorated with ovals and denticles. Here there is more freedom and wealth than in the preceding *hôtels*; the other façades are also decorated with garlands and draperies.

The Hôtel de Beaulac has preserved its handsome wrought-iron winding staircase and its interior decoration; in the Louis XIV salon the painting by Sébastien Bourdon and Nicholas Loir, who worked at Montpellier at the close of the 17th century, are framed by pilasters.

The *hôtel* of the adviser to the Cour des Comptes, Jean Deyde, at No. 8 of the street of the same name, is the work of d'Aviler. It consists of a main building flanked by two wings connected, on the street, by a balustraded terrace which frames an elegant porch, whose lintel is replaced by an acutely elliptical arch and whose crowning consists of a triangular pediment and, above it, a head of Hercules enclosed by draperies.

D'Aviler's influence is again found in the Hôtel Bonnier d'Alco at No. 3, Rue Fournarie. It has a graceful sculptured pediment with figures of Cupid playing around a vase encircled by garlands and draperies.

The Hôtel de Cambacérès-Murle at No. 3, Rue Saints-Croix, was built by Jean Giral to whom we owe the Château de la Mosson and the episcopal palace. Forsaking the orders given him, he was content to decorate the keystoned windows with masculine or feminine heads and elegant wrought-iron balconies.

The Hôtel du Trésorier-de-la-Bourse at No. 4 of the street of the same name is also the work of Jean Giral. It has a magnificent open balustraded staircase and figures of Cupid adorning the doors.

The Hôtel de Saint-Côme, founded by Doctor la Peyronie for the surgeons, was built by Jean-Antoine Giral, Jean's nephew, from 1752 to 1757. The amphitheatre is in the form of a rotunda, octagonal on the exterior and circular in the interior, each side of the octagon being pierced by a very high bay framed by four pilasters. The whole is surmounted by a lantern-turret and a balustraded cupola. The *hôtel* has a façade overlooking the Grand'Rue, whose ground storey with its lattice work consists of a slightly projecting central section framed by twin Doric columns. Above, three large curved bays with twin Ionic pilasters are fronted by handsome wrought-iron balconies. The staircase has a beautiful wrought-iron handrail.

This *ensemble* of wonderful classic architecture is completed by the remarkable design of the Promenade du Peyrou. In 1688 the city council decided to lay out an esplanade for an equestrian statue which had been commissioned to Mazeline and Hurtelle to glorify Louis XIV. Afterwards a decision was taken to replace the ancient drawbridge which leads to this esplanade by a monumental entrance bridge on which a triumphal arch was to be erected in honour of the sovereign.

Dorbay had supplied the design and d'Aviler, who had just arrived at Montpellier, was commissioned to do the work which he executed from 1691 to 1693. The Triumphal Arch, greatly inspired by the Porte Saint-Martin in Paris, consists of a large gate flanked by two smaller ones which are false. Constructed in ornamental fashion, it is decorated with medallions which we owe to Philippe Bertrand. It is surmounted by an entablature with triglyphs and metopes and by an attic bearing an inscription. The statue, overthrown in 1792, was replaced by the bronze one which we now see.

As the square seemed empty merely with the triumphal arch and the statue, the city decided to complete its decoration. Various projects were requested of the local architects and submitted to Soufflot. The one by Jean-Antoine Giral was selected and after certain modifications was executed in 1767.

Since there had been a decision to construct an aqueduct which would bring water from the Lez on to the Peyrou, the extremity of the terrace was raised and there a water tower was erected opposite the triumphal arch, the statue lying midway between the two. On the other hand, the width of the terrace was diminished. Accordingly two low connected terraces, behind the water tower, were overhung by a third terrace planted with trees and embellished with ornamental ponds.

The whole is pleasantly designed and the water tower itself is very elegant with its arcades framed by fluted, twin columns decorated with shells and nets filled with fish. It is one of the most graceful urban creations of the 18th century, one that can best serve as example for our modern town planners, so skilfully has the harmony between the different components been planned.

There remains to be seen the Cathedral of Montpellier, an ancient abbatial church of the Monastery of Saint Benoît whose creation was decided upon by Urban V in 1364. This Benedictine, who had been a professor at the University of Law at Montpellier, cherished the town where he had taught. Work was actively carried out and dedication took place three years later.

The Church of Urban V consists of a single nave bordered by side-chapels which open between the inner buttresses of each bay. The nave terminated at the chevet in a regular pentagon. Then, as now, the principal façade was fronted by a peristyle consisting of two round, massive pillars terminating in conical pepper-pot style and supporting a vault with heavy ogival ribs in four sections. A large Gothic portal, which was destroyed by the Protestants, represented the Virgin holding the Child and surrounded by the Twelve Apostles, while the bas-reliefs traced scenes in the life of Saint Benedict and his disciples, Maur and Placide. The portal is framed by two large square towers. It was a characteristic construction of southern Gothic and, thanks to Urban V, it received a magnificent decoration. The stalls were the work of his *fustier* and 56 panels painted by Giovanni de Viterbe relate the life of Saint Benedict. The vermeil altar-piece on the high altar is the work of the Pope's goldsmith, Barconcelli, and the enamel painting is by Jacques de Verceil. The other altars are decorated with silver statues.

In 1536 the episcopal seat was transferred from Maguelone, where the climate then was very insalubrious, to Montpellier, and the church of the Monastery of Saint-Benoît became a cathedral. Unfortunately the Protestant revolts were to prove disastrous to the art treasures of the new cathedral. In 1561 they succeeded in seizing the building, pillaged and destroyed everything, tearing down even the sculptures of the portal. A second revolt occurred in 1567. Barricaded in Saint-Pierre as in a fortress, the Catholics held out for 48 days and did not surrender until faced with famine. One of the towers collapsed; this time the destruction was complete.

Restoration work was not finished until 1634. Then in 1773 the choir being too small, it was replaced by two bays in the classic style designed by Audran. At the Revolution the wood-panellings, the stalls and the statues were again burnt and the monastery was transformed into a prison. In 1855 the Classic choir was demolished and replaced by a transept and a large neo-Gothic apse which are even worse!

It now remains for us to glance at the façade and the first bays of the nave. The ancient monastery buildings were transformed at different times. The façade, which is still crowned by machicolation, was modified by Jean Giral when the ancient buildings were occupied by the archbishopric.

All that remains of the old 14th-century cloister is a gallery which has been transformed into a chapel.

We should not miss seeing the Musée Fabre, one of the richest museums in France, before visiting the handsome *châteaux* in the environs of Montpellier; their beautiful classic architecture completes an *ensemble* with the urban *hôtels* which we have just seen.

We leave by the D. 127 in order to see first of all the CHATEAU D'EAU, commonly known as the Château d'O, on the road to Grabels, built by M. de Saint-Priest who was Intendant from 1750 to 1786. It is especially remarkable for its well-designed park adorned with statues from the Château de la Mosson which we will soon see. To feed the large artificial lake which is surmounted by a belvedere, Saint-Priest did not hesitate to divert some of the water from the Saint-Clement aqueduct which fed the town.

We will retrace our steps and take, on the right, the small road to Celleneuve which crosses the Montpellier aqueduct and passes in front of the Château d'Alco, which was built by Joseph Bonnier's eldest brother who completed the residence of la Mosson begun by their father, and which we will shortly visit. The *château* of Antoine-Samuel Bonnier, who died in 1737, had already been constructed in 1734.

We will make a left turning and follow a small road which emerges on the N. 100 almost facing the CHATEAU DE LA PISCINE, perhaps the most elegant of all the *châteaux* in the Montpellier district.

The façade, which rises at the end of the entrance courtyard, is fronted by a flight of steps flanked by two sculptured dogs. It is a small building with a single storey over the ground storey; the main building is surmounted by a triangular pediment with a large aperture between hunting trophies. The bays at each end are framed by corner stones. The façade facing the gardens is in the same style, but the pediment crowns three apertures on each storey instead of one.

The staircase, which begins at the vestibule, has a very pretty wrought-iron balustrade and the salons have preserved

PEZENAS, LA MAISON CONSULAIRE.

CHATEAU DE CASTRIES.

their plasterwork and panelling which date from the time of Louis XV or Louis XVI. The gardens are designed in their original French style.

The Château de la Piscine may possibly have been built by Jean Giral for Richer de Belleval, President at the Cour des Comptes.

We will follow the N. 109 as far as CELLENEUVE where we will stop for a few minutes to see the small Romanesque church with its single nave in semicircular vaulting and rounded apse which dates from the 12th century. It was fortified in the 14th century: and the walls were then raised and surmounted by machicolation.

On the left, we find the CHATEAU DE LA MOSSON, which has been left in a sad state of neglect, but which was the first and the most magnificent of all the *châteaux* of the wealthy families of Montpellier. It was built by Joseph Bonnier. His father came of a wealthy line of cloth merchants, and had tried his hand at finance by purchasing the office of Receiver and Payer of the Etats du Languedoc.

The Château de la Mosson, built from 1723 to 1729 by the architect Jean Giral, was decorated by the painter Jean Raoux and the sculptor Nicholas-Sébastian Adam: but Joseph Bonnier did not live to see its completion, for he died accidentally during a fête held there in 1726. His son, who inherited his office, completed the *château* where he also gave some magnificent fêtes. He died in 1744 and the *château*, sold ten years later, was dismantled and stripped of its wealth which became destined for the embellishment of new residences.

The *château* lies on the left bank of the Mosson. The first courtyard of outbuildings was bordered by two long parallel buildings connecting two pavilions with projecting angles with which they were harmonised by a curve. A stone bridge crossing a large moat and closed by a beautiful wrought-iron grille, which is now at the Château de l'Engaran, leads to the *cour d'honneur*. The *château* itself consisted of a main building which is still standing and two wings which have been demolished. The design of the main building depends upon

c

Tuscan columns which support Corinthian columns surmounted by a pediment, while, overlooking the gardens, we
have a rounded façade decorated with pilasters whose pediment has preserved sculptures of Nicholas-Sébastian Adam.

In the interior, which has been transformed into a wine-
making plant, there is the large reception room, two storeys
in height, with an upper gallery. The walls are still decorated
with Corinthian pilasters and the panels adorned with some
fine sculptured medallions; again we find the two subjects—
Aurora and Cephalus and Diana and Endymion—which
Adam used in his decoration of the oval *salon* of the Hôtel de
Soubise.

The gardens were magnificent. They were adorned with
statues which have disappeared, vases, benches and artificial
lakes. There remains, at the end of a vista, a large fountain
which is quite handsome in spite of the state of neglect in
which it has been left.

We will cross the Mosson and take, on the left, the D. 5E
which winds among vineyards and leads us to the last
château, that of L'ENGARRAN, built about 1758, in the
pure Louis XV style. The entrance façade is quite delightful
with its projecting main building, which is toned down in
quarter-round, as well as at the angles, with its decoration of
stone tying and its large central wrought-iron balcony,
supported by two telamones.

The façade which overlooks the gardens is straight but
equally gracious, and the French flower beds are embellished
with vases, statues and groups from the Château de la
Mosson, also with the grille which we have seen on entering.

We will go back as far as Juvignac where we will take the
D. 127E as far as Saint-Georges-d'O, then the D. 5E which
leads us to the ABBAYE DE VIGNOGNOUL, which in
the 12th century was a joint community of men and women,
a dependency of the Bishop of Maguelone. In 1178 Pope
Alexander III suppressed the community of men and
imposed on the women the Cistercian reform. The abbey,
which was attached to Valmagne, was very prosperous in
the 13th century.

The church consists of a single nave with three bays of the 13th century. Originally it probably had a timbered roof which in the 15th century was raised and had prismatic ogival ribbed vaulting resting on very short brackets. The choir, which was built about 1250, includes an ogival-vaulted straight bay and a sectioned apse whose vaults rest on eight ogival ribs and a lierne radiating around a keystone adorned with foliage. An elegant triforium extends from the straight bay. The choir is flanked on either side by a chapel with a bay which terminates in a circular apse in the interior, sectioned on the exterior, with ogival vaulting. The small gables pierced by their circular windows above each section of the apse produce a very picturesque effect. On the south, a side door, which led to the cloister that no longer exists, is decorated with a semicircular archivolt with a double moulding resting on twin columns on either side.

This pretty little edifice has nothing southern about it and belongs rather to the Gothic art of northern France. There is also the 16th-century rood-screen.

By way of Pignan, an old town which has preserved its picturesque mediaeval aspect, with its feudal towers, its ancient houses and its church which is partly Gothic, then Laverune whose episcopal *château* is enclosed by a park planted with exotic trees, and Saint-Jean-Vedas, we rejoin the N. 108 where, on the left, we will take the D. 185 and N. 586 which lead us to MAGUELONE, lying on the narrow stretch of land which separates the lagoons from the sea.

Instead of finding a unique little fortified town as we might have done, with, around a cathedral which itself was a fortress, the cloister, the episcopal buildings, the town dwellings and the wall fortifications, we see nothing except the imposing, stark mass of the cathedral, which itself has been despoiled of its defensive elements.

In 1663 Louis XIII ordered the dismantling of this place so that it would no longer serve as a stronghold for the Protestants. The buildings, then still standing, were in turn demolished in 1708 during the construction of the Canal from Sète to the Rhône.

The ancient cathedral, which is enclosed by clumps of pine and eucalyptus trees, now rises, solitary, facing the sea and the lagoons, sole evidence of the illustrious past of the famous city which was first destroyed in 737 by Charles Martel when he wished to deprive the Saracens of this vantage place.

The first known Bishop of Maguelone was Beotius who assisted at the Council of Toledo in 589. After its destruction by Charles Martel, the town was left in a state of abandonment until about 1030 when the Bishop Arnaud rebuilt the cathedral. The bishopric of Maguelone soon became prosperous and Bishop Gautier (1104–1129) undertook the construction of a larger cathedral. The choir, the apsidioles and the transept were raised by Gautier and his successor Raimond (1129–1158), while the nave was rebuilt afterwards by Jean de Montlaur (1158–1190). A tower, which belonged to the 11th-century cathedral, was preserved on the south side of the nave up against the transept.

An edifice of great unity, it is one of the most beautiful productions of southern Romanesque art. Narrow apertures which allow for a proper degree of lighting, and admirable equilibrium of masses and proportions, capitals decorated with acanthus leaves of great purity, characterise this grand edifice which must have been even more impressive when it still had its towers and its machicolation.

The single nave has only three semicircular bays but they are of impressive proportions. An aperture leads to the Chapel of Saint-Augustin, which is arranged in the ground floor of the ruined 11th-century tower. The bay of the transept has pointed barrel-vaulting and the arms are covered by ogival ribs. Some oven-shaped apsidioles have been designed in the thickness of the right wall. Also the apse, pierced by three circular bays, includes a decorative design consisting of blind arcades and ornamental mouldings. A storey forming a tower rises above the north transept.

We can see a marble sarcophagus of the 5th century, different pieces of sculpture fastened to the wall, and several tombs.

Like the Cathedral of Agde, the church near Vic, or the Palace of the Popes at Avignon, the church was surrounded by large pointed arches which supported machicolation and rested on buttresses. All that remain are the toothing-stones of these arches, except on the façade, where one of these has recently been restored above the portal. It consists of a lintel decorated with rosettes imitated from the antique and an inscription of 1178, together with a tympanum which presents a Seated Christ Blessing, on the right, and surrounded by the Tetramorphy, which cannot be earlier than the 13th century. On the jambs two set-back bas-reliefs, which represent Saint Peter and Saint Paul kneeling, seem to date from the middle of the 12th century, as also do the consoles decorated with two heads of the Apostles which support the lintel.

A building known as the Bishop's Palace, itself fortified by large arches carrying machicolation, was set against the north façade in the second half of the 13th century, and it acted as a tower. Its two storeys, which formerly had ogival vaulting, have collapsed.

We will return to Villeneuve where the church is partly pre-Romanesque and partly from the 13th century, and taking the D. 116 which passes through Mireval we will visit the little church, which also is fortified, of VIC-LA-GARDIOLE on the bank of its lagoon.

It is an edifice dating from the close of the 12th century, forming a long rectangle divided into four bays, of which only the first has preserved its semicircular vaulting on cross ribs. On the exterior the large arches with machicolation, most of which are reduced to ruins, rest on buttresses which have the aspect of pilasters with imposts. Around the church terrace there is a watch path bordered by a crenellated parapet which has been rebuilt. Small apertures, pierced somewhat at random between the buttresses, give the nave a niggardly amount of light.

Taking the D. 114E we rejoin the N. 108 which passes through Frontignan, renowned for its muscat wine, whose church is an interesting 14th-century edifice. A large nave

without side-aisles and with pointed vaulting is followed by
a polygonal apse flanked by two square apsidioles. A heavy,
square, fortified steeple completes the edifice.

We reach SETE where we can visit the old port, which is
quite picturesque, and climb Mont Saint-Clair from which
there is a splendid panoramic view. We can see in passing the
Church of Saint-Louis, which was built in 1712 from
d'Aviler's design, and the marine cemetery that was dear to
Paul Valéry.

We will come back as far as la Peyrade and, thanks to the
D. 2, we can rejoin the N. 113 which we will leave about
eight kilometres away in order to visit two interesting
churches at LOUPIAN.

Saint-Hippolyte is a charming little Romanesque church
dating from the middle of the 12th century, with a single
nave of three bays terminating in a five sectional apse. The
walls are reinforced by three semicircular blind arcades. The
sections of the chevet are pierced by semicircular bays and at
each angle a slender column is lodged to receive the ribs of
the vault. They are very awkwardly erected, but they have a
very charming effect on the oven-shaped vaulting whose
stones are imbricated with fish bone decoration. The capitals
are quite archaic and the west portal is curious with its
slightly projecting moulded archivolt and its arch stones
divided into scrolls.

The church was fortified in the 14th century, and the
arcade and apse are flanked by corbelled watch-towers
which add to its picturesqueness.

Sainte-Cécile is a pretty 14th-century Gothic church, with
its single nave, oblong bays and very projecting buttresses
which form flying buttresses. The four bays of the nave are
extended by a choir bay which is narrower and by a polygonal apse. The two portals are adorned with moulded cusps.

Slightly further on we will take the D. 161 and the D. 5E
which lead us to the ABBAYE DE VALMAGNE which
was founded in 1138 and affiliated with Cîteaux in 1145.

The present church, which replaced an early Romanesque
edifice, was undertaken in 1252. The nave and transept date

from the second half of the 13th century, but the high vaulting was not finished until the 14th century. The choir, the ambulatory and the fore-nave also date from this period. It is less a sober, austere Cistercian church than a cathedral of northern France, elegant and refined with its façade flanked by two steeples.

A nave with side-aisles of seven bays, fronted by a porch and flanked by chapels along the north aisle, is followed by a transept and a choir which terminates in an apse and is enclosed by an ambulatory whose seven-sectioned chapels are preceded by two square ones which open on to the transept crossing. It is a construction of great lightness.

The conventual buildings are also worthy of interest. The 14th-century cloister still partially exists. Each arcade includes a tympanum which is pierced by a large oculus and supported by four small semicircular arcades which rest either on a small rectangular pillar or twin columns. The lavabo is an 18th-century design of the early building. The monks' building, which dates from the early 13th century, also underwent later transformations. The armarium and the sacristy have semicircular vaulting, while the chapter-house has ogival vaulting which dates from the 16th century. A door, which is framed by two semicircular bays whose arches are supported by three small columns, leads to the cloister.

After the reception room with its barrel-vaulting, the other rooms have been transformed in the 17th century, as also was the refectory in the 15th century with its three ogival-ribbed vaults. Of the building of the lay brothers all that exists is the refectory, also Gothic.

We will follow the very picturesque road overlooked by the Dentelles de Valmagne, thin chalky jagged strips of mountain, to Montagnac, where we find the N. 113 which leads us to Pézenas.

A Molière or a La Fontaine merely had to use a mocking phrase for a small provincial town for it to become synonymous with ridicule. This is what happened to Landerneau, to Quimper-Corentin and to Pézenas.

There was once a time when, if PEZENAS were mentioned, people would smile, thinking of a wicked town where Molière, while being shaved by the barber Gély, noted ridiculous episodes which he could use in his plays. But there are Marquises d'Escarbagnac everywhere and Pézenas should not be ashamed, but should feel honoured for having furnished the author of *Les Précieuses Ridicules* with some amusing characters.

A.-P. Allies (1868–1935), a local scholar, realised this and made his fellow citizens again feel proud of their little town. In his book *Pézenas, Ville d'Etats*, he related its history and its beauties, created the *Société des Amis de Pézenas*, organised fêtes and exhibitions. In 1922 he arranged for the Comédie-Française to come to Pézenas to celebrate the 300th anniversary of Molière's death. It was done with such brilliance that, in the place of the ridiculous picture people had of the town, he substituted that of the charming reality which we are about to discover.

Pézenas is one of those small French towns which have preserved their ancient character. It was fortunate so far as we are concerned (though for its inhabitants this was not so fortunate) that it remained at some distance from the railway lines, and that its business which was formerly quite active soon became depressed. One by one, it lost its factories which produced linen, hats, nitre, verdigris, sulphur and leather goods. All that remained was a small commerce in wines and spirits and a distillery, a modest survival of that great market which was formerly held in the Place des Trois-Six and which set the price of spirits throughout Europe.

Since Pézenas is entirely surrounded by vineyards, it is natural that, at least, this activity should continue. During the vine harvest its picturesqueness increases, with its barrels and red half-barrels of tannin which are piled beneath the Gothic porches or in the Renaissance courtyards, the pungent smell of which must instantly seize you. The rustic character of the ancient capital of Languedoc has been intensified and the fine opulent *hôtels*, with their sumptuous staircases, with their double flights and stone balustrades, appear to us still more poignant in their decay.

The origin of Pézenas is very ancient and dates from the time of Roman colonisation. Caesar sent his sick to *Piscenae* (Pézenas) to recover when he had his camp at *Cessero* (Saint-Thibéry), seven kilometres away. Pliny the Younger praised the waters of the Peyne for the glossing of cloth which was even then a commercial activity at Pézenas.

During the feudal period, Pézenas belonged to the Counts of Toulouse, then to their vassals, the Viscounts of Béziers and of Agde.

In 1261 St. Louis repurchased the Château de Pézenas and made it once again part of the royal domain. In 1362 Jean II raised it to a county in favour of the Count of Artois. When the latter revolted, the county was confiscated in 1368 and once again annexed to the Crown.

During the Middle Ages, when important commercial activity flourished at Pézenas, Jacques Coeur established a bank there about 1432; his house still exists in damaged state.

In 1562, not far from the town fortifications, the Duke of Joyeuse defeated the Baron Jacques de Crussol, seigneur of Beaudine, who commanded a Protestant Army which had seized Pézenas and which, in spite of its defeat, held out in the castle until 1574. Two years later the Huguenots burned down the Convent of the Observance on the right bank of the Peyne.

In 1456 the Etats Généraux du Languedoc held their first assembly at Pézenas. They returned several times afterwards, in fact 44 times during the 16th and 17th centuries, which justified the name of *Ville d'Etats* (Town of the States) given to Pézenas. Moreover, its importance grew for other reasons and its wealthy bourgeoisie and fastidious nobility built beautiful dwellings. In 1597 Henri IV instituted a College which was given first to the Jesuits, and later on to the Fathers of the Oratoire. Some of its professors are famous: Massillon, Barême, Mascaron, Thomassin, Plantade, and others.

The Governors of Languedoc established their residence at Pézenas, first the Constable Henri de Montmorency, who inhabited the old feudal castle built on a summit around which the town was built, and then his son, who was to be beheaded at Toulouse, and finally Armand de Bourbon, Prince de Conti, at the Château de la Grange-des-Prés, outside the city.

The Fairs and the assemblies of the Etats du Languedoc brought a joyful animation to Pézenas. They were accompanied by fêtes which gave rise to processions and spectacles. Molière wrote *Les Précieuses Ridicules* at Pézenas and it was there also that his first plays were given during the sessions of the Etats du Languedoc.

But even when in the 18th century Pézenas ceased to be the place of assembly for the Etats du Languedoc, and the Château de la Grange the seat of the Court of the Conti, the town remained animated and active. It was not until the 19th century that it began to slumber. Its aristocratic dwellings fell into the hands of commoners, its art treasures were pillaged by antique dealers and junk merchants who, not satisfied with carrying off curios and paintings, removed the wrought-iron balconies and the sculptured stones of the façades. It fell into an ignoble decay.

Tourists ignore Pézenas which lacks a first-class monument to draw them there—its castle was razed in 1633 on Richelieu's orders after the revolt of the Duke of Montmorency and its Church of the Templars collapsed in 1733—but, on the other hand, it possesses an *ensemble* of mediaeval houses and *hôtels* dating from the Renaissance and the 17th century which makes it one of the best preserved architectural gems in France. It has a charm all its own with its ancient ghetto, its huddle of narrow streets, many of which still preserve their doors with sculptured pediments and, owing to not having been rejuvenated in the 17th and 18th centuries, their mullioned windows and pretty wrought-iron balconies. At one place an arch spans the street, at another there is an angle turret, then a richly-decorated niche, farther on a courtyard with a magnificent balustrated staircase. The streets have an unusual diversity and an unceasing picturesqueness.

Let us, therefore, discover, one after another, the hidden beauties of Pézenas by making a methodical visit, starting from the Promenade du Pré, which is planted with three rows of plane trees and adorned with stone benches dating from the time of Louis XV. It was presented to the town by the Commanders of Saint John of Jerusalem in 1538. It was formerly the promenade of the elegant women of the town and it was here that the consuls received the royal highnesses when they came to Pézenas. For its former visitors include Louis VIII, Louis IX, Francis I accompanied by Queen Eléonore of Austria in 1533, Charles IX, Louis XIII in 1622 and 1632, and Louis XIV in 1660.

Let us enter the huddle of the narrow streets by taking the Rue des Chevaliers-de-Saint-Jean. Immediately, on the right, at No. 6, Rue Francois-Oustrin, we find the Hôtel du Baron de la Coste with its synthesis of those features which characterise the *Ville d'Etats*. This 15th-century house is remarkable for its elegant staircase with Gothic ribbed-vaulting which was remodelled in the 17th century and adorned with stone balustrades, and its Renaissance windows. On the first floor there is a fine beamed ceiling. It was in this *hôtel* that Armand de Bourbon-Conti received Louis XIV.

This street leads us to the ancient Place de l'Hôtel-de-Ville, the most ancient part of the town with, at the far end, the belfry dating from 1693, which flanks the old Maison Consulaire, now the Tribunal de Commerce, built in 1552, whose façade was rebuilt in the 18th century, with its large triangular pediment decorated with a coat-of-arms of Louis XV framed by flags and military accoutrements. This pediment is supported by four Doric pilasters and is broken by a large wrought-iron balcony which rests on four consoles and supports the entire façade. In the interior there can be seen a fine stone staircase which leads to an elegant 16th-century door, which gives access to a chapel dedicated to Saint Roch. A lateral façade has preserved a beautiful

Renaissance mullioned window. The celebrated session of the Etats du Languedoc, in which the revolt of Henri II de Montmorency was decided on, took place in this edifice.

Opposite, we find at No. 1 the shop of the barber Gély; on the right, at No. 3, Rue Alliés, the Hôtel Saint-Germain with its beautiful Renaissance façade, which on the second storey has preserved its mullioned windows, but whose portal and noble storey were remodelled during the time of Louis XV, the windows having then been enlarged and adorned with wrought-iron balconies. This *hôtel* was transformed into a museum and restored with rather excessive zeal.

On the left, the Hôtel de Flottes de Sébassan, which has retained in the interior the remains of its 15th-century ogival construction, has on the exterior an elegant Louis XV façade with a splendid central balcony and at the angle a delicately sculptured niche dating from 1511, which is one of the most precious decorations in Pézenas.

Near by, after we have passed beneath the porch of the Impasse Simon-Ducrois, we see the Louis XIII door and the picturesque courtyard of the Hôtel de Plantavit, where Mazarin stayed, then, taking the Rue Canabasserie, which was that of the weavers, canvas and hemp merchants, but which after undergoing several demolitions lost much of its character, we see, at No. 1, the Hôtel de Juvenel de Carlencas, whose courtyard has retained some 15th-century arches; while, opposite, the Maison du Châtelain de Boudoul has a Louis XIII door and mullioned windows. The Rue Montmorency, where there can be seen, in a Henri II niche, a 15th-century *Pietà* in varnished terracotta, leads to the old castle, of which, once we enter the gate, we find no trace, for it is now a garden, from which there is a pretty view over the town and its surroundings.

If we descend by taking the Rue du Château, we find at No. 9 the Gothic tower of the Hôtel de Graves and here and there a few ancient vestiges, such as doors, door knockers, coats-of-arms; then at No. 8, Rue Alfred-Sabatier, the Maison des Pauvres (Poorhouse) with its vestibule and double-landing staircase with wrought-iron railings and its coat-of-arms on a double monumental arch, which dates from the 17th century and recalls the engravings of Piranesi.

The Rue de la Triperie-Vieille has retained its picturesque aspect with its 15th-century meat stalls and the high vaulted passage which spans it. At No. 11 there are a Gothic vestibule and a 15th-century spiral staircase which was altered to the taste of the time in the 17th century by the addition of a twin, stone balustraded stair-head.

We next take the Rue de la Foire, which has retained the pretty Renaissance windows of the Hôtel de Wicque. A monumental fireplace and some beautiful stained-glass windows of the same period were transported to the Château de Saint-Pierre. In the courtyard there can be seen four façades with 15th-century windows and Renaissance medallions with, at the far end, a gallery which is also from the 15th century with a beautiful sculptured keystone.

The Hôtel de Nisas at No. 16 has a Renaissance façade with a Louis XIII door and its courtyard is dominated by a beautiful Gothic tower with machicolation which contains a spiral staircase. A stone staircase with a flight of stairs to the right leads to an outer gallery, then to a loggia. Every one of the houses in this street has retained some typical detail; at No. 17, an ogival door; at No. 22, above the door, a pretty 18th-century bas-relief which represents child musicians; No. 26 was the home of Venel, 18th-century doctor and chemist, who invented Seltzer water.

The Rue de la Conciergerie, which is now called the Rue Emile-Zola—the Municipality would do well to rename the streets of the old town as they were before—retains, at No. 7, the Maison de Jacques Coeur who, as we have said, had a bank at Pézenas. Its beautiful 14th-century façade has been stupidly mutilated. However, there are still some brackets which are nicely sculptured; some represent a dog gnawing a bone, others a musician, a captive in chains, and farther on a miller on his ass with a sack of wheat over his shoulder, a *Christ*, a greyhound. Opposite, at No. 10, in the courtyard, there is an old watch-tower and a Henri II door with fluted moulding.

We reach now one of the most picturesque corners of old Pézenas: this is the vault which leads to the ghetto and, at the side, the beautiful gate placed slantwise known as the Old Consular Prison, whose lintel is adorned with rosettes and bucranes. The streets of the ghetto do not seem to have stirred since the 14th century. Not a single shop: a sad and fatalistic silence reigns. . . .

We go through the Porte Faugère, rebuilt in 1597 and one of the ten fortified gates of the old ramparts of Pézenas, which were partly demolished in 1627 by the Duke of Montmorency, who erected on this site a large promenade known as the Quai, which in 1883 was named the Cours Molière and has since become the Cours Jean Jaurès.

It is bordered by fine *hôtels* in which we admire not only the noble façades but, above all, in their courtyards the extraordinary staircases of the time of Henri IV with double flights of balustraded steps and porticos. The most magnificent is, at No. 20, that of Grasset or le Grand Cercle. We should see also that of No. 18, the Hôtel de Landes de Saint-Palais, and, at No. 37, that of the Hôtel de Latude. The Hôtel de Bezons has a charming 16th-century door with pediment and fluted columns.

The new town, which was created at the close of the 16th century by the Constable de Montmorency, extends from the other side of the Cours Molière. The Rue des Capucines (or Rue Henri-Reboul) has in the centre a pretty door with rounded pediment from the ancient church of the Black Penitents of 1590 where the Etats du Languedoc often met. After the Revolution it was transformed into an entertainment hall and has finally become the Municipal Theatre of Pézenas.

Slightly farther on, we find the old Chapel of the Ursulines of the 17th century, which retains in the centre of a large wood-gilt altar-piece *The Black Virgin and Child*, a 12th-century statue in cedar which was brought back from the Crusades by a Commander of Saint John of Jerusalem and which became the object of veneration by the people of Pézenas.

At No. 13, the Hôtel du Connétable de Montmorency, which is terribly mutilated, recalls the stay made by Louis XIV and Mazarin in 1660: a large stone arch in the courtyard, some Renaissance windows and a guardroom with its large canopied fireplace are mute witness to the event.

Farther on, a Louis XIII door, which is surmounted by a *Virgin and Child* of the 18th century, leads to the Hôtel de Paulhan de Guers, later the Convent of the Ursulines and transformed into a hospital. Its former guests include such famous persons as Louis XIII in 1622 and 1660 and Queen Marie-Therèse, while her husband lived next door. The pharmacy is decorated with jars and old pots from the Saint-Jacques Hospital; a magnificent Renaissance chest can also be seen.

Retracing our steps as far as the Place Ledru-Rollin, we find the Louis XIII door adorned with the heads of angels from the Théâtre des Variétés and a large stone *hôtel*, which is interesting for its iron work, its large staircase with landings and 18th-century wrought-iron banisters.

Taking the Rue Marceau we reach the College of the Oratoire which dates from the early 17th century. The Hôtel de Ville is in the right wing. There are first of all two splendid chests which belonged to the Fathers of the Oratoire, the one from the time of Henri II, and the other from that of Louis XIII, representing episodes in the life of Alexander and Julius Caesar. The Chapel of the Oratoire, with its tri-angular pediment which is supported by four tall Ionic pilasters, contains different sepulchres and a 17th-century altar-piece with twisted columns. The old College was demolished in 1886 and rebuilt in a less elegant style, without any real necessity other than that of destroying a rather attractive *ensemble*.

We reach the old Rue de Béziers, which has become the Rue Anatole France, where at No. 18 there is a stone *hôtel* with wrought-iron balconies and curious masks; at No. 24 the sombre façade of the Convent of the Dames de Sainte-Ursule, which was founded in 1618 but replaced shortly afterwards by the Blue Penitents; and here and there some beautiful 16th-century doors.

The Rue Danfert-Rochereau where formerly stood the Hospital and Church of Saint-Jacques, leads us to the Rue de la Fronde where at No. 9 there is a Louis XIII door, and then the circular windows of the Monastery of the Dames Hospitalières, then to the Hôtel Malibran, which I think is one of the most remarkable buildings in Pézenas.

Here again we have a building which was remodelled in the 18th century. The door is Louis XIII, the windows on the first and second storey are fronted by magnificent wrought-iron balconies and surmounted by some finely sculptured heads, and the third storey consists of a row of circular windows. The staircase with its columns and balustrades is one of the most elegant staircases in the Henri IV style in all Pézenas.

Taking the Rue de la Ferronnerie, which is at the corner of the Hôtel Malibran, we reach the Rue Victor-Hugo. First of all there is a beautiful stone door; then, at No. 13, the Hôtel de Grasset which has retained its noble staircase and its garden; and at No. 9, a charming 18th-century façade with its sculptured heads and wrought-iron balconies.

After admiring the Fountain of Vedel, which dates from the 18th century, we take a small street leading to the Place des Sauvages, now the Place du Quatre-Septembre, which is bordered by fine stone buildings with ornamental doors and sculptured window keystones which retain their 15th-century spiral staircases. The theatre where Molière played formerly existed in a nearby street the Rue du Jeu-de-Paume.

Taking the Rue Baraterie we reach a horrible iron market, an imitation of those in Paris, which replaces the ancient Place Couvert which was erected in 1617 on the site of ancient ramparts. The demolition of the old covered place has been on a par with the transformation of its surroundings, where the fine shops were the meeting places of Pézenas. A short distance away, in the Cours Jean-Jaurès whose beautiful harmony we have admired, the Caisse d'Epargne (Postal Savings Bank), making a mockery of the old *hôtel*

CLOITRE DE L'ABBAYE DE
FONTFROIDE.

6. CHATEAU DE SALC

where it ought to have been installed, had this demolished in order to construct a building whose ugliness is quite unimaginable.

The Rue Kléber leads us to the Collegiate Church of Saint-Jean. In passing, there can be seen in the narrow and picturesque little Ruelle de la Fromagerie-Vieille, a watch-tower and a door dating from the time of Louis XIII with a lozenge work of great originality in its robust simplicity, and quite near by, transformed into a shop, is the Hôtel du Chatelain de Grasset with its sculptured frieze, its windows with *cabochons*, balconies and wrought-iron impost. Opposite, the Hôtel of the Commanders of Saint John of Jerusalem, which dates from the 16th century but which replaces an old House of the Templars of the 13th century, is one of the most original buildings in Pézenas. It has a high façade rounded off at the angles and a beautiful ornamental door with a broken pediment.

The Collegiate Church, opposite, has replaced the ancient Church of the Templars which collapsed, as we have said, in 1733, crushed by the fall of its steeple. It is built in a rather heavy but sombre Tuscan style and has three vaulted naves. The choir is decorated with carved wood-panellings dating from the time of Louis XVI and several chapels are adorned with statues, the most interesting being *The Virgin and Child* in white marble by Coustou, which is in the Chapel of the Virgin. But already, when this church was built, the splendour of Pézenas had passed away and we no longer find the wealth worthy of the noble dwellings we have just visited.

As a consolation, we enter, immediately on the right as we leave, the courtyard of the Sacristy of the White Penitents, one of those charming corners of Pézenas which has retained all its flavour. Here the 17th century has left no mark: the door and the gallery are Gothic and finely sculptured, a small twisted column and some windows are Renaissance.

The Rue des Commandeurs leads us to the Place des Trois-Six, where the market for spirits took place every Saturday. Its animation is now gone, so also for several years has the *Hôtel de la Paix*, which was one of the oldest hostelries

D

in southern France. Pope Pius VII gave his benediction to its reconstruction in 1814 when, returning from Paris, he alighted at the *Hôtel du Tapis Vert*, almost facing it, whose façade is decorated with malicious looking sculptured heads.

The Rue des Selliers, now the Rue Jean-Jacques Rousseau, has retained, at No. 20, the Hôtel de Marimond with its coats-of-arms still visible on the wrought-iron balcony; at No. 18, the old Hôtellerie des Singes, which was rebuilt in the 18th century but which has retained its mediaeval façade with its remarkable sculptured motifs. Slightly farther on, on the left there is a painted *Virgin* which still adorns the angle.

We reach two of the most impressive dwellings in Pézenas. First of all, at No. 34, the Hôtel de Conti, adorned by a frieze with modillions and wrought-iron balconies with a monumental corkscrew staircase of monolithic stone, while the apartments are decorated with 18th-century plasterwork. Then the Hôtel d'Alfonce, at No. 36, which is the most original construction in Pézenas. The first vault leads us to a courtyard remarkable for the twisted columns of its terrace. A second vault leads to the old gardens which are overlooked by a marvellous Renaissance façade with a portico supporting two storeys of loggias in the Italian style adorned with balustrades. Unfortunately, the twisted columns of the terrace disappear behind a glass partition; the loggia cannot be seen because the present owner thought it a good idea to build some shops and hangars on the site of the old gardens. However, the Hôtel d'Alfonce is precious not only for its architecture, but also for the memories which are associated with it. Here, on November 8, 1654, the Prince de Conti received homage from the deputies of the Etats du Languedoc and that same evening Molière played in one of his comedies. The Fine Arts Administration ought to have classified this dwelling which is so elegant and so rich in memories; there still can be seen a curious 15th-century service staircase with a grooved shaft.

After the princely *hôtels*, we come to the less noble hostelries of travellers, pilgrims and boatmen; at No. 38, is the old

Hôtellerie du Griffon d'Or, which dates from the 17th century and has retained its fine wrought-iron balconies and its picturesque courtyard with galleries and arches; at No. 42, is the Hôtellerie du Bât d'Argent, whose courtyard is no less inspiring with its circular gallery and in the centre its well with its curb. The downstairs room of the inn has retained its large Henri II fireplace and we can imagine Molière chatting with Dassoucy while he poked the fire, for they both stayed here.

There are some remains of fortifications on the outskirts of this quarter and if we head for la Grange-des-Prés, we can see, on the left, along with some houses which have been built on to the old fortifications, a large machicolated tower which dates from the 15th century and which is known as the keep.

After crossing the Peyne over the old Pont de l'Observance which was rebuilt in 1836, we find ourselves in the Faubourg des Cordeliers with, on the left, the old Convent de l'Observance which has been disfigured in the most odious fashion.

The church, which is in the ogival style, with its sculptured keystones, was transformed into wine shops and is in a pitiful state, so also is the charming cloister which houses several families who have partitioned it as they pleased. The Etats du Languedoc assembled here several times and, during the Revolutionary period, clubs held their meetings here. A kilometre away lies the Château de la Grange-des-Prés where Molière played.

If the countryside around Pézenas has been deprived of its most remarkable *châteaux*, there nevertheless exists a real garland of them in the valley of the Peyne which is worth visiting.

We will rapidly list that of Larzac where Lord Clive, Governor of India, sojourned in the 18th century. His Indian cooks were responsible for the recipe of little Pézenas *pâtés* of sweet meat which became famous; then farther on, the Domain of Saint-Jean, whose orangery is adorned with a door dating from the time of Henri II; then the Hermitage of Saint-Siméon which was founded in 1658 and whose church is the object of a pilgrimage. Slightly higher up, lies the Grangeot des Peintres, which Jean Pillement inhabited for several years during the Revolutionary period.

There is also the Château de Fondouce with, opposite, the small farm of Saint-Palais, the Château de Montpezat, that of Roquelune, that of Le Parc, which was a hunting pavilion of the Montmorency and the Prince de Conti. Louis XIII and Louis XIV were guests here. Crossing the woods, we reach the Tour de la Maréchale of the 16th century and a small mediaeval *château*, that of Loubatières, where according to tradition Ninon de Lenclos stayed.

We head in the direction of Agde, taking the D. 13 which passes through Conas with its 12th-century mill and then through Nezignan-l'Evêque whose church dates from the 14th and 16th centuries.

SAINT-THIBERY, which is the ancient *Cessero*, where we next arrive, is built in the midst of a basaltic ring, the crater of an ancient volcano. There can be seen the ruins of an old abbey whose church, which lost part of the nave, dates from the 15th and 16th centuries. There remain merely some toothing stones of a portal which must have been magnificent, stayed against a solid square tower. There are some beautiful High Gothic windows. Downstream on the Hérault can be seen four ruined arches of a Roman bridge which was part of the Domitian Way.

We go through Bessan which has preserved the rest of its fortifications, a large house and a 13th-century mill, also a Romanesque chapel known as the Guinarde, and we reach AGDE.

The ancient Phocaean colony *Agathae Tychae*, which became the Roman *Agatha*, was the seat of a bishopric as early as the year 400. In 506 a Council was held in the suburban church of Saint-André. A cathedral was first built between 848 and 872 within the walls. The present building was undertaken at the close of the 12th century and was fortified to serve as a defence against the Saracens for the same reason as those of Vic and Maguelone, which we have just seen.

The Cathedral of Agde, which is built of lava stone, like the other buildings in the town, is a curious edifice because of its "T" shape design. The very impressive single nave, with pointed barrel-vaulting, rests against a transept which is not at right angles and has no apse. The side walls are reinforced by large semicircular engaged arches which are borne by pilasters. In the 17th century all the bays were enlarged except the second bay which is semicircular, very narrow and splayed only in the interior. It is curious that the arch of one of them is elliptical.

Outside, the walls are reinforced by pilasters supporting semicircular arches which are independent of the foundation wall and form machicolation. The wall mounted on these arches is crenellated and forms the parapet of the watch-path. The two transept arms serve as the base of the two towers, one of which was raised later than the main building and which, with its machicolation and watch-towers crowning the last storey, constitutes a real keep.

The cathedral, pillaged by the Protestants, was restored in the 17th century and the design was entirely modified: the high altar was installed in the west section and a door was pierced in the wall of the ancient chevet. The original design was restored at the close of the last century, the ancient façade was freed and a door was pierced in the façade, which was blind.

On the south side are some remains of a Gothic cloister, which was stupidly demolished about 1860, arranged into a chapel.

There still can be seen the 12th-century Hôtel de Ville, the 15th-century Church of Saint-Sévère with its panelled nave, its ogival vaulted lateral chapels, its polygonal apse and apsidioles and the rest of its fortifications which date from the 13th century with a fragment of the ancient Greek wall.

We will take the N. 112 which passes through Vias where we can see an elegant little 15th-century church which is built of lava and also fortified. The façade is blind and there is a watch-path around the edifice. The apse has seven sections and the choir is flanked by chapels, which thus form a false transept. The nave is in the southern Gothic style; it is larger and higher than the choir. The steeple is surmounted by a stone spire.

We then pass through Villeneuve-lès-Béziers where the church is Romanesque. The nave has semicircular vaulting resting on columns and the side-aisles have transversal vaulting. The steeple is a curious mixture of Romanesque and Gothic.

We reach BEZIERS which is the capital of that red wine known familiarly as "*gros rouge*". At Béziers I have seen the largest and most impressive cafés in the world, with thousands of tables in huge rooms, their walls covered with mirrors reflecting them a thousand times over, in the gardens and beneath the clumps of trees. An entire nation could come here to drink. I have seen them empty, but I suppose that on certain occasions they are full.

In the midst of this prosperity, what has become of the ancient Béziers, the *Colonia Julia Septimana Biterrae* of the Romans which was pillaged by the Vandals in the 5th century, the city of the Viscount of Béziers which was stormed by Simon de Montfort and his Crusaders who massacred all the inhabitants without exception and they numbered 60,000? It was the most atrocious episode of the Albigensian War, which saw many terrible ones, and we would like to see some memorial in the town which would recall this barbarism, so that the memory of these past crimes would prevent men from committing new ones.

The town, which lies between the railway station and the acropolis on which old Béziers is built, has retained nothing of its heroic past; but when, from the other side of the Orb, near the Pont-Vieux, we see the mass of the fortified cathedral rising on its hilltop, we rediscover the silhouette of the ancient city as, in its general lines, it must have appeared from this site two or three centuries ago.

The sloping streets which lead to Saint-Nazaire have retained a certain picturesqueness, without their ancient houses moreover having much character, for they have been too disfigured for this.

Saint-Nazaire is one of the most beautiful fortified churches in France. Massive and powerful, with its crenellated towers and its machicolation, its Gothic cloister, its decorated apse flanked by a square tower, which is as impressive as a keep, it forms a fascinating *ensemble*. Burnt by the Crusaders, the Romanesque cathedral was rebuilt in the Gothic style in a larger design. The nave with two bays which are flanked by chapels is completed by a transept and a very deep choir which terminates in a seven-sectional apse. On to the north arm of the transept there has been built the Chapel of the Virgin which terminates in a five-sectional apse flanked by the 15th-century Chapel of Guillaume de Montjoie with its magnificent ribbed vaulting. There is also the handsome 14th-century cloister with the ancient chapter-house which is surmounted by a second chapter-house built in the 15th century. A 10th-century crypt consists of an apse whose sections are adorned with columns which are surmounted by pilasters.

In the Place des Albigeois, some old houses surrounding the apse with its ancient bishop's palace form a setting which is not without poetical charm; here alone the past has not been obliterated by the din and vulgarity of modern life. A few trees, the museum which has been installed in a near by house containing some first-class paintings, an atmosphere of tranquility and meditation, all this is far removed from the tragedy of 1209. We should descend as far as the Church of the Madeleine whose Gothic steeple is resting on a Romanesque base; most of the population who had sought refuge in the church were massacred there.

The Church of Saint-Aphrodise which is partly Romanesque, the small Church of les Récollets with its charming Gothic portal, and a few handsome 17th-century *hôtels*, are still of fascinating interest to the tourist; but the inhabitants of Béziers are especially proud of the Allées Paul Riquet, of the Plateau des Poètes and of the solid, comfortable buildings which border the new arterial roads.

Proof of their lack of interest in the vestiges of their past is furnished by the curious fact that some old *hôtels* have been demolished, not in order to build apartment houses, but to build other *hôtels* in imitation of the old ones without having their beauty—over-elaborated pastiches in the Louis XV or Louis XVI style are proof, not only of the architects' bad taste, but also that of the owners who had accepted the designs. Sometimes the courtyard has remained intact and the façade facing the street appears all the more ridiculous. It is the reign of foolishness and ignorance.

But here is the height of this idiocy. Beside the Hôtel de Ville, which is an elegant 18th-century construction with a straight high façade surmounted by a very gracious and original square bell-tower, a building which is similar in style to the Galeries Lafayette department store in Paris has been constructed, complete with dome and big-bellied balconies, and it is quite incongruous.

Would it not be possible one day to diminish this building by two storeys and remove the dome and its balconies so that its agressive ugliness no longer crushes the small masterpiece adjacent to it?

To console ourselves, we will visit a pretty piece of decoration: the five-sectional polygonal apse of the Church of Saint-Jacques, which was the abbatial church of a monastery of the Order of Saint Augustine. The rest of the edifice was remodelled and disfigured in the 18th and 19th centuries, but this apse of the early 12th century has a quite remarkable decoration imitated from the antique and it is comparable to the apse of Alet. Four projecting buttresses are adorned with quarter-round projecting mouldings and support short columns where capitals are adorned with ornamental foliage, palmettes and interlacing of Oriental inspiration. Above, a very projecting antique cornice is decorated with denticles, ovals and modillions.

We will follow the N. 9 as far as NISSAN-LES-ENSÉRUNE where we will visit the Ensérune excavations.

The pre-Roman *oppidum* of Ensérune is the only one in France to have been methodically excavated and thus gives us a clear idea of the evolution of civilisation in France from the Second Iron Age until the close of the 2nd century B.C.

The hill was indeed constantly occupied from the 6th century B.C. onwards and there can be seen three distinct phases. The first is represented by huts of puddled clay built in extended order without fortified protection. Silos were dug in the tufa near these dwellings to serve as storage places for food. This phase is characterised by the rarity of metal and the use of a crude pottery. But soon this indigenous civilisation started to evolve, thanks to contact with Greek commerce.

The second phase manifested itself at the close of the 5th century by the creation of a real town whose buildings were designed in chessboard pattern along narrow streets built at right angles. The silo was replaced by a *dolium* sunken into the soil of the dwellings which remained modest with a single room and with the hearth directly on the ground. The town was enclosed by gigantic fortifications which also included a funerary field. Henceforth there was an abundance of iron as well as pottery which was imported from the Hellenic world.

The third phase began in the second half of the 3rd century with the arrival of the Gauls. A new quarter was erected on the site of the necropolis. Roman influence was seen in the creation of large cisterns and sewers, in the paving of the houses and in the coating of plaster given to the walls.

A museum, which has been installed at the summit of the hill, contains all that has been disclosed by excavation: arms, jewellery, coins and ceramics. There are especially the everyday pottery of Neolithic inspiration known as Iberian pottery and, among the more artistic ceramic pieces, some beautiful vases of the 5th and 6th century B.C., decorated with figures.

We will continue to follow the N. 9 as far as NARBONNE which was the former capital of *Gallia Narbonensis*, whose buildings, judging from the praise they received from Austone and Sidonius Apollinaris, were sumptuous. Although no important ruins remain, none the less the lapidary museum, which has been installed in the church of the old Benedictine priory in the Boulevard Ernest-Féroul, is rich enough to rival the one at Arles. It contains several *cippus*, sarcophagi, funerary steles, statues and fragments of monuments.

The edifice itself is worthy of interest. The façade and the south portal are of the 12th century, the nave of the middle of the 13th century; and the choir was raised about 1280 under the episcopacy of Pierre de Montbrun whose coat-of-arms can be seen in several places. The nave is quite large, bordered by side-chapels which are set between the buttressess. The roof rests entirely on the back of the stone arches which act as principal rafters and an inner gallery where people could move about runs above the chapels. Beneath the high windows is the triforium. The apse is fortified and flanked by a tower with an adjoining spiral staircase.

But there is a much more interesting church at Narbonne, that of Saint-Paul-Serge, which dates from early Christian times. In fact, an early Christian oratory was erected on this site in the middle of the 3rd century bordering the Domitian Way by Saint Paul-Serge, first Bishop of Narbonne, who was buried there. A Christian necropolis was created around it and the oratory was enlarged and reconstructed. The present edifice, so far as the nave is concerned, dates from the 12th century. The construction of the choir, which was undertaken in 1224 involved the rebuilding of the transept. In 1364 a fire necessitated rebuilding the vaulting of the nave, and in the 15th century it was extended by two bays which were fronted by a porch. Different other works were undertaken in the 16th century, such as the reinforcement of several pillars of the nave and the construction of the steeple above the porch and that of the polygonal chapel on the north side. In the 19th century it was necessary to prop up the nave with three stone arches.

The triforium of the third and fourth bays, which dates from the 12th century and whose semicircular arcades are lighted by small windows, is one of the oldest examples of clerestory. The ambulatory with Champagne vaulting is enclosed by five seven-sectional chapels with a clerestory above, like the cathedrals of Le Mans and Bourges, similar to the one above the choir arcades. There can be seen also some beautiful 5th-century Christian sarcophagi and a 12th-century capital which represents *The Last Judgment*. All that remains of the cloister is a gallery which has been transformed into a sacristy where two beautiful 12th-century tombs can be seen.

Finally, we should not miss descending to the underground galleries which have recently been opened and where an entire section of the ancient Christian necropolis has been discovered.

Quite near by, at the corner of the Rue des Trois-Nourrices and the Rue Edgar-Quinet, there is a beautiful house of 1558 with caryatid windows. We then head for the two principal buildings in Narbonne, the Cathedral and the ancient Archbishop's Palace.

The Archbishop's Palace again offers the occasion to regret the mania of Viollet-le-Duc for collaborating with the mistakes of the past. It is to him, alas, that we owe the building in the Gothic style which is set between the two towers of the façade and which houses the principal offices of the Hôtel de Ville. There was sufficient room in the constructions already existing without having to erect this pastiche which ruins an *ensemble*, for it was then quite remarkable as is witnessed by romantic engravings.

Let us therefore disregard this modern wart and admire the three square towers. The thickest, that on the left angle, built between 1290 and 1310, is a real keep which could have been isolated. Its four vaulted rooms are surmounted by a platform which is flanked by four watch-towers commanding the canal and the bridge. The Tour Saint-Martial, in the centre, was constructed in 1375 by the Archbishop Pierre de la Jugie. The tower on the right, built in 1273, is known as the Tour de la Madeleine because of the twin chapel of which it forms the extremity.

Between the Tour Saint-Martial and the Tour de la Madeleine there opens, beneath a vault, the Passage de l'Ancre, a kind of fortified street which separates the palace into two sections. On the right, is the old palace whose foundations are Gallo-Roman. There is a main building which is Romanesque of the 11th and 12th centuries, with an 11th-century steeple which belongs to the ancient cathedral. On the left, the new palace consists of 14th-century constructions which were remodelled in the 17th century. A section of the buildings is devoted to a museum rich in paintings and ceramics.

On its other sides, the Archbishop's Palace, on the exterior, is flanked by four round towers, like a fortress. Just behind rises the Saint-Just Cathedral, which although unfinished is nevertheless an important edifice because of its style and its influence in southern France and Catalonia.

Work was begun in 1272 with the choir, which was finished in 1340 and whose buttresses, terminating in turrets, are connected by huge arches having a crenellated watch-path. It is flanked by two square towers with watch-towers whose crowning dates from the 15th century. In the 18th century an archbishop wanted to finish the edifice, but he was able merely to raise two bays which have remained unfinished.

The choir, which is enclosed by an ambulatory and 13 pentagonal chapels connected by a passage, is related to the style of the great Gothic cathedrals of northern France which later inspired those of southern France: Clermont, Limoges, Narbonne, Toulouse. The chapels contain many works of art which we will not attempt to enumerate. We will limit ourselves to indicating the tomb of the Cardinal de la Jugie and in the seventh chapel some very handsome bas-reliefs representing scenes in Hell which were hidden by some modern panels and which someone decided to uncover.

Taking the beautiful 15th-century chapter-house with its vaulting resting on four columns, we ascend a spiral staircase to the treasure chamber which contains some remarkable works of art: an Arabian 10th-century ivory box, an 11th-century missal, a 12th-century ivory plaque, three portable altars of the 13th century and a magnificent 16th-century Flemish tapestry.

We should also visit the cloister which was built from 1350 to 1417 on the site of the 11th-century cathedral whose steeple we have seen. Its large tierce-point arcades are surmounted by balustrades and flanked by pinnacled buttresses, forming along with the towers of the Archbishop's Palace and the Cathedral a very picturesque *ensemble*.

We leave Narbonne by the N. 113 which we will follow for a distance of five kilometres, then take the N. 613 and after seven kilometres we take the road which leads to the ABBAYE DE FONTFROIDE.

Founded about the close of the 11th century, before 1097, by Aymeric I, Viscount of Narbonne, it was annexed to Cîteaux in 1146. In a charter of 1157, Ermengarde, the donator's grandaughter, delimited the domain of Fontfroide. It is one of the most sumptuous Cistercian abbeys and one that is furthest removed from the simplicity prescribed by Saint Bernard. We are far from the rigour of le Thoronet, all the more so since it was further embellished in the 18th century.

The entrance portal dates from this period and the courtyard which follows is bordered on one side by terraced gardens and on the other by the ancient guest chapel. We then enter the beautiful storeroom which dates from the close of the 12th century, with its crossed ogival-ribbed vaulting with heavy square profile; the fireplace dates from the 15th century.

The cloister, where some fragments of an earlier cloister of the 12th century have been re-used, dates from the middle of the 13th century and was finished in the early 14th century. The galleries have ogival-ribbed vaulting of Doric profile resting on brackets which are adorned with crockets or foliated forms and, towards the exterior, on slender columns with capitals having crockets or clusters of leaves. The south gallery is the oldest and has some very curious vaulting with a longitudinal lierne. Each bay opens on to the ambulatory by four small arcades which rest on twin slender columns of marble, supporting a high tympanum which lies beneath a large pointed relieving arch and which is pierced by three oculi in the south gallery and by a large rose-window in the west and east galleries. The one on the north side was rebuilt in the 17th and 18th centuries.

The church, which was built in the second half of the 12th century, consists of a nave with side-aisles—with five chapels which were built on to the south aisle in the 15th century—a transept and a rectangular choir which terminates in a five-sectional apse flanked by two chapels on each side, the first rectangular, the second much deeper, terminating in a five-sectional apse, like that of the choir. A large rectangular chapel extends the second chapel of the south transept arm. The door of the sacristy and the staircase of the dormitory are at the far end of the north transept arm, and that of the lay brothers, which opens onto the street, is in the first one. The portal is Romanesque; it is quite simple with, on the tympanum, some small 15th-century sculptured panels.

The chapter-house, which also dates from the close of the 12th century, is very elegant with four slender columns of marble whose splayed capitals support the ogival-vaulting and the elliptic cross-ribs of the vaulting.

It is well worth going for a stroll in the admirable gardens which have been tastefully designed by M. Fayet to whom we owe the restoration of Fontfroide. If only we had more people in France like him, lovers of beautiful things bent on restoring these ancient abbeys which are too often left in a pitiful state of abandonment and which can be saved from ruin by a little love—and a great deal of money!

We return to the N. 613 and three kilometres away we pass at the foot of the ruined fortress of Saint-Martin-de-Troques with its keep which dates from the time of St. Louis. Then taking the V.O. 1, the D. 123 and the N. 611 by way of Saint-André-de-Roquelongue and Montséret, which overlooks the ruins of another fortress, we reach the N. 9 which we will follow as far as SALCES where we will see one of the finest military constructions of the 16th century.

An ancient fortress, built in 1165 on the site of a Gallo-

Roman villa, was rebuilt of beautiful reddish stone from 1497 to 1504 by the Spanish engineer, Ramirez, to prevent the French from entering Roussillon. In fact Salces, which lies between the Etang du Leucate and the mountains, commands the passage to the plain.

In spite of certain remodelling in the 17th century, notably by Vauban, it is the most complete and intact example we possess of the transitional defensive system where the use of towers built for artillery enters into the general plan of defence.

The design consists of a parallelogram flanked on each angle by a tower. Two of the frontal ones are covered demi-lunes. A keep, which is the ancient keep of the fortress, occupies the third side and a demi-lune forms a projection on one of the angles. The walls are casemated and the towers and demi-lunes are crowned by platforms for artillery use. Moreover, small cannon were set in battery in the lower storeys of the towers to rake the trenches.

The demi-lunes are veritable isolated flanking towers open at the neck and connected with the casemates of the curtain walls by caponiers or covered galleries, pierced by embrasures for rifle fire.

The castle is surrounded by a moat measuring 45 feet in width and 21 feet in depth; it could have been inundated up to the level of the castle courtyard and even higher. It communicates with the castle by narrow posterns. Other outlets, which were open on to the counterscarp, no doubt communicate with the exterior, for the Chevalier de Beaulieu in his leaflet on Salces says, "There are more lodgings underground in this castle than outside it, since it is entirely casemated and counter-mined, and to go outside one has to pass beneath the moats . . .". Some casemated galleries communicated with a covered passage behind the counterscarp, some galleries having been found dug in the moat and from there to the exterior, protected by advanced works of earth.

As the place was dominated by the last buttresses of the Corbières mountains and the towers and demi-lunes were open to view both from behind and in enfilade, the parapets of the towers were raised on this side and some parados were set in the necks of the towers opposite.

We enter the castle over a drawbridge, fronted by a barbican, which leads to a gate which is flanked by two turrets. Of the earlier buildings there remain the palace of Pedro I of Aragon and some Roman baths.

We will take the N. 9 again and after 15 kilometres we reach Perpignan.

7. ABSIDE DE LA CATHÉDRA
D'A

8. DONJON D'ARQUES.

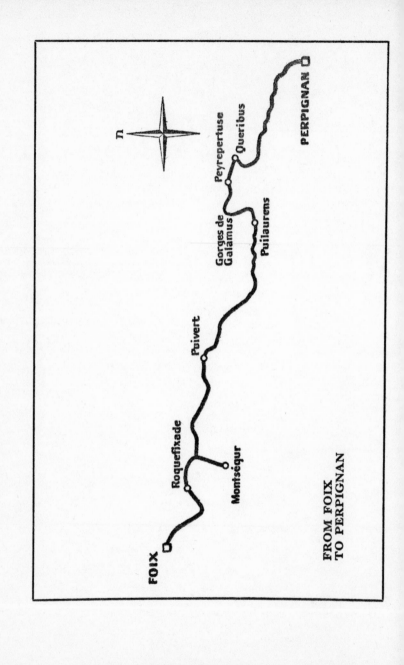

FROM FOIX
TO PERPIGNAN

FOIX

Roquefixade

Montségur

Puivert

Gorges de
Galamus

Puilaurens

Peyrepertuse

Quéribus

PERPIGNAN

n

ITINERARY II
FROM FOIX TO PERPIGNAN

*Foix — Roquefixade — Montferrier — Montségur —
Puivert — Puylaurens — Gorges de Galamus —
Perapertusa — Quéribus — Espira de l'Agly —
Perpignan.*

THIS itinerary may be regarded as the eastern part of
an itinerary from Bordeaux to Perpignan, the first part
of which, from Bordeaux to Foix, I shall be describing
later on. The usual route between these two places consists in
following the valley of the Garonne along the N. 127, 123 and
20, travelling from Bordeaux to Toulouse by Agen and
Moissac, then the N. 113 by Castelnaudary and Carcassone
as far as Narbonne, where, taking the N. 9, we can travel
south as far as Perpignan. But for those who are already
familiar with the town of Carcassonne, the old *hôtels* of
Toulouse, the cloister and portal of Moissac, I propose to
indicate alternative itineraries which are hardly longer and
which are as rich in little known beauties as in picturesque
landscape.

They will enable us to discover small towns which have a
charm all their own, like Condom and Saint-Bertrand de
Comminges, Larressingle, Saint-Lizier and Montjoie, and
likewise a number of *châteaux*. Some of those on the first part
of the route, like the Château de Cadillac and the Château
de Villandrault, are familiar, while others, like the Château
de Xaintrailles and the Château de Durban, are less well
known.

But the road which we are now going to take from FOIX
to Perpignan may be called the route of the fortresses. We
will see Roquefixade, Montferrier, Montségur, Puivert,

Puilaurens, Perapertusa and Quéribus which are the most famous and best preserved fortresses in France.

This road which extends along the flanks of the Pyrenees is rich in attractive mountain landscapes and in steep gorges, such as those of the Galamus.

The Château de Foix, proudly set on its rock, is one of the most impressive sights I have ever seen. Its isolation has preserved it from destruction and its three towers rise bravely to the sky surrounded by vestiges of its fortifications. The Tour du Nord dates from the 12th century. It is the oldest yet the lowest; it is square and divided by beams of wood. The second tower, which is also square, dates from the 14th century; it is higher and flanked by a projecting turret. It consists of three ogival-vaulted rooms, the last on twin bays. The third tower, isolated, is the keep which is 126 feet in height, whose construction, although attributed to Gaston Phoebus, does not seem to date prior to the 15th century. It consists moreover of a cellar and four beautiful six-sectional ogival-vaulted rooms.

We can still visit the Church of Saint-Volusien, which is an ancient abbatial building. In fact, Foix was originally an oratory founded by Charlemagne which in the 10th century became the Abbey of Saint-Volusien where the remains of Saint Volusien, who was Archbishop of Tours and who had been massacred near Varilhes in 497, were placed. The abbots remained the seigneurs of the bourg under the suzerainty of the Counts of Carcassonne until about 1012 when Bernard Roger constructed an early castle. His son Roger took the title of Count of Foix in 1036.

The Church of Saint-Volusien is fronted by a heavy square tower forming a porch which is surmounted by a triangular steeple-wall. The church was rebuilt in the 14th century in the Gothic style, but of the ancient Romanesque church there remains a part of the south wall of brick with an ornamental arcade and a beautiful Romanesque door with historiated capitals. The single nave is followed by a poly-gonal choir enclosed by rectangular chapels and fortified on the exterior. Blind arcades of brick placed between the

powerful buttresses support a watch-path with some small
Gothic windows, while beneath the roof there is a trefoiled
gallery.

The town contains many timbered houses of the 15th and
16th century, a beautiful 17th-century house facing the
church with, on the first storey, some Ionic columns which
are surmounted by Corinthian ones and caryatids and,
behind, a Renaissance octagonal tower.

Lying on the junction of the Ariège and the Arget, Foix is
lacking neither in charm nor picturesqueness, and those who
are fond of grottoes may visit that of l'Herm, le Mas d'Azil
or the underground river of Labouiche, lying 9, 28 and 5
kilometres away respectively.

From Foix, taking the N. 20 and N. 117 which follow the
Scios Valley, we will go as far as Nalzen, where, on the left,
we will take a little road which leads us to ROQUEFIXADE
where we are at an altitude of 2,100 feet. The village is
overlooked at a height of 3,000 feet by a crest with enormous
grey rocks on which, in the 13th century, a castle was built
with its wall sheer above the precipice. It was rebuilt in the
16th century and its ruins are still impressive.

We will return to the N. 117 and at Lavelanet, a small
weaving town which is dominated by the ruins of its Château
de Castelsarrasin, we will take the D. 109 which passes
through Villeneuve-d'Olmes and Montferrier, two other
small weaving towns. The Church of Montferrier was built
in 1212 and the castle was a powerful fortress, but all that
remain are some thick ruined walls. We enter a gorge and
soon see rising before us in a setting of proud solitude, 600
feet above the village of MONTSEGUR, on a peak which
rises straight up like a column, the fortress which was the
last refuge of the Catharists. These curious people were, like
the Albigenses, a religious sect of mediaeval times, whose
members were called *Parfaits* and *Parfaites* from the word
"perfect" or "pure".

The Fine Arts Administration has had the happy idea of
restoring this fine fortress, which was the object of one of the
most epic sieges in history.

A lieutenant of Simon de Montfort, Enguerrand de Boves, was the first to besiege Montségur, but he was repulsed by Raymond de Pereilhe and the Seigneurs of Mirepoix and Lavelanet. Later on, after the Battle of Muret, Simon de Montfort besieged the fortress in vain. But after his death, when the royal troops gradually began to destroy all resistance from the different regions of southern France, it appeared that Montségur was once again going to be invested. Consequently Arnaud du Villar, a well-known fortress engineer, pupil of the celebrated Escot de Linard, put the citadel in combat state, reinforced the barbicans and built an engine of war. His two sons, Jordan and Hugo, remained in the fortress with the *Parfaits* and *Parfaites*, the Catharist bishops and the defenders, who were led by the Chevaliers Raymond de Pereilhe and Pierre Roger de Mirepoix.

The troops of the King of France, under the command of Hugues des Arcis, Seneschal of Carcassonne, had already established themselves on the wooded slopes of Serrelongue and at l'Aire de l'Espagnol at the foot of the castle, shutting off the surrounding valleys. They were accompanied by Pierre Arnul, Archbishop of Narbonne and Durand, Bishop of Albi. The besieged made furious sorties and epic combats took place. Some redoubtable moveable towers were built in the French camp and the siege tightened. Bertrand d'En Marti, the Catharist archbishop, gave the besieged the *convinenza*, a preparatory rite for the *consolanentum*, administered when the dying person could no longer speak; then he set himself up as an object of worship.

The besieged tried several times to set fire to the Tour de la Chatte, which was the most formidable of all the moveable French towers, but they failed. Dragged on an armoured chariot, it was gradually advanced towards the citadel; it took five months to move it 1,500 feet. Several Catharist seigneurs died during these combats—Guilhem de l'Ile, Bertrand de Bardenac, Ramon de Carcassonne, Clarey and Jordanet.

Contrary to the hopes of those besieged in the citadel, the

winter was a mild one. Snow did not interrupt the assault
until January and already in February the Tour de la Chatte
was able again to attack the fortifications and soon reached
the barbicans. The Catharists set fire to it and merciless
hand-to-hand fighting took place.

In the citadel, the *Parfaits*, surrounded by the aged and
children, remained unmoved, calling upon God to come to
their aid.

One dark night a brave troop led by some Alpine men left
the Lasset ravine and scaled the east edge of the Pic de
Montségur. They surprised the sentinels, killed them and
then seized the advance works of the Roc de la Tour. The
Catharist situation became desperate and surrender seemed
inevitable. Some had already fled the previous night, no
doubt along a difficult path. The knights were spared, but
200 heretics who refused to abjure were burnt alive including
several Catharist bishops and many *Parfaits* of Catharist
nobility. Philippe Sicre has written a very enthusiastic book
on the subject, *Le Château de Montségur*.

We cannot help but feel a certain emotion when we visit
these stones which have been the witnesses of the heroic
Catharist defence with the remains of the keep and the large
room where the *Parfaits* met.

We will return to Lavelanet and the N. 117 and, by way of
Belesta, which is dominated by the ruins of the Castel
d'Amont, we reach the Col de Babourade from where there
is a magnificent view over the Rivel and Hers Valleys and the
Château de Puivert which, standing out on its peak against the
surrounding forests, overlooks the town spread out at its foot.

Dr. Jean Girou, who has written a very detailed book on
the land of Aude[1] that is our principal source of information,
tells us that the CHATEAU DE PUIVERT was famous
long before the Albigensian War. It was the meeting place of
the troubadours and in 1150 it was the scene of the Court of
Love where a poem by Pierre d'Auvergne received a prize:
"At le Puy Verd in the torchlight assemblies where stories

---

[1] *Itineraire en terre d'Aude.*

and *fabliaux* (short stories in verse) were recited in an
atmosphere of play and laughter."

But war drove out poetry. Simon de Montfort sent Pons de
Bruyère at the head of 6,000 men to pursue the Albigenses
who had taken refuge in the Kerkorb and the Pays de Sault.
The Albigenses concentrated their troops in Puivert. Pons
approached the fortress from the north and no sooner had he
established his camp than he attacked. But he was repulsed
before he could approach the ramparts and, when night fell,
combat ceased. Two mornings later he again attacked and
was turned back. He regrouped his troops and, axe in hand,
led the assault. The ramparts were scaled and the fortification towers surrendered. Surprised by this sudden offensive,
the besieged took refuge in the keep. The Crusaders followed
them, penetrated into the lower room and were astonished
to find it empty; a subterranean passage had enabled the
Albigenses to reach the Plateau de Nabias. Pons took his
revenge on the wounded and had them hanged from the
summit of the keep.

Of the Château de Puivert, which was built in the 12th
century but remodelled in the 14th century, there remain
only the formidable ruins which are enjoyable to visit. A
stone bridge has replaced the ancient drawbridge and the
entrance door is adorned with the coat-of-arms of the
Seigneurs of Bruyères, "the lion with its forked and knotted
tail", for the Baron de l'Ile-de-France had received Puivert
and Chalabre in reward for his services. He raised Puivert
from its ruins and installed himself there in 1210.

The gate was defended by a square tower with machicolation, a portcullis and wooden swing-doors. After the gateway
we enter a huge *cour d'honneur*, measuring 240 feet in length
and 140 feet in width, where tournaments and assemblies
were held. It is enclosed by curtain walls and towers; one
angle tower, the Tour Quayre; two side towers, the Tour
Bonne and the Tour Gaillarde; and in the middle the keep,
isolated, with the residential dwellings and the out-buildings
behind.

The keep, which is 105 feet in height, has two beautiful

sculptured windows. We enter through a postern to which we gain access by stones set along the wall. A spiral staircase leads to the three superimposed rooms. The one below with semicircular vaulting is a sober, military-looking guardroom which communicates with an underground room which is itself connected with the prisons, the cisterns and the underground passages. Above the guardroom, there is a beautiful Gothic room lighted by two windows and with fine ribbed vaulting whose keystone represents *The Crowning of the Virgin*, while the ribs rest on brackets which are embellished with monks and Biblical figures. Near the window is a niche with delicate mouldings and fine slender columns forming a fountain. Access to the upper storey is through a monumental door adorned with the bust of a man-at-arms and a woman with a falcon on her wrist. It is the chamber of state known as the "Musicians' Chamber". In the keystone of the ribbed vaulting are the twin coats-of-arms of the Bruyère and the Melun, while the brackets represent musicians playing the hurdy-gurdy, the lute, the harp and guitar as well as the tambourine and pipes.

There was formerly a lake adjacent to the castle which contributed as much to its beauty as to its defence. In 1279 Jean de Bruyère, second Seigneur of Puivert, attempted to drain the lake and utilize the ground it occupied. Unfortunately the base of the dam gave in, water rushed down the valley and the town of Mirepoix was entirely destroyed. The land reclaimed by the draining of the lake was distributed to the men-at-arms of the castle and hamlets were created which still bear their names.

We pass by way of the Col du Portel, through Quillan where the *mairie* occupies the ancient *hôtel* of the Seigneurs of Espezel of the 18th century, and we follow the wonderful Défilé de Pierre-Lys. The road, carved out of the rock which overhangs the left bank of the Aude and which passes in gallery-fashion beneath three tunnels, was begun in the early 19th century by a *curé* of Saint-Martin-Lys, and that is why it is known as the Trou du Curé.

At the hamlet of Lapradelles, at the junction of Magnac

brook and the Boulzanne, we see sticking out on a steep rock
the ruins of the CHATEAU DE PUYLAURENS, *castrum
de podio laurenti*, which is relatively well preserved and whose
merlons still extend towards the sky. We should not miss
taking the D. 22 which brings us to it.

This fortress, which was attacked in vain by Simon de
Montfort and also by the King of Aragon, remained impreg-
nable and resisted until the end of the Crusades. Its seigneur,
the Vicomte de Fenouillèdes, obstinately resisted the armies
of the North and Simon de Montfort, master of the entire
South, never succeeded in capturing the three fortresses of
Puylaurens, Fenouiller and Perapertusa. Puylaurens was
later owned by the King of France and became one of the
defensive positions on the frontier of the Kingdom of Aragon.
This explains why its defences were reinforced in the time of
St. Louis.

Mademoiselle Annie de Pous, who has written an excellent
study of the *châteaux* of the Perapertusan district, has established the date of the different constructions which are still
standing. The square tower of the keep, whose different
floors were not vaulted and which lies on the culminating
point of the rock, dates from the 11th century. The *enceinte* of
the keep and the different buildings which are adjacent to it
are built of medium-sized stones and date from the 12th
century. They dominate a lower courtyard enclosed by a
huge, very high surrounding wall, which is crenellated by
small merlons without loopholes and flanked on the south
by a semicircular tower open at the gorge. Two posterns lead
to this esplanade.

The constructions subsequent to the time of St. Louis
appear in the ornamentation of a round tower at the north-
west angle and in the near by curtain wall which is pierced
by three large machicolations with pointed arches. This
tower is also open towards the interior and entrance to the
ground floor is by a corridor which begins at the gate of the
keep.

A final campaign of building, which was marked by an
embossed construction, affected the south-west and east

towers, the latter being furnished with an interesting
speaking-tube conduit at the same time as the south tower
of the esplanade was built. There is finally the ribbed-
vaulted room on the ground floor in the south-west tower.

We return to the N. 117 which leads us to Saint-Paul-de-
Fenouillet where, on the left, we will take the D. 7 which
follows the Gorges de Galamus which are some of the most
desolate and impressive gorges that exist. After ascending
through blackish schistous hills, the road, which has been
hewn out of the flank of a great chalky wall, enters the cutting
dug out by the Argy at a height of 1,500 feet. We pass the
grotto-chapel of the Hermitage of Saint-Antoine-de-Galamus
half way up, as we take the winding corniche road. There
are tufts of grass on the white cliffs and, if we look over the
edge, we can see the green water of the torrent right at the
bottom.

At Cubières we will take, on the right, the D. 14 which
passes through Soulatgé. We leave, on the left, Rouffiac des
Corbières whose Romanesque church was remodelled in the
14th century, and on the right we see a rocky ridge whose
steep cliffs constitute an inaccessible bastion for the fortress
of Perapertusa whose walls blend with the rock.

The origin of the fortress of PERAPERTUSA goes back
no doubt to the 9th century during the struggle against the
Saracens and, as early as 1020, mention is made of a *castrum*
of Perapertusa held for the Count of Besalu by the Constable
Séguier. Entrance is solely by a stairway hewn out of the
rock, thanks to a natural fissure: for the cliff constitutes a
vertical wall measuring 100 to 250 feet in height and 900 feet
in length. The platform thus constituted hardly reaches 180
feet in width in its narrowest part.

We will follow the plan which has been set out by
Mademoiselle Annie de Pous. Two independent keeps face
each other at either extremity of the ridge; between them
there extend two esplanades which are separated by an inner
curtain wall; they enclose several buildings and are limited
by the wall which follows the edge of the cliff.

The castle, which was built in the early 11th century by

the Count of Besalu, consisted of a rectangular two-storey construction which was flanked by a round tower enclosing a cistern and forming a keep. There were two vaulted rooms on the ground floor and a large one on the first floor, the whole built in a construction of small stones.

Another *ensemble* of buildings dates from the time, the year 1111, when Perapertusa passed into the suzerainty of the county of Barcelona. A chapel was raised on the north and below the keep; and a crenellated curtain wall connected the tower with the cistern. The chapel had semicircular vaulting and the apse oven-shaped vaulting.

At the close of the 12th century, a long rectilinear curtain wall was erected on the north-east front. It is flanked by two semicircular towers open at the gorge and by a salient which contains the sole entrance to the fortress. Archery windows have been pierced on the ground level and the crest has a crenellated watch-path which can be plugged. An inner curtain wall connects this rampart with the chapel. The entrance door with its pointed arch leads to a zig-zagged corridor commanded by the keep.

After Perapertusa had become French, St. Louis in 1242 undertook new work on this fortress also, which made it the principal fortress on what was then the frontier with the Kingdom of Aragon. The ancient *castrum* was reinforced and set into the centre of new constructions. A large semicircular tower with two storeys with oven-shaped vaulting and sur-mounted by a platform, flanking a curtain wall crenellated by loopholed merlons, pugged and pierced by a postern with a pointed arch, was built on to the east side. The chapel was raised with two storeys and given a watch-tower, while a pentagonal tower forming a spur was built at the edge of the platform.

Moreover, at the other extremity, near the enormous mass of the San-Jordy Rock, there was built another keep, known as the San-Jordy Keep, whose curtain walls, pierced by a tiers-point gate, rested against the rock. They were flanked by three towers and were reached by a stairway known as the St. Louis Stairway, whose 100 steps are hewn out of the rock.

The Historic Monuments Administration had the fortunate idea of restoring this magnificent fortress, whose situation is really admirable, as well as the Château de Quéribus which we are now going to see. The work undertaken on these two fortresses has, among other things, made the paths which leads to them more practical.

To go to Quéribus, we will continue to follow the D. 14. We leave Cucugnan on our left, and we find at the top of the col the track which, on the left, continues towards the fortress whose spur rises directly before us.

Situated on a high crest commanding the Crau de Maury, it has always depended on the Seigneurs of Perapertusa. In 1255, the Seneschal of Carcassonne laid seige to it, as the last Catharists had sought refuge there. When the governor of the castle, Chabert de Barbaira, had submitted, Louis IX took possession of it and increased its defences.

In 1020 QUERIBUS, then known as Popia Cherbucio, was nothing more than a simple observation post the trace of which is still found, according to Mademoiselle de Pous, at the foot of the south side of the keep where it is pierced by three small loopholes of rather crude design.

In the 12th century, an *enceinte* defended the south side, which was the only accessible one. It consists of a very simple thick wall pierced by a gate which was later surmounted by a bartizan. A three-storey residential building is set against this wall.

In the 13th century a second *enceinte* in medium-sized stones was built at the foot of the escarpments. In some places it has a twin row of ornamental shaped stones and is pierced by loopholes.

Finally, the ancient keep was rebuilt in medium-sized stones and its walls are almost 9 to 12 feet in thickness. A large room which measures 21 feet on one side occupies the interior. It is lighted by deep windows and its vaulting rests on ribs which meet in a central pillar. The keep is flanked by a square tower which contains a spiral staircase. A small room belonging to the early keep contains an excavation which communicates with an underground passage, which winds around the keep and emerges at the base of the cliffs in a watch-tower which is equipped with archery windows. A mobile ladder made it possible to use this exit.

From the terrace of the keep there is a fine view over the entire Roussillon landscape, with, beyond, the Albères and the chain of the Pyrenees, from the Capeir to the Canigou.

Taking the D. 19 we rejoin the N. 117 at Maury. This follows the course of the Agly and descends into the plain. We pass through Estagel, but we should not miss seeing, on the left at ESPIRA-DE-L'AGLY, the beautiful Church of Notre-Dame, consecrated in 1130 but rebuilt in 1211 when it was given to a priory of canons of Saint-Augustin. Its single nave of four bays, marked off by blind arcades in the lateral walls, has pointed barrel-vaulting without cross ribs and terminates in paired apses. There is a remarkable Romanesque portal whose tympanum is framed by six elegant columns of white marble with magnificent capitals decorated with monsters, birds, and foliage and supporting some splendid arch mouldings. Another door, very simple this time, leads to the cloister whose vestiges remain. The steeple is in four storeys with ogival apertures.

We reach PERPIGNAN, where it is worth seeing the Castillet, a remarkable military construction in brick built about 1360 and remodelled in 1478; the Loge, built in 1397 to house the Bourse and the Sea Consulate, but remodelled in 1540, and now occupied by a café; the Hôtel de Ville adjoining, with its pretty arcaded courtyard dating from the 16th and 17th centuries; and then the 15th-century Deputation Provinciale with its large semicircular doors with enormous arch-stones and its charming twin windows with fine slender columns.

Several ancient houses are also worth seeing: the Maison Julia dating from the Renaissance in the Rue des Fabriques-Nodot which has a beautiful loggia courtyard and staircase, another in the same style at No. 7, Rue du Théâtre, where again, at No. 10, is a Renaissance dwelling.

But we should visit, above all, the Saint-Jean Cathedral

with its altar-pieces, its fine Rhenish *Christ* of the 13th century, the ancient Campo Santo of the 14th century and the portal of Saint-Jean-le-Vieux.

Finally, we should not miss seeing the ancient Palace of the Kings of Majorca, which dates from the 13th and 14th centuries, which was long occupied by the military who had transformed it into barracks, and which the Fine Arts Administration is now having restored. The beautiful arcades in the courtyard have been freed and several magnificent apartments and the two-storey chapel have been restored.

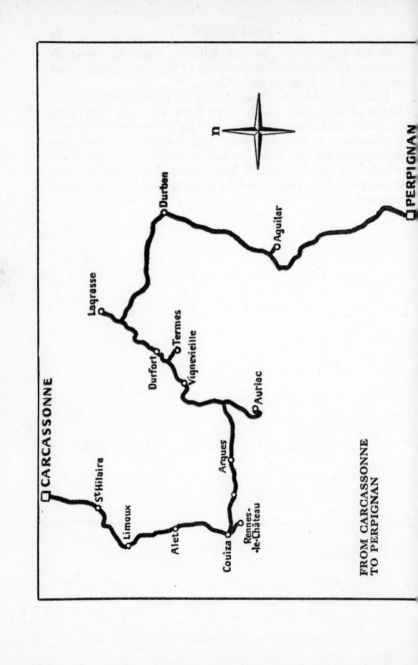

CARCASSONNE

St Hilaire
Limoux
Aleto
Couiza
Rennes-
le-Château
Arques
Auriac
Vigneveieille
Durfort
Termes
Lagrasse
Durban
Aguilar
PERPIGNAN

N

FROM CARCASSONNE
TO PERPIGNAN

OUR DE L'ABBAYE DE LAGRASSE.

10. TRIBUNE DU PRIEURÉ DE
SERRAB

10

ITINERARY III

FROM CARCASSONNE TO PERPIGNAN

Saint-Hilaire — Limoux — Alet — Couiza — Arques — Auriac — Termes — Durfort — Lagrasse — Durban — Aguilar.

THE country which we are now crossing is the county of Razès or Country of Rhedez, the *Pagus Rhedensis*, whose ancient town of *Rhedae* became the Visigothic capital of which not a stone remains intact and whose site lies not far from the small village of Rennes-le-Château, above Couiza, which we will soon pass. *Rhedae* meant "travelling chariots", and thus a nomadic encampment first occupied this plateau which lies at the junction of the Aude and the Sals, where the road emerges coming from Carcassonne towards the Pyrenees. When Clovis turned back the Visigoths in the direction of Spain where they established their capital at Toledo, they retained the Septimania (the littoral of southern Gaul) and *Rhedae* was then an important place, Carcassonne remaining their frontier fortress.

We will leave Carcassonne by the D. 104 which follows the right bank of the Aude. We pass through Cavanac, a small village enclosed by vineyards, dominated by the square tower of a Romanesque church and that of a castle, which has preserved its spiral staircase. We then traverse Leuc in the pleasant Lauguet Valley whose seigniorial *château* dates from the middle of the 14th century. It was built by Pierre de la Jugie, Archbishop of Narbonne, and modified in the 16th century. We leave, on the right side of the road, the little 11th-century Chapel of Saint-Laurent, then on the left, the Château de Pech where during a battle the Count Roger invoked Saint Hilaire: his prayer was evidently granted since he became the protector of the abbey which we are about to see.

This famous ABBAYE DE SAINT HILAIRE was founded in 550 by Saint Hilaire, the first Bishop of Carcassonne, who is buried there. It was first of all under the invocation of Saint Saturin, apostle of the Languedoc, but later on it took the name of its founder because of the miracles he accomplished. In 970 when the relics of Saint Hilaire were being transferred, Count Roger le Vieux and Adélaïs, his wife, made the vow to conform to the rule of Saint Benedict. In the presence of a solemn assembly, which included several bishops and abbots of the region, the body of Saint Hilaire was exhumed and laid out on the high altar for the veneration of the faithful. It was then set into a rich sarcophagus of white marble whose sculptures represent the martyrdom of Saint Sernin. This sarcophagus, which still exists and which we will see in the right apsidiole of the church, although it merely dates from the 12th century, is a curious imitation of 6th-century Gallo-Roman sarcophagi. It is attributed to the Master of Cabestany of whom we will have occasion to speak in greater detail. It seems that in asking the sculptor to imitate an antique sarcophagus, the monks in doing so wanted to authenticate the relics it contained. This would make a curious case of artistic falsification! Roger le Vieux and Adélaïs were in their turn buried in the church of the monastery, but their rich mausoleum was destroyed during the Wars of Religion. Thanks to numerous donations, the prosperity of the abbey reached its height in the middle of the 13th century.

The monastery has retained its *enceinte* which we cross through a gate that was formerly fortified. The church, which was built of beautiful ochre sandstone, consists of an apse flanked by two apsidioles in the Provençal Romanesque style of the close of the 12th century. The nave, which was built afterwards in the 13th century, consists of two bays which also would be Romanesque, if they had not been covered later on with ogival-ribbed vaulting.

The cloister forms a vast irregular trapezium with

galleries covered with wooden framework and whose pointed arcades, which number 16 on the large sides and 12 on the small, rest on high twin slender columns. The capitals, which have been treated with vigour and elegance, are decorated with foliage, monsters and heads of monks, and a powerful flying buttress shoulders each angle. Large trees give a very poetic atmosphere to the cloister.

The refectory, which also dates from the 14th century, has preserved its reader's seat which has been designed in the thickness of the wall and covered by a groined vault, while the ruined kitchen beside it still has its large fireplace. The remains of the chapter-house and the old abbatial dwelling, which has become the presbytery, with a handsome *salon* whose ceiling was painted about 1520—the coffers are an admirable symphony of white, green and red, decorated with allegorical subjects, coats-of-arms and *fleurs-de-lys*—can also be seen.

We will continue to follow the D. 104, which winds through slopes which produce the fruity wine known as *Blanquette de Limoux* and we descend at Pieusse, to the Aude Valley. The village was formerly fortified and the castle which overlooked the Aude belonged to Raymond Roger, Count of Foix, brother of the celebrated Esclarmonde who had herself received as a *Parfaite*. A large Catharist assembly was held at Pieusse under the presidency of the Bishop of Toulouse, Guillabert de Castres. It consisted of more than 100 *Parfaits* and ordained Benoît de Termes, who was consecrated Bishop of Razès. We can stop for a few minutes to see the church which is Gothic with a five-sectional apse and a very elegant porch.

We then pass near the Sanctuary of Notre-Dame-de-Marceille which is approached, on the right, by a paved path known as "The Sacred Path". Half way along, at the side, flows a fountain which was held in repute for being miraculous; and, near it, André Chénier is said to have lived for a time, when he was a child.

The 14th-century chapel was modelled after the churches of the lower town of Carcassonne. Two chapels form a false transept and are decorated with pretty 17th-century wood-panellings. In the one on the left, there can be seen *The Black Virgin* which is the object of great veneration throughout the region; it is protected by a beautiful 17th-century wrought-iron grille.

We reach LIMOUX where we will stop to drain a half-bottle of sparkling wine along with a *touron* which is a regional speciality; it is a nougat which rivals both the nougat of Montélimar and the Spanish *touron*. We will also visit the town which was formerly built on the Régat mountain, but which was destroyed during the Albigensian Crusade and rebuilt on the plain in 1262. It lies on the two banks of the Aude which is crossed by three bridges, two of which are ancient, the one from the 15th century and the other from the 16th century. The Church of Saint-Martin has preserved a Romanesque portal with historiated capitals and, in the side-aisles, some engaged columns dating from the 12th century. The choir terminates in a seven-sectional apse enclosed by an elegant 14th-century ambulatory on to which some five-sectional radiating chapels have been built. The nave is in the late Gothic style of the 16th century, lighted by oculi and flanked by side-aisles and lateral chapels. A beautiful 14th-century octagonal tower, which is surmounted by a notched spire, rests on a much older base.

The square is very picturesque with its arcades bordering it on three sides, several dating from the 15th and 16th centuries. It was on this square that the Fête des Fécos took place at carnival time. A pretty timbered house dating from the 16th century in the Rue de la Trinité is also of interest.

Before continuing our route, we will visit, if we really want to, at a distance of four kilometres along the N. 626, the cloister of the Convent of the Carmelites of Perpignan, which a poet and playwright, who was also an Academician and above all a man of taste, Alexandre Guiraud, saved from destruction and had transported into the park of the Château de Villemartin. The Convent of the Carmelites was converted into barracks, just as was the Palace of the Kings of Majorca, and the military decided to demolish the cloister in order to enlarge the courtyard. Guiraud had transported here this charming 14th-century Gothic cloister, with its delicate trefoiled arcades of marble. An inscription indicates that it was begun in 1333 and finished in 1342. With the arcades of red and green marble, Guiraud put together a Romantic chapel which opens on to the cloister. We will come back to Limous and take the N. 118 which climbs the Aude Valley which begins to narrow, then to widen again when we reach Alet, where we will cross the river over a handsome 15th-century bridge up stream from an ancient Roman bridge of which there remains some vestiges.

ALET, the ancient *Electa*, as early as 813 was the seat of an abbey which was founded by Béra, Count of Razès, and raised to a bishopric in 1317. Its titular in the 17th century was Nicholas Pavillon who dared to side with Port-Royal and on whom Richelieu imposed this modest, distant bishopric. After serving as bishop for 38 years, Pavillon died at Alet in 1677 after giving the greatest proof of virtue. He never, however, officiated in the cathedral, which had been pillaged and destroyed by the Protestants in 1577. As we travel through France, we can see how much the Wars of Religion have been prejudicial to the survival of our religious monuments. Wherever the Protestants held power, they not only set fire to the paintings and wood-panellings and mutilated the statues, but they destroyed the buildings themselves. They would often refrain from this, however, if the inhabitants offered fine sacks of *écus* in return for their churches. Once the Protestants had left, the churches were often repaired or rebuilt, but at Alet the cathedral was too vast and too important for this modest bourg and funds were lacking.

One is all the more given to express these bitter considerations since the ancient cathedral was a quite remarkable edifice erected in the second quarter of the 12th century and very characteristic of the Provençal Romanesque style which long retained the memory of antique classical art. The ruins, embellished with that beautiful golden tint often found in the stones of southern France, are the more poignant as they still seem impregnated with a former joy and fullness. Entrance is through the porch of the parish church.

The nave had semicircular vaulting and high tribunes, in quarter-circle vaulting, were erected above the side-aisles which had groined vaulting. If the vaulting has mostly disappeared, the walls as a whole are still standing with their semicircular arcades. The fairly well preserved apse has retained its vault and its five niches which are enclosed by some beautiful semicircular arcades, as well as its triumphal arch which rests on some magnificent Corinthian capitals. Its outer decoration greatly resembles the one we saw at the Church of Saint-Jacques at Béziers, the same very projecting antique cornice inspired by Roman monuments and resting on half-columns. Around the apse rises a Gothic 14th-century ambulatory which has been left unfinished. The two south lateral doors have a rich decoration which unfortunately has been mutilated.

Of interest also is the chapter-house (which has been converted into a stable), dating from the 14th century; and which has preserved its 12th-century door flanked by two semicircular bays.

The parish church, which dates from the close of the 14th century, is a modest edifice of the traditional southern Gothic type, whose framework is supported by diaphragm arches similar to those of the Church of Lamourguier at Narbonne. The interior contains some 15th and 16th-century frescoes.

We should not miss strolling in the narrow streets of the old town, which is rich in ancient timbered and corbelled houses with their sculptured motifs: they are adorned with vines, leaves and rose patterns, giving a very country-like aspect to the whole place. Near the Porte de la Cadène, which is part of the *enceinte* erected at the close of the 12th century, there can be seen a 13th-century house which has preserved, beneath the plaster and distemper, its large arcades on the ground floor and its semicircular twin windows on the first storey. A much-corbelled storey on beams is an addition which dates from the 15th or 16th century. Alongside, a house of 1673 has beneath the cornice of the roof the inscription, *Vive moi, le maître!* This is a good deal better than our villas called *Mon Désir* or *Ça me Suffit*, for it dates from the time when everything was built with feeling and dignity and when the buildings were not only useful but also beautiful, because the simplest mason had a natural taste.

Alet is also a watering place, where you can have your digestive tract attended to. But, none the less, we will take the N. 118 which continues to ascend the Aude in a rather desolate defile and we will stop at COUIZA at the junction of this river with the Sals. We will visit on the bank of the river the castle of the Dukes of Joyeuse whose severe outer *enceinte* is flanked at each angle by a heavy tower. This fortress changes in the interior into a Renaissance *château* with its square courtyard, whose entrance façade is well decorated with its windows framed with fluted pilasters on the first storey, with Ionic columns on the second and Corinthian columns on the third, each storey being surmounted by a frieze with masks and arabesques. A beautiful monumental staircase, the French ceilings and the sandstone fireplaces in certain rooms, can also be seen.

After belonging to the Joyeuse, the castle passed into the hands of the Guise, and it is now occupied by studios and shops where hats and sandals are made.

On leaving Couiza, we will take a small road which ascends the plateau where Rennes-le-Château, the ancient capital of the Razès, was built. The houses are in ruins, so also is the fortress, and the villas we see are, alas, modern with verandas and pergolas which well illustrate the bad taste of our time in a place like this, where it was sufficient to restore the ancient dwellings. If we continue to climb the plateau as far as the escarpment overlooking the valley of the Sals, we will find the site of the ancient Visigothic town which numbered 30,000 inhabitants and which was razed in 1170 by the troops of the King of Aragon. We must be satisfied with the admirable view we have from the belvedere with, facing us, on the other side of the Sals, the ruins of the

Château de Coustaussa, those of Blanchefort and a landscape
of valleys and mountains.

We redescend to Couiza where we will take the N. 613
which follows the valley of the Sals, a chalky defile between
rocky points. We leave, on the right, the road which leads to
Rennes-les-Bains where Blanche de Castille came to cure her
scrofula, and we continue to ARQUES where we will see, on
the left, before entering the village, the handsome castle
which Gil de Voisins began to build in 1280 and which was
completed in 1316 by his son, Gil II. The keep, which is one
of the masterpieces of the military art of the time, measures
65 feet in height; it is well preserved and has been restored.
It is a square construction, flanked, like many Spanish keeps,
by four corbelled turrets set on the angle buttresses in which
fall-traps have been arranged. The keep is enclosed by a
rectangular *enceinte*, which is mostly in ruins. It contains
several buildings which also are in ruins: the *salle de justice*,
the seignioral dwellings, the chapel and others.

We will continue to follow the N. 613 which passes over the
Col du Paradis and traverses the cedar forest of Rialsès, with
its splendid views over les Corbières and the wooded slopes
of Fortous. At the Pont d'Orbieu, we will take, on the right,
the D. 212; we descend into the valley of the Orbieu and
find, on a rocky escarpment which overlooks a steep ravine
in which a magnificent cascade falls in three breaks, the
CHATEAU D'AURIAC which was sold in the 10th
century by Rongarde, Countess of Carcassonne, to
Raymond, Count of Barcelona. In the 12th century it
became the apanage of the Cadets of Termes. In 1173
Bertrand, brother of Pierre-Olivier de Termes, was its
seigneur. It was restored in the 15th century as a defensive
element on the Spanish border.

An irregular-shaped keep with its cistern, its walls of uncut
stone, and its fish-bone courses of masonry can be seen. It is
enclosed by an *enceinte* of medium-sized stones. The façade,
more recent, is fairly well preserved. It is flanked by a three-
storeyed tower which houses a large unvaulted room heated
by two fireplaces with the light coming from three windows.

A small tower built with handsome medium-sized stones, which is embedded in the north curtain wall, has preserved its spiral staircase.

We will rejoin the D. 212 which we will follow beyond le Pont d'Orbieu and which is going to descend the desolate and picturesque Gorges of the d'Orbieu. We pass through Montjoi whose Gothic church is not lacking in interest, then through Vignevieille where the church is partially Romanesque and overlooks the ruins of the keep of the ancient castle with, at its base, a covered passage, and on the right, we take the D.40 which follows the narrow Gorge du Sou. After le Moulin de la Buade, we will enter two tunnels which have been dug out of the great chalky escarpment at the summit of which lies the CHATEAU DE TERMES. From the village a path leads to this powerful fortress which, together with Queribus, Perapertusa, Puylaurens and Aguilar, forms the "five sons of Carcassonne" and which, after the annexation of Languedoc to France, defended the frontier on the side of the Kingdom of Aragon. The castle and its *enceinte* occupied an area of 50,220 square feet.

In the 13th century, during the Albigensian War, after the fall of Carcassonne, Termes became one of the principal citadels of Catharism, together with the Château de Cabaret at Lastour which commanded the Haut-Cabardès. For this reason, Simon de Montfort decided to seize it. He besieged Termes with an army of 15,000 men, in spite of the raids from Cabaret which attacked his convoys and especially the one which was bringing his war machines from Carcassonne. Besieged in August, by November the castle had resisted all attacks and the Crusaders, discouraged, were about to raise the siege when they saw the white flag floating above the keep. The Crusaders agreed to allow the besieged to keep their possessions. But that night a heavy rain fell and filled the cisterns: and Raymond de Termes decided not to surrender. Unfortunately, the besieged abused this gift of water: they drank too much and were stricken with dysentery. Simon de Montfort, who had received fresh troops from Lorraine and had succeeded in making a break in the walls, decided on a general assault for the following day. Realising their danger, the besieged made their escape that night along the mountain paths, but they were pursued by the Crusaders and massacred. Raymond de Termes had also made his escape, but, having returned for some precious jewels he had forgotten, he was made prisoner. He died in a dungeon of one of the towers of Carcassonne. On November 23, 1210, Simon de Montfort entered Termes where only the women and the sick remained.

Confiscated, the castle was then given to a French knight, Alain de Roci, but later on, as reward for his services in the Holy Land, Olivier de Termes, companion of Joinville, regained possession of his father's property.

Of this powerful fortress there remains hardly more than a heap of débris. The early *enceintes* enclosed the dependencies of the castle, dwellings, shops and stables which formed a veritable village. The large *enceinte*, above, is better preserved; it consists of a wall measuring 12 feet in thickness with two watch-paths: the one inside for the use of a first rank of archers, the other on the summit behind the crenellation. This circular *enceinte*, whose plan has been revealed by Mademoiselle A. de Pous, was merely flanked by two round towers, tangent to the curtain walls, very close to each other and now razed to the level of the palisade. The opposite angles were supported by buttresses surmounted by watch-towers. The west front was pierced by three large pointed machicolations. The keep, set in the centre and at the summit of the rock, has collapsed.

We rejoin the D. 212, where we soon see, on a steep wooded peak, a veritable peninsula of rock measuring 120 feet in height surrounded by the Orbieu, the fortress of DURFORT, which was the advanced sentinel of the Château de Termes with which it communicated by the intermediary of a signal tower lying above the Gorges of the Orbieu. It extended its length by taking for its walls the edge of the platform on which it sits and which is consolidated by some powerful buttresses. The castle is in ruins, but the angle towers and the corbelled watch-towers can still be seen and different rooms, the chapel and the guard room can be recognised.

As we continue to follow the D. 212, the Défilé de l'Orbieu becomes somewhat wider, and in a turn in the river we see Saint-Martin-du-Puits with its modest Romanesque church whose portal is of 1179, then Saint-Pierre-des-Champs which overlooks the ruins of an ancient fortress in which some dwelling houses have been installed. The village also has a Romanesque church and, in the Grand'Rue, perpendicular to the quay, there can be seen an old house built of cut quarry stone which has preserved its semicircular portal and its twin windows.

We continue along the D. 3 as far as Lagrasse where the Orbieu meets the Alsou, which emerges from its narrow gorges.

LAGRASSE, which was formerly celebrated for its abbey whose vestiges we are going to see, is a very characteristic mediaeval town with the remains of its fortifications. Its old accentuated "ass's back" bridge which formerly had three towers, its old houses reflected in the waters of the Orbieu, the roofs of the monastery, with their rose-coloured tiles, form a delightful *ensemble* rich in memories and legends.

These legends are marvellous: they tell of hermits who lived in this valley which was scantily inhabited before the passage of Charlemagne, of battles with the Saracens and of other romantic events. It seems quite certain, however, that it was Charlemagne who founded the abbey in 778 or at least confirmed its foundation by the Abbot Ninfridus. The Benedictine Abbey of Lagrasse received important donations from Charles the Bald and only recruited among noblemen. It exerted a profound mediating influence between France and Aragon and during the period of the Albigensian Crusade. Reformed in 1665 by the Fathers of Saint-Maur, it was suppressed at the Revolution.

Its constructions, which extend along the left bank of the Orbieu and which date from the 10th to the 18th century, are now divided into two foundations, a home for the aged and the orphanage for the children of holders of military medals, and both may be visited. The monastery was formerly enclosed by ramparts flanked by towers and the Abbot of Levis-Mirepoix had a keep erected, which made it a veritable fortress.

The home for the aged occupies the buildings which enclose the *cour d'honneur* and which were rebuilt in 1745. Three semicircular doors give access to the monastery and a vaulted corridor leads to a monumental staircase whose wrought-iron banister adorned with beautiful shell decoration is a magnificent work of the Regency period. We then enter a cloister which was rebuilt in 1760 and from where a door allows us to enter the church which dates from the 14th century and of which only the nave and the side-aisles remain. A small door leads us to the steeple through the early 10th-century chapel whose three apsidioles can still be seen. In the 14th century, this chapel became one of the arms of the transept of the new edifice. We pass near the cover of a 6th-century sarcophagus and reach the foot of the steeple which dates from the 16th century and which, although uncrowned, still measures 132 feet in height. On a square base there rises an octagonal tower which is flanked at each angle by buttresses crowned by pinnacles. Taking the turreted staircase, we can climb to the summit from where there is a beautiful view over the Orbieu Valley.

The part occupied by the orphanage includes the ancient abbatial building with a cloister of the 11th and 13th centuries whose timbered roof is surmounted by a wooden storey. Facing this cloister is a huge 14th-century room which is an ancient refectory or a cellar. On the first floor is the chapel of the abbot, dated 1290 according to an inscription set above the door, whose walls are covered with frescoes portraying *The Last Judgment* and *The Tree of Jesse*, this latter being formed of vine branches, since we are in the country of vineyards. The paving of enamelled and polychrome stones of the 13th century is remarkable. There still can be seen the monks' dormitory of the 13th and 14th centuries whose roof rests on pointed arches and the room known as the "Guardroom" of the 15th century, which has preserved its beamed ceiling and a beautiful 16th-century fireplace.

We will retrace our steps in order to follow, on the left, the D. 23 which rejoins the N. 613 and at Talairan we will take the D. 323 as far as Coustouge and later the D. 106 and the D. 40 as far as Durban. The village is dominated by the ruins of the Château de Gélon, an important fortress which overlooks the valley of the Berre. It was captured, however, in 1390, by the Infante Don Juan, son of the King of Aragon.

We will follow the N. 611 which ascends the valley of the Berre and at the end of 10 kilometres we will see the path which leads to the ruins of another fortress, the CHATEAU D'AGUILLAR.

It was the last defence point of the French lines of le Perapertuse. From its rocky peak measuring 450 feet in height, it commanded every path of entry to the region and it communicated by means of eye signals with the other fortresses. It consists of a square, 12th-century keep which was completed in the 13th century by a polygonal construction forming a much more powerful keep. Around this retreat rose an *enceinte* flanked by six round towers. A second *enceinte*, of which only the foundations remain, encompassed the Chapel of Saint-Anne, isolated from the castle, and the west flank of the knoll.

At Tuchan, we will take the D. 39 then the D. 12 which descends into the plain and reaches Rivesaltes, the birthplace of Marshal Joffre. We rejoin the N. 9 and reach Perpignan.

FROM PERPIGNAN
TO PUIGCERDA

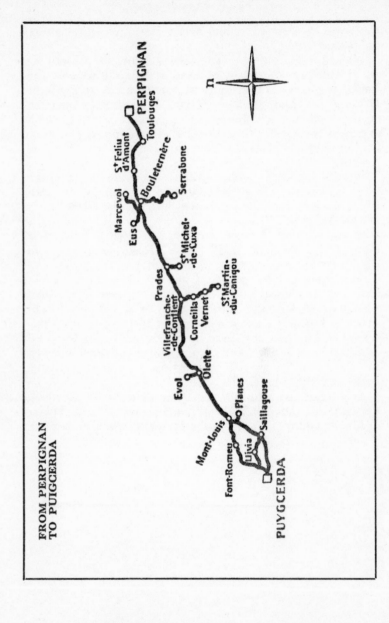

ITINERARY IV

FROM PERPIGNAN TO PUIGCERDA

*Toulouges — Saint-Féliu-d'Amont — Prieuré de
Serrabone — Eus — Abbaye de Saint-Michel-de-Cuxa —
Villefranche-de-Conflent — Corneilla — Abbaye de
Saint-Martin-du-Canigou — Olette — Mont-Louis
— Planès — Puigcerda.*

THE aim of these itineraries starting from Perpignan is
to enable us to discover the Romanesque art of
Roussillon, that pleasant and fertile countryside which
has seen so many vicissitudes over the centuries. The recent
work of such Catalan archaeologists as José Gudiol Ricart
and such French archaeologists as Marcel Durliat, have
greatly enhanced the interest in this and shewn us its
importance. That is why we will leave Perpignan by taking
the N. 612 which we will follow as far as TOULOUGES
where we will see the Romanesque portal of the church. It is
framed by four columns whose capitals support two arch
mouldings with heavy torus having on the exterior a small,
rather archaic frieze containing figures of monsters. One of
the columns and one of the capitals have disappeared. The
three others are adorned with foliage, mermaids and lions,
while the tympanum, which is sculptured in low relief, seems
to represent the struggle of Saint Michael and the Dragon.

We will take the D. 39 which rejoins the N. 116 at le Soler
and we will stop at SAINT-FELIU-D'AMONT whose
Romanesque church, remodelled, has preserved a beautiful
door adorned with 12th-century iron fittings whose framework is remarkable. It is a work of beautiful proportions,
restrained and severe, with its moulding set off by a line of

indentations. On the tympanum, two angels support a medallion depicting a lamb which has been severely damaged.

We will now follow the N. 116 which ascends the valley of the Têt and, 27 kilometres away, at Bouleternère, we will take, on the left, the N. 618, which follows the picturesque Gorges du Boulès. Eight kilometres away, we will find a forester's lodge where we can ask for the keys of the PRIEURE DE SERRABONE, and we will ascend the little road which is accessible to motorists, at any rate those with small cars, in spite of some rather sharp turnings.

Of this ancient priory of the canons of Saint Augustine, lying in a desolate site at the top of the mountain, there remains little more than the church, but it is of extraordinary interest. The nave is of the 11th century, while the transept and the apse, which are flanked by two apsidioles built onto the arms of the transept, date from the 12th century. In the 12th century as well, the nave was flanked by galleries; and at the entrance an entire *ensemble* of arcades has been erected to form a tribune whose sculpture is of outstanding quality. One might have thought that this kind of low chamber resting on six groups of pillars (the three arcades of the entrance are resting against coupled columns) was not destined for this place, nor even for Serrabone, but came from another edifice. It might well have been that it was transported from Saint-Michel-de-Cuxa in 1870. By comparing certain elements of this decoration with those framing the door which at Cuxa leads to the cloister, one may form the conclusion that the door of Cuxa and the tribune of Serrabone belonged to the same building. But it is also possible that the tribune of Cuxa may have inspired the one of Serrabone. The monumental character of the fine historiated capitals and the elegant decorative friezes make this *ensemble* one of the masterpieces of Romanesque sculpture in Roussillon.

The lateral gallery which acts as an ambulatory opens on to the exterior by two series of three arcades resting on twin columns, whose capitals are very differently treated, but are

ÉGLISE DE CORNEILLA-DE-
CONFLENT.

12. ABBAYE DE SAINT-MARTIN-D
CANIC

CLOITRE   DE   SAINT-MICHEL-DE-
CUXA.

14. CLOITRE DE MONASTIR-DEL-
C.

equally beautiful. They are mostly decorated with lions and fantastic animals.

We rejoin the N. 116 and at Marquixanes we take the D. 35 which ascends to the picturesque village of Marcevol, which has preserved its old fortifications and whose Romanesque church, an ancient abbatial building, possesses a door famous for its fittings.

Before returning to the N. 116 we can visit, at the other end of the D. 35 and still on the same bank of the Têt, another old village, that of EUS which, with its two churches, the one Romanesque of the 12th century and the other of the 18th century, and its old ruined castle, is proudly set on its hill.

At Prades, to which the N. 116 next leads us, we can see the Church of Saint-Pierre, which is Gothic with a Romanesque steeple in the Lombard style, decorated with one of those gigantic Baroque altar-pieces which abound in the region. Then we will take, on the left, the D. 27 which leads to the ABBAYE DE SAINT-MICHEL-DE-CUXA.

If this Benedictine abbey, one of the most famous in Roussillon, was founded in 878, a community already existed on this site from before 860. An early Church of Saint-Germain, erected in 866, was rebuilt in 953. The large Church of Saint-Michel, constructed in 941, was rebuilt in 956 and 975 during the time of the Abbot Watinus or Guarin. In a sermon addressed to Oliba, Bishop of Vich, Abbot of Cuxa and Ripoll, the monk Garsias gave an enthusiastic description, stating that there was a nave with side-aisles, that its pillars were as massive as the wall sections, that the stones were of great dimensions and carefully carved. He also praised its carpentry and its striking ornamentation; that is to say, the frescoes which covered its walls.

According to the famous Catalan archaeologist, J. Puig i Cadafalch, there perhaps date from this period the remains of the paintings which decorate the opening of five windows and which, he thinks, are earlier than the transformation that would have occurred between 1009 and 1040, when the

G

chevet was amplified and the ciborium was erected. It is regrettable that, during the work which was undertaken recently, an ignorant labourer damaged the most interesting of these paintings, a bird of Sassanid type within large concentric circles.

Although remodelled at different times, the choir especially was rebuilt in the 16th century, and although the church was long left in a state of abandonment, it has preserved most of its early design with the thick courses of heavy pillars which separate the nave from the side-aisles and its walls made with small stones. Certain architects and archaeologists contest its Mozarabic character, which none the less cannot be in doubt. Its horseshoe arches, without imposts, resting directly on the foundation wall, are arranged in the Cordovan fashion with an extended semi-circle whose stones are arranged vertically as well as horizontally. The nave, which is large, measures almost 30 feet. It is longer than the side-aisles, as is the case at Lourosa in Portugal. Two oven-shaped, deep, chapels have been built on to each transept arm. The very long and rectangular choir was enclosed, later on, by an ambulatory in the form of corridors. On the corridor at the far end there opened three chapels containing the altars which had been erected on the tombs of the martyrs Valentinus, Flamidianus and Nazarius whose bones had been preserved.

In the outcome, in the 17th century, all these additions had been demolished and had made way for a single chapel behind the choir.

As a Mozarabic church, Saint-Michel-de-Cuxa is extremely interesting, for it is the sole example in Roussillon; but in Catalonia there are several small buildings which resemble it, like San Miguel de Olerdula, San Quirce de Pedret and Santa Maria de Marquet, all from the 10th century.

Another two-storey circular church, Saint-Germain which also dates from the 10th century, is found in front of the principal church. Of the upper church, the basic structures have recently been found: a semicircular apse and some projecting niches opening on to the circular church. The lower church is intact with its annular nave encircling an enormous pillar. It is fronted by a small straight nave of a somewhat later date.

Finally there were two steeples at either extremity of the transept arms; the one has collapsed, but the other is still standing. It is a handsome steeple in the Lombard style whose base ought to be reinforced by a more solid mass of masonry.

At the door entrance leading to the cloister there has been reset a beautiful marble decoration which was originally part of the baldachin in the interior and which was described by the monk Carsias in his famous letter of 1042. When the monastery was despoiled in the 19th century, some of the elements of this baldachin were reset around the door of the monastery and others were taken to the United States. It was thought that some had been transported to Serrabone and utilized with the capitals and columns which came from one of the two cloisters. The elements placed around the door of the monastery have been reset here. The same decorative elements used at Serrabone are rediscovered here: indented mouldings, scroll work and rosettes sculptured in a similar marble.

After allowing the monastery to be pillaged for a century, the Fine Arts Administration has decided to save what remains and even to rebuild two galleries of the great cloister with the elements which have remained in the region, in front of the church of Prades and in several private dwelling places. This is a courageous initiative which deserves praise. Unfortunately, the remains of the columns and capitals purchased at a low price by American breakers-up are now in the Cloisters Museum in New York. It is worth remembering that Grey Barnard in 1913 purchased the two galleries which had been reset in the courtyard of a bathing establishment at Prades. There was great concern, the Fine Arts Administration had granted a subsidy, an action of classification had been instituted: but, for want of 3,000 francs and on account of the War, the cloister was shipped to New York, while the large basin which adorned the centre emigrated to Philadelphia.

The capitals which once more are in place at Cuxa are among the most remarkable pieces of sculpture in Roussillon. Some have acanthus leaves which are stylized in a large and monumental manner, others lions and monsters, arranged with an absolutely astonishing decorative sense.

Monks have once again taken possession of the monastery, at least of the buildings which are still standing, such as the abbatial building of the 16th century.

We will retrace our steps and, shortly before reaching Prades, we will take, on the left, a small road which rejoins the N. 116 a short distance before Ria.

Five kilometres farther on, we reach the walls of the small fortified town of VILLEFRANCHE-DE-CONFLENT.

I confess that nothing enchants me more than an ancient little town slumbering within its walls and preserving only the happiest and most charming recollections of the past: symbols and attributes which have lost, not only what was magical and fearful, but also what was reassuring both for this life and the hereafter, the fortified *enceinte*, the castle and the church.

These are no longer authoritarian buildings—the church is so small!—so that they no longer frighten us, they no longer impose themselves on us like the authoritarian buildings of our own time: the school, the barracks, the prison; they are no more than a gracious and fairylike *décor* which incites us to reverie.

Unfortunately, the number of towns in France which have preserved their fortifications can be counted on the fingers of both hands: Carcassonne, Saint-Malo, Avignon, Aigues-Mortes, Guérande, Brouage, Provins. . . . People generally forget Villefranche-de-Conflent, this small town of 600 inhabitants lost in the valley of the Têt at its junction with a brook which descends from Corneilla.

A bastion was founded there in 1095. Its walls, if they do not go that far back, at least date from the Middle Ages—the Tour du Diable, for example, was built from 1431 to 1454—

but they were remodelled in the 16th century and perfected by Vauban who, not far from there, further up the valley of the Têt built those of Mont-Louis.

The utilitarian character of these fortifications enabled them to come down to us intact. We should be happy, for, thanks to them, the small town greets us with all its ancient grace and in the full radiance of its picturesqueness.

The valley of the Têt, from Mont-Louis to Prades, is quite beautiful with its foaming river, its wild gorges and its mountains with their rocky ridges. On one of them, the Belloch, has been built the fort which overlooks Villefranche with, below, a much older castle connected to the small stronghold by a winding path, an underground staircase and an old bridge, the Pont Saint-Pierre, which dates from the 13th century but whose fortifications were rebuilt in the 17th century.

All this creates a truly astonishing *ensemble* in a rocky setting with meadows bordering the river. As for the town, it remains enclosed by its fortifications divided by watch-towers which are connected by a partly covered watch-path. Here and there rise the mediaeval towers, the ruins of the early *enceintes*, some round, others square, generally dating from the 14th and 15th centuries.

The town is formed by two parallel streets which extend from the Porte d'Espagne to the Porte de France. The houses are ancient and of the Catalan type, the majority dating from the 14th, 15th and 16th centuries. They have a severe aspect with little artistic character, but it is true that many have been modernised. Some, however, with their Gothic windows have preserved their entire flavour. One of them is especially characteristic with its two semicircular arches, its indented lintel and its fine slender columns.

The church dates from the 12th century, but it was remodelled in the 14th century and is rather curious with its high crenellated tower and its two naves of unequal height, with pointed barrel-vaulting, without cross ribs, flanked by Gothic lateral chapel and communicating by four arches of varied width, one being especially large.

The two portals with their historiated capitals and their arch mouldings are among the richest in the region. In front of the church there is a charming square planted with trees with, on one side, the crenellated tower and, on the other, the steeple which is surmounted by a stone spire, the top having been truncated.

Our own epoch has intervened at Conflent merely to suppress the moats and the *glacis* of the ramparts, so that the road passes directly beneath them. The chains of the draw-bridge, before the very simple gates, owed no doubt to Vauban, hang to the ground. But this is a small evil! The cosy little town, with its torrent, its rocky mountain *décor* and its castle is one of those pure jewels of the past of which a few still remain on our soil, far from the great urban centres and beyond the industrial regions.

We should not leave Conflent without visiting, two kilo-metres away, after climbing the Gorge du Riu Major, the beautiful Romanesque Church of CORNEILLA-DE-CONFLENT which dates from the 12th century and which is very well preserved.

In the 11th century, Corneilla was the centre of the private domain of the Counts of Cerdagne. Guillaume-Jourdan in 1097 founded a convent of the canons of Saint-Augustin to which he granted many privileges. The canons erected the church which we see, by utilizing the steeple of the ancient edifice. It has three naves with a large transept on to which open five oven-shaped apses whose principal one is circular on the exterior, while the others terminate in a straight wall.

First of all, there is the admirable crenellated façade in white marble with its richly-sculptured portal framed by six columns and surmounted by a tympanum decorated with an admirable *Virgin in Glory* dressed in a robe of long folds and worshipped by two kneeling angels; the 12th-century folding panels with their fittings; the tower built of small stones with fine arcading; the magnificent decoration of the apse with its windows with slender columns and its ornamental arcades with modillions; and finally the nave with its heavy square pillars and the pointed barrel-vaulting without cross ribs, while the side-aisles have quarter-circle vaulting.

The Church of Corneilla contains several interesting works of art, such as the tombstone of Ermengaud de Lupia and a *Virgin* in carved wood, but especially its altar-piece of Maître Jacques Cascall, dated 1345, sculptured in high relief, one of the most interesting works of Catalan art of this period.

We will continue along the N. 116A which passes through Vernet and as far as Casteil. From there we will climb on foot the rocky path which in 35 minutes leads us to the ABBAYE DE SAINT-MARTIN-DU-CANIGOU which doubly deserves our attention: first because of its extraordinary position in a grandiose mountain setting, on a spur of rock, at the foot of the Canigou, and also because of the exceptional interest of its pre-Romanesque architecture of an archaic quality which is still barbarian.

The abbey was founded immediately after the year 1000 by the Count Guifred de Cerdagne who professed himself of the Order in 1025 after the death of his second wife, and died there in 1049. The church was consecrated in 1009 and in 1026. It dates therefore from the 11th century and was built by a monk named Sclua who came from the monastery of Saint-Michel-de-Cuxa. We can compare it to the ancient church of la Cluse which we shall see in the next itinerary.

Like this church, the Basilica of Saint-Martin-du-Canigou has three naves which are preceded by a narthex. It is built of small size stones with material from the mountain, without a transept, and has barrel-vaulting. But its originality stems from its strange portly columns whose cubic capitals, which are extremely splayed and without abacus, present a very archaic flat decoration.

Beneath this church there exists a second one which has the same surface area and which also has three naves, but the bays are twice the number of those in the upper church and the barrel-vaulting is on cross ribs except in the east section which has groined vaulting.

The steeple, pierced on the ground floor by a corridor

which was the entrance to the abbey, is square, massive and suitable to defence. It recalls those of Elne and of several Catalan churches of the same period.

In 1428 it was overthrown by an earthquake which destroyed also a part of the church and the monastic buildings. The damage was then repaired, but the monastery declined into a bad state during the centuries which followed and, suppressed before the Revolution in 1783, it slowly fell into ruin.

When in 1902 it was decided to restore the monastery, three-quarters of the vaulting of the upper nave collapsed. But, if the church has been faithfully restored, the same does not hold true for the cloister of which only three sides remained standing. Since it had probably been raised by one storey in the 12th century, the fourth side was erected with the capitals belonging to this gallery. They are moreover remarkable for their vegetal and animal decoration. They are related to those of Saint-Michel-de-Cuxa, but appear of a less perfect technique. They are rich in extraordinary monsters. Different interesting sculptures, especially some 14th-century tombstones of different abbots of the monastery, have been rediscovered. But the most impressive one is that which the founder of the abbey had dug in the rock himself, surmounted by an 11th-century inscription. It was flanked by two other tombs, also dug in the rock, those of his two wives, the Countess Guisla and Countess Elizabeth.

We should climb to the rock overlooking the monastery for a view which displays its entire beauty. The constructions embrace the rounded ridge of the peak on which they have been raised, forming a block above the precipice, surrounded by chestnut trees and broken stones.

The monasteries lying in even the most gradiose or wildest sites, like Mont Saint-Michel or Baume-les-Messieurs, are surrounded by pleasant landscape as compared to the wild *décor* of Saint-Martin-du-Canigou.

We pass through Vernet-les-Bains whose sulphur springs have made it a small but pleasant watering place. The old town no longer has any important character, its church contains nothing remarkable and the castle, which was dismantled by the Prince de Conti in the 17th century, has become private property.

We will return to Villefranche-de-Conflent where we will continue to follow the N. 116 which ascends the valley of the Têt which becomes increasingly wild. We pass through Serdinya whose church has preserved a 15th-century vermeil reliquary and two handsome 14th-century Primitives, in front of the two crenellated towers of the Château de Labastide, and we reach OLETTE which stretches out in a long street on the mountain side. On a terrace there can be seen some Romanesque capitals which supposedly come from the Château d'Evol; and this makes us want to climb to this picturesque village lying two kilometres above Olette.

The church, which is Romanesque, also has two fine altar-pieces of the School of Roussillon, the one depicting the Life of Saint John the Baptist and dated 1330, the other dated 1578. Higher up we reach the small Chapel of Saint-Etienne and the ruins of the castle.

After Olette, the road enters the narrow and rocky Défilé des Graus, passes not far from les Bains de Canaveilles, which is in a very picturesque site at the bottom of a fissure in the mountain where the Têt flows, then we pass through the oasis of Thuès-les-Bains with its springs of hot water, its gardens and its Gorges de la Carença, a narrow canyon which, if we so wish, we can ascend on foot as far as the Lac de la Carença in an astonishing mountain site near the Spanish border.

The valley becomes increasingly wild, the road makes a winding ascent and we reach the *glacis* of the fortified town of MONT-LOUIS lying on a narrow plateau which commands the different cols leading to the high valleys of the Têt, the Aude and the Sègre, which form the country of the Cerdagne, now popular with holiday-makers with its woods, lakes and trees. The strategic strength of this place inspired Vauban to erect a fortress here.

The ramparts which he erected have remained intact, but trees have been planted on the *glacis*. The village, which we enter through the Porte de France, consists of eight straight streets laid out at right angles, with an 18th-century church in the main square. An esplanade separates the town from the citadel, which we enter through a gate with a pediment which is surmounted by a bell-tower. It is all characteristic of the restrained and massive architecture of the fortresses created by Vauban; this example dates from 1692.

From Mont-Louis we can reach Puigcerda either by way of the N. 618 which passes through Font-Romeu, Angoustrine, Ur and the Tour de Carol, or by way of the N. 116 which passes through Saillagouse. But before doing so, we should not miss seeing the little church of Planès whose design has perplexed archaeologists. It is an equilateral triangle in which a circumference has been inscribed which acts as the base for a cupola on whose sides there are three projecting apses. The rough, unpolished style of the edifice has given rise to the thought that it might be a *marabout* (shrine) dating from the time of Moorish occupation, but it is more generally thought to be a church inspired perhaps by the symbol of the Trinity and dating no later than the 15th century.

Moreover, in addition to the two very picturesque routes which I have just indicated to travel from Mont-Louis to Puigcerda, I will also point out the variant by way of the Spanish enclave of Llivia, after leaving Saillagouse. LLIVIA was the Roman *Julia Livia* and the capital of the Cerdagne until the 11th century.

This small town has remained Spanish by reason of a grammatical subtlety. The Treaty of the Pyrenees in 1659 ceded to France 33 Cerdange "villages", but Llivia having the title of "town" remained Spanish.

Its narrow streets bordered by balconied houses are huddled at the foot of a hill around a fortified church whose porch is flanked by two huge towers, pierced by fall-traps, and a castle of which nothing remains but vestiges and whose walls are of Roman origin.

The last French town, which was formerly called La Guinguette, received the name of Bourg-Madame in honour

of Madame Royale when in 1815 the Duc d'Angoulême
re-entered France along this route.

PUIGCERDA, which was the capital of Cerdagne, is a
very lively place whose Plaza Mayor with its arcaded houses
has a great deal of charm.

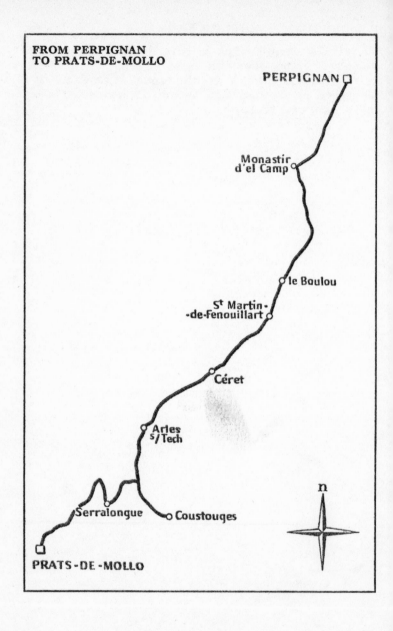

FROM PERPIGNAN
TO PRATS-DE-MOLLO

PERPIGNAN

Monastir
d'el Camp

le Boulou

St Martin-
-de-Fenouillart

Céret

Arles
s/Tech

Serralongue   Coustouges

PRATS-DE-MOLLO

n

ITINERARY V

FROM PERPIGNAN TO PRATS-DE-MOLLO

Prieuré de Monastir del Camp — Le Boulou — Saint-Martin-du-Fenouillar — La Cluse — Céret — Arles-sur-Tech — Coustouges — Serralongue — Prats-de-Mollo.

WE leave Perpignan by way of the N. 9 which is the direct route for Barcelona. Eleven kilometres away at Rameylbes, we take, on the right, the D. 37A which leads us to Villemolaque where we will take the D. 2. A kilometre farther on, a plaque on the right indicates the ancient **PRIEURE DE MONASTIR DEL CAMP**. It is private property, but a visit can be arranged.

In the midst of vineyards we will find a two-storey rectangular building (the second storey being a later addition) with, on the first storey, some beautiful twin windows and a crenellated tower on one angle. A slightly-pointed portal, which is flanked on each side by two columns having historiated capitals, leads to the single nave church. In the centre of the building there is a charming cloister whose fine slender columns support trefoiled arches which have great elegance. The *ensemble* dates from the 13th century. A church built by the Rocaburti was given at the close of the 11th century to the Bishop of Elne who established a community of regular canons of Saint Augustine there.

It is a typical and well preserved example of these priories which were destined for a restricted community. The cloister with its palm trees is delightful.

We rejoin the N. 9 and at **LE BOULOU** we will visit the church for its fine Romanesque portal which has a very restrained but charming decoration with the pretty frieze resting on corbels. We recognise the work of the Master of Cabestany whom we have already met at Saint-Hilaire and whose famous tympanum we will see in the next itinerary. He has proved himself especially skilful here by designing in this narrow frieze several Biblical themes in an art which is perfectly suitable to them.

The interior contains some fine 15th-century Primitives and a large Baroque altar-piece.

We will rejoin the N. 9 and three kilometres farther on we will see, on the right, a plaque which indicates the small path leading to the little church of SAINT-MARTIN-DU-FENOUILLAR, whose frescoes are so famous that copies of them may be seen at the Fresco Museum of the Palais de Chaillot in Paris.

They date from the first quarter of the 12th century and decorate the two walls and the vaulting of a very narrow nave of a small edifice whose architecture perhaps goes back to the 10th or 11th century. The *Pantocrator* has its place on the vaulting where also *The Assumption of the Virgin* has been painted, while on the two walls the cycle of the Childhood of Christ and the theme of the Old Men of the Apocalypse form two superimposed records which are separated by winding bands. The substructure is decorated with a drapery forming festoons and enriched by *cabochons*.

These paintings in very subdued tones, in an excellent state of preservation, are among the most remarkable in Roussillon and are related to numerous Catalan frescoes which have been discovered in the small churches on the other side of the Pyrenees and taken to the Barcelona Museum. There is the same force of expression, the same rough and savage energy of certain faces whose prototypes appear in *The Apocalypse* of Gerona.

Taking the N. 618 shortly afterwards, on the right, we reach Céret, but before this we can do the three kilometres along the N. 9 which separate us from l'Ecluse in order to visit the little Church of la Cluse which also has some frescoes similar to those of Saint-Martin-de-Fenouillar.

L'ECLUSE or, rather, la Cluse or les Cluses, takes its

name from the *cluses* and defiles, which the road follows as it
leads from France into Spain. This route already existed in
Roman times, as is witnessed by different vestiges which we
see at the bottom of the ravine and which lead to a deep
opening between two Roman walls. Here was the fortified
gate which barred the *Via Domitia*. This gate was commanded by two forts crowning the peaks which rise on each
side of the defile. The east peak is occupied by the ruins
of a fortress in whose *enceinte* we find the Romanesque
Church of la Cluse and a few houses which constitute the
hamlet of l'Ecluse-Haute. The Roman fort, a rectangle
flanked by square towers, is still recognisable above the
church on the summit of the peak.

The other peak is also occupied by a fort, but a much
larger one, whose north section is Roman. It was probably
enlarged during the Visigothic period. It is thought that it
was on the west peak that in 70 B.C. Pompey erected the
monument commemorating the victorious termination of the
war in Spain and which is called the Trophy of Pompey.

The Church of la Cluse, which is mentioned in several
documents during the 10th century, has three narrow naves
which terminate in three apses. The barrel-vaulting is
gathered beneath a single saddle-roof accentuated on the
façade by a large gable. They are separated by four arcades
and fronted by a narthex which is now in ruins. The window
which opens on the pediment presents a trapezoidal capital
with interlaced design. This little church is the type frequently found in this region and is related to the Churches
of Santa Margarita de Tossa de Montbuy, San Miguel de
Campmajor and Castelloir.

We come back as far as the N. 618 which we will now
follow as far as CERET, a small town which is not lacking in
charm, where we should see the old bridge over the Tech,
known as the Pont du Diable, which was built from 1321 to
1341 and which, in spite of important restoration in the
18th century, is one of the most beautiful ancient bridges in
France. The bold single arch in the form of a curve creates
an admirable design.

We then join the N. 115 which passes through **Amélie-les-Bains** where the modern baths have little in common with the ancient thermals. Four kilometres farther on, we reach ARLES-SUR-TECH which owes its origin to its Benedictine abbey, mentioned as early as 802.

The abbey, consecrated in 1046, was an edifice of the Provençal type with three naves which in the 12th century underwent profound modifications. The apse was placed at the opposite end to that which is usual, namely at the west, the pillars were doubled and the vaulting rebuilt. A new consecration took place in 1157. The façade, decorated with Lombard bands, is very simple. It is pierced merely by a single rectangular door surmounted by a small cross enclosing, between an interlacing design, like a Byzantine ivory, the *Christ in Majesty* set off by the symbols of the Evangelists, while there are two animals rampant above a framework. A small window somewhat higher is enclosed by a pretty decoration. Another window, no less richly decorated, has been transported to a private dwelling. All these decorations are related to the School of the sculptors of Saint-Génis-des-Fontaines.

On the left of the façade, there still can be seen a 5th-century marble sarcophagus, the tomb of Saints Abdon and Sennen who, it seems, had the ability to produce, at any time, a limpid water which was distributed to pilgrims. Above, the very handsome figure of a man with his arms crossed over his chest forms the funerary monument of the Chevalier Guillaume Gaucelme, who died in 1210.

The interior has three naves with pointed vaults without cross ribs and semicircular vaulting in the side-aisles. In the first chapel, on the right, there is a very rich wood-gilt altarpiece of the 17th century, which contains the relics of the two martyred Saints, Abdon and Sennen. There are also some 15th-century silver busts, and some beautiful Romanesque frescoes which M. Ponsich has recently discovered behind the tribune.

A door on the left leads to a large Gothic cloister which is quite charming with its elegant arcades resting on twin

ATHÉDRALE D'ELNE.

AINT-ANDRÉ-DE-SORÈDE, PORTAIL.

slender columns. It has a lean-to roof and was built between 1261 and 1303.

At Arles we can also visit the Church of Saint-Sauveur whose Gothic nave is flanked by a beautiful Romanesque tower: and, if we are fortunate enough to visit at festival time, we may see pretty girls dressed in the local costume riding richly-harnessed mules and the *juglars* leading the inhabitants in a dance of their traditional *sardañas*.

The route continues to ascend the valley of the Tech. The green Vallespir is very beautiful with its chestnut, its cork-oak, its green oak trees and its fern. After five kilometres we will take, on the left, the D. 3, the side road which leads us up to Coustouges, then later the D. 44, the further side road which takes us to Serralongue and Lamanère.

These routes are worth taking for the fine panoramic views they offer and also for a few edifices which are not without interest. SERRALONGUE is dominated by a pretty Romanesque church and Lamanère by the three towers of Cabrens or the Château de Serralongue of the 13th and 14th centuries. But we should especially see the very curious Romanesque church of COUSTOUGES.

Founded by the Pope Damascus about 370, it was destroyed by the Arabs, then rebuilt in the 9th century. The present church which was consecrated in 1142 consists of a nave, fronted by a narthex added afterwards, and a semi-circular choir much lower. We enter the nave by a magnificent portal which is flanked by four columns, two with spiral fluting, whose capitals are adorned with foliage and scroll work. The semicircular archivolt consists of a torus and five rows of moulding adorned with pine needles, male heads, animals, interlacing, flowers and garlands.

The nave has three bays with pointed vaulting on cross ribs which rest on pilasters. Three arcades, the pointed one in the centre much larger, the two others narrow with raised arches, rest on two heavy short and thick-set columns of red sandstone with heavy cubic capitals. They separate the nave from the choir. This is divided into three sections; the lateral sections form chapels and their ogival-vaulting has

H

ribs which rest on consoles embedded in the walls. The choir properly speaking, which we enter by several steps, has semi-circular vaulting which is joined to the oven-shaped vaulting of the apse. On the exterior the fine apse has a pretty cornice with blind arcades and a beautiful semicircular window which is enclosed by slender columns supporting an archivolt with a flower ornamentation. A high three-storeyed square tower built on to the south side of the nave is pierced by semicircular windows which are paired on the last storey. It is crenellated and part of a defence system which included the apse, which is pierced by loopholes. Thus it was com-manded by a captain in the 14th century.

We rejoin the N. 115 and after the Défilé de la Baillanouse we reach the very picturesque little town of PRATS-DE-MOLLO, an ancient fortress which has preserved its ramparts in Vauban's style. They date from 1673 and are pierced by four gates and flanked by watch-towers.

The church, also fortified, was rebuilt from 1649 to 1681 after the annexation of Roussillon, but a part of the walls of the Romanesque church and the crenellated steeple of the 13th century, surmounted in 1634 by a pyramid, have been preserved. The door fittings are Romanesque and the interior contains several 17th-century altar-pieces.

A vaulted underground passage from the church and a fortified path lead to the fort of la Garde, built by Vauban around a 13th-century watch-tower on the mountain overlooking the town.

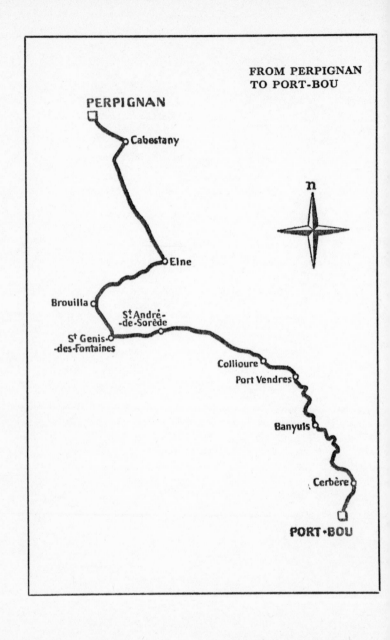

FROM PERPIGNAN
TO PORT-BOU

n

PERPIGNAN

Cabestany

Elne

Brouilla

St André-
-de-Sorède

St Genis-
-des-Fontaines

Collioure

Port Vendres

Banyuls

Cerbère

PORT·BOU

ITINERARY VI
FROM PERPIGNAN TO PORT-BOU

Cabestany — Elne — Brouilla — Saint-Génis-des-Fontaines — Saint-André-de-Sorède — Collioure — Port-Vendres — Port-Bou.

WE will leave Perpignan by the D. 22 in order to visit, four kilometres away, the Church of CABESTANY whose 12th-century tympanum is famous for its sculptures representing *The Resurrection, The Assumption* and *The Replacing of the Virgin's Girdle*. Its force, its expression, and its exaggerations—the unusual length of the hands—its barbarian, immature character, all contribute to make it a very surprising work of art. Some, like Marcel Robin, have wondered if there were not some element of Catharism concealed beneath these sarcastic and parodical attitudes, and the effeminate Orientalism of the Virgin with her slits of eyes whom he compares to a lost houri. But this would be going too far; it has, on the contrary, a tormented Baroque quality, an exasperated expressionism such as is fervently admired today.

According to certain archaeologists like Jose Guidol Ricart, the Master of Cabestany was not from Roussillon. Other works have been attributed to him, like the Portal of le Boulou and the sarcophagus of Saint-Hilaire, which we have seen in our previous itineraries, a door and some capitals at the Church of Rieux-Minervois in the Aude, the marble *Lamb* of the tympanum of San Pedro de Roda in Catalonia and that of Errondo in the Navarre Pyrenees, now transported to some American collection, also the figure of the musician of the tribune of Cuxa, now in the Cloisters Museum in New York. We recognise him also at the Abbey of Saint-Pons de Thomières, at San Esteve de Bas and at San Pedro de Besalú.

We rejoin the N. 114 which we will follow as far as ELNE where we will find the ancient Cathedral of Sainte-Eulalie, which is one of the most important Romanesque edifices in the South of France, together with its cloister whose capitals are among the masterpieces of Roussillon sculpture. The barbarians who have dismembered so many admirable cloisters in this region have not entirely spared the one of Elne; the upper gallery is in the hands of an antique dealer who should be ashamed of possessing a part of such an admirable *ensemble*. But the stone-plundering antique dealers are no more ashamed of their evil doings than are the directors of the American museums who profit by them.

Elne is the ancient *Illiberis* which was founded by the Celtiberians. Hannibal camped within its walls during his march on Rome. Ruined by the invasions, it was rebuilt during the 4th century by the Empress Helena who gave it her name and in 571 it became the seat of a bishopric. But in 1602 this was transferred to its rival city Perpignan, which had increased in prosperity while Elne had declined.

Today, whereas Perpignan has a population of 72,000 inhabitants, Elne has no more than 4,000 and slumbers on its hill, the high town still being enclosed for the most part by its ancient ramparts flanked by towers.

The Cathedral of Sainte-Eulalie was built in the middle of the 11th century, following the plan of Provençal Romanesque churches, without an ambulatory. It consists of a nave of seven bays flanked by two side-aisles and terminating in an apse between two apsidioles. On the south side, on the side opposite the cloister, a row of chapels was later erected.

There is no triforium. The semicircular vaulting is slightly pointed above the arcades and the arch of the cross ribs is somewhat elliptical. The pillars on the east are separated into pilasters with engaged columns, the bases are crude and the capitals archaic. The *ensemble* gives an impression of strength and restraint.

The façade, crenellated later, has a beautiful bronze colour and is flanked by two towers also crenellated, which are in the Lombard style. Only the one at the right is ancient. It is a veritable keep in which the inhabitants took refuge in 1285 when Philip the Bold captured the town. They were, just the same, all massacred.

The cloister was built in the second quarter of the 12th century, as is witnessed by the sepulchre of Guillaume Jorda, who occupied the episcopal seat of Elne from 1171 to 1186 and who began the cloister about 1175. The south gallery adjoining the church is the most ancient and its capitals are remarkable. Next is the west gallery. For those of the north and east, the 14th-century image-makers took their inspiration from the scenes represented by their predecessors, but the School of Roussillon was then in complete decline. The design of each bay includes, between two thick rectangular pillars, three semicircular arcades resting on two pairs of twin slender columns. Large historiated friezes adorn the pillars, while the capitals are decorated with historiated subjects or fantastic animals.

The vaults on the wall side rest on rectangular panels sculptured in half-relief in the 14th century and representing scenes in the life of Christ. Moreover, here and there, in addition to the recumbent figure of the founder, there have been discovered some tombs of bishops of the 12th and 13th centuries and three 6th-century sarcophagi adorned with foliage. It is while admiring these masterpieces of mediaeval utilitarian sculpture that we can understand the confusion of our present-day artists who have no other outlet than the isolated statue to be placed in a public square or a garden, in the vestibule of an apartment or on a mantelpiece. Before endeavouring first to be good workmen, they must at any price show the marks of their genius and for one who is truly an artist, how many others are merely worthy practitioners? But they want to be geniuses and refuse to shape a capital or sculpture a tombstone.

These harmonious cloisters, such as that of Elne, offer us an inspiring lesson if we care to take it: they could be the setting for meditation for those who can still think for themselves in our noisy and dangerous traffic-filled cities. But are we anxious that this sort of thing should survive? It is so much simpler to govern men who no longer respond to anything except passwords and slogans and who, between the factory, the radio, the television, the cinema, the newspaper and the stadium, no longer have occasion to find in themselves any individual thought.

Taking the D. 40 we will reach BROUILLA where we will find a modest Romanesque church dating from the second half of the 12th century, which is related to an entire group of Roussillon churches which have been very well studied by Marcel Durliat. This one is a single-nave edifice with five bays. Two semicircular chapels, which open on to the last bay which is larger than the others, together with the apse, give the chevet a trefoiled design.

The portal in white marble is set against the south façade and crowned by a cornice with palmettes. The tympanum is uniform and without mouldings, so also are the relieving arch and lintel.

"The exterior arch", says Marcel Durliat, "consists of two concave mouldings, the one adorned with laurel leaves, the other with a garland of palmettes and rosettes held in a diamond-shaped design. These are the motifs of the ancient door of the abbatial building at Cuxa. Interlacing designs are developed on the torus, as at Villefranche-de-Conflent and Serrabone. The capitals reproduce also the motif of the small door of Villefranche. The entire sculptured *ensemble* is therefore closely related to the art of Serrabone and Cuxa".

From Brouilla we will take the D. 2 which leads us to Saint-Génis-des-Fontaines where we will have the bitter pleasure of counting the vestiges which have survived the spoliation of the ancient ABBAYE DE SAINT-GENIS-DES-FONTAINES. I have already told of the passionate interest evoked by the Romanesque art in Roussillon. Here was not only the most complete *ensemble* of this architecture and sculpture, but also together with that of Saint-Michel-de-Cuxa one of the oldest; yet people have managed to pillage it and scatter its pieces. The lintel, which is still in place on the portal of the Church of Saint-Génis-des-Fontaines, dates from 1021, the oldest dated sculpture in France. If it were not a part of the church wall; if it had been, for instance, in the cloister, it would now no doubt be in Philadelphia.

In the early 11th century there was a workshop of sculptors at Saint-Génis connected both with the marble industry of the Pyrenees in the 6th and 7th centuries and with the Mozarabic art which was then manifesting itself in Catalonia at San Pedro de Roda. At this time there was also felt the influence of the ivories of the Carolingian tradition, and that of the East through the medium of Cordovan art. We have seen that at Saint-Michel-de-Cuxa the horseshoe arches of the church which were not trimmed are similar to those of the Mosque of Al-Hakem. The ornamental arcades of the lintel of Saint-Génis, like those of the lintel of Sorède which we will shortly see, are elliptical. At Saint-Génis they enclose six Apostles, at Sorède four Apostles and two Seraphim frame a *Christ in Majesty* in an almond-shaped glory held by two kneeling angels with large wings. The one of Saint-Génis is dated by an inscription from the 24th year of the reign of Robert II, son of Hugues Capet, that is to say, from 1020 to 1021. Different other sculptures, including two tombstones, are placed in the wall of the façade on either side of the door.

The abbey was founded in the early 9th century. The lintel of the door has been re-used in the present church which was consecrated in 1153. This consists of a single nave with three bays and a transept on to which three oven-shaped apsidioles open. The nave has pointed barrel-vaulting on semicircular cross ribs, while the transept has semicircular vaulting which is perpendicular to the nave. The two square steeples are from the 16th or 17th centuries. The base of the south steeple is circular and may be a vestige of the early church.

It is regrettable that the façade has been given such a horrible coating of plaster. As for the abbatial buildings, they have been terribly disfigured and the cloister has been demolished. It was of marble and consisted of four angle pillars and four middle ones connected by some arcading,

resting on isolated columns whose capitals are decorated
with monsters, eagles, serpents and foliage. Some are
historiated. It is contemporary with the present church and
was sufficiently advanced in 1197 for the Abbot Raymond II
to be buried there, near the door of the church. There has
been an attempt to distinguish the work of two workshops in
the capitals of the cloister, some from the second half of the
12th century, the others from the early 13th century.

This magnificent cloister was shared among four inheritors.
Three have sold the arcades and the sculptures which were
part of their share. Only one has refused and has built
a dwelling-place on the part of the cloister which he kept. In
order to see these arcades, we must therefore enter the house
and they form the angle of the room in which we enter.
Three other arcades are in the Louvre Museum. But, to see
the rest, we would have to go to Philadelphia.

I am not going to speak of what the Americans have taken.
They are not affected in any way by the idea of returning it;
which also holds true for Cuxa. They have gone so far as to
refuse Mme. Copper-Royer, the present owner of the
Château de Biron, her request to have a cast made of the
Pietà which was sold in 1904 by the owner and transported
to the Cloisters Museum in New York. The original was
clandestinely sold by an unworthy owner and its loss is
hopelessly prejudicial to the remarkable *ensemble* of the
Chapel of Biron. They have even refused to give a museum
conservator photographs of the capitals of Saint-Génis-des-
Fontaines, which he needed for a study.

Even if we disregard the sculptures which are now in the
Philadelphia Museum, we can still go some way towards
reconstituting the Cloister of Saint-Génis-des-Fontaines, if
the Fine Arts Administration will take the initiative.

Not far from Saint-Génis, at le Mas Cabanes, we can visit
the ancient church of an abbatial domain at the far end of the
Allée des Moines. It has a nave and a transept whose arms
are less elevated than those of the nave. The apse is in ruins.
There are four handsome capitals in white marble belonging
to the transept which, so Marcel Durliat has stated, are

similar to certain capitals of Saint-Martin-du-Canigou, with
its crude masks above foliage or the figure embracing the
neck of two eagles.

Taking the N. 618 we will do the four kilometres which
separate us from SAINT-ANDRE-DE-SOREDE where we
will find another Romanesque Benedictine church contemporary with that of Saint-Génis-des-Fontaines. The
entrance door is surmounted by a lintel imitated from the
one we have just seen at Saint-Génis, but the *ensemble* of the
decoration is much more complete. The lintel is surmounted
by a tympanum decorated with a cross and higher up by a
very remarkable window framed by a marble decoration of
leaves and interlacing design, and by its frieze on which the
symbols of the Evangelists are represented in a sumptuous
and decorative manner. Beneath the gable there is a blind
arcade showing Lombard influence.

The Church of Saint-André-de-Sorède is formed by a nave
with three bays preceded by another bay which is very
narrow and flanked by side-aisles, also narrow and having
semicircular vaulting, as at San Pedro de Roda. Two large
apsidioles of extra-circular design open on to a large
transept, and the same is true of the apse which they
enclose. The pointed barrel-vaulting has heavy semicircular cross ribs which rest on strong pillars flanked by half
columns.

This church was consecrated in 1121. The abbey was
founded in 814, then reformed in 1109, and it was then that
the new edifice was undertaken. The sculptures of the façade,
the lintel and the window are elements which have been
taken from the earlier church. The same is true of the altar
which is set against the wall and the holy-water basin,
supported by a column adorned with an interlacing design
and whose capital of white marble decorated with lions is
now at Saint-Martin-du-Canigou. All these elements date
from the early 11th century.

If we have sufficient time, we can take the side road from
Sorède to see the ruins of the Château d'Ultrera and the
Hermitage of Notre-Dame-du-Château. The Château

d'Ultrera, mentioned as early as 673, was demolished by the French in 1675 during a war. It was then that the chapel, mentioned as early as 1100, and which was then in ruins, was re-erected. But the mason who was in charge of this work had no taste at all and he arranged on the façade above the door everything that he had found in the ruins of the castle: some capitals, shafts of columns which he sliced like sausage, white marble stones, resulting in a grotesque and ridiculous puzzle.

We come back to the N. 114 at Argelès and we will stop at COLLIOURE. This small port, with its lively coloured boats drawn up on the beach, between the castle and the church, is one of the most charming I have ever seen. The church is shouldered by a round tower, one of the ancient defence towers of the town, surmounted by a small cupola which shows a slight Moorish influence. Another tower, this time crenellated and with machicolation, appears behind the red roofs of the fishermen's houses. The whole is very colourful and picturesque.

We should visit the church which dates merely from the 17th century, but it contains an extraordinary group of Roussillon Baroque altar-pieces, all carved and gilded, with twisted columns with angels and saints.

This church was built in the 17th century when Vauban, in order to construct the fort which encompassed the ancient castle of the Kings of Majorca which had been erected in the 12th century by the Templars, destroyed the ancient church and the *quartier* which enclosed it. Of the ancient castle which was then disfigured, there remain different buildings which the Fine Arts Administration is having freed and restored, now that the military have abandoned the fort. The large chamber of the palace has been rediscovered and the arcades of the courtyard have been freed. If the resurrection will not be as sensational as that of the Palace of the Kings of Majorca at Perpignan, at least so far as its situation is concerned, the ancient castle of Collioure will be an additional and major attraction for this already attractive town. To enjoy its charm, we merely have to stroll in the old *quartier* of le

Mauret, behind the church, with its old cobwork and shingle houses with their galleries and exterior staircases.

We will continue to follow the N. 114 which extends along the coast which is very broken with magnificent views of the sea and the rocks. We first pass in front of the ancient Gothic church of a Dominican convent and we see on a hill the ancient Fort Saint-Elme, built about 1550 by order of Charles V. Then we descend to PORT-VENDRES, the ancient *Portus Veneris*, the "Port of Venus", for a temple dedicated to the goddess existed here as early as the 6th or 7th century B.C. But the port had completely fallen from its ancient glory when Louis XIV ordered Vauban to restore it and enclosed it with fortifications which were completed by the Comte de Mailly, Intendant of Roussillon under Louis XV. It is now a charming resort devoted to the pleasant modern pastime of yachting.

Although Port-Vendres lacks the charm of Collioure, it none the less offers some pleasant views.

We will continue towards Banyuls and on reaching the Cap de l'Abeille we will stop for a moment to contemplate the magnificent view we have with, on one side, the entire coast of Roussillon as far as the Cevennes and, on the other, the jagged coast of Catalonia as far as Cap Creus.

We quickly descend to Cerbère, the last French town, to reascend again as far as the last cape from where we will descend to Port-Bou.

The Spanish *corniche* has many descents and sinuous ascents, but it is extraordinarily picturesque. If we follow it, we should not miss seeing, in spite of a rather difficult ascent, the ruins of exceptional archaeological interest of San Pedro de Roda which is related to the *ensemble* of Romanesque art which we have just seen at Saint-Génis-des-Fontaines, Saint-André-de-Sorède and Saint-Michel-de-Cuxa.

SOUTH-WEST FRANCE

ITINERARIES VII–XI

From ORLEANS to FOIX,
JACA, and RONCEVAUX
by way of PERIGUEUX and BORDEAUX

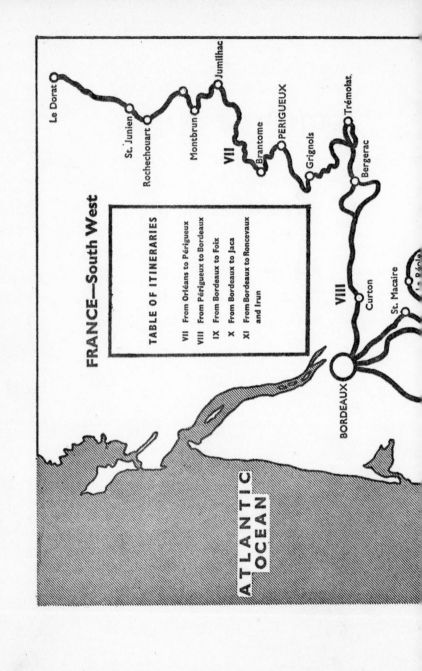

FRANCE—South West

TABLE OF ITINERARIES

VII   From Orléans to Périgueux
VIII From Périgueux to Bordeaux
IX   From Bordeaux to Foix
X   From Bordeaux to Jaca
XI   From Bordeaux to Roncevaux
      and Irun

Le Dorat

St. Junien

Rochechouart

Montbrun

Jumilhac

VII

Brantome

PÉRIGUEUX

Grignols

Trémolat,

Bergerac

VIII

Curton

St. Macaire

La Réole

BORDEAUX

ATLANTIC
OCEAN

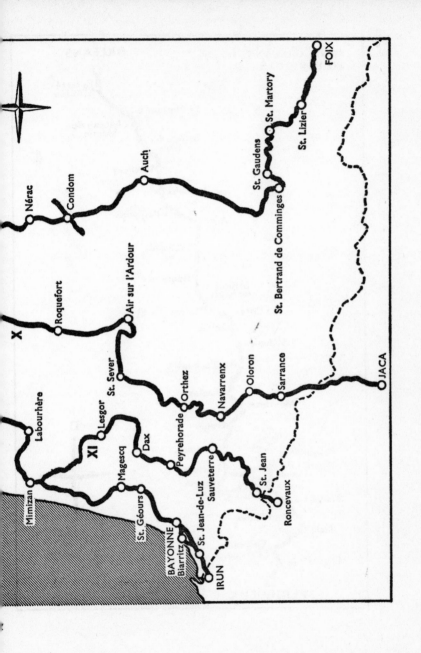

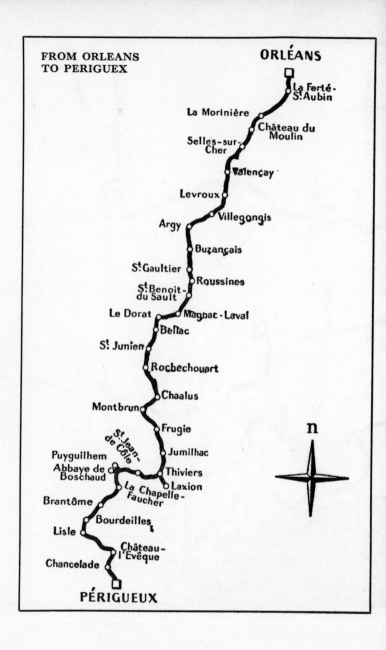

FROM ORLEANS
TO PERIGUEX

ORLÉANS

La Ferté-
St.Aubin

La Morinière

Château du
Moulin

Selles-sur-
Cher

Valençay

Levroux

Villegongis

Argy

Buzançais

St.Gaultier

Roussines

St.Benoit-
du Sault

Le Dorat

Magnac-Laval

Bellac

St.Junien

Rochechouart

Chaalus

Montbrun

Frugie

St.Jean-
de Côle

Jumilhac

Puyguilhem

Thiviers

Abbaye de
Boschaud

Laxion

La Chapelle-
Faucher

Brantôme

Bourdeilles

Lisle

Château-
l'Evêque

Chancelade

PÉRIGUEUX

n

ITINERARY VII
FROM ORLEANS TO PERIGUEUX

La Ferté-Saint-Aubin — Château de la Morinière — Château du Moulin — Selles-sur-Cher — Château de Valençay — Levroux — Villegongis — Argy — Saint-Gaultier — Saint-Benoît-du-Sault — Le Dorat — Saint-Junien — Rochechouart — Chalus — Château de Montbrun — Château de Frugie — Château de Jumilhac-le-Grand — Thiviers — Château de Laxion — Saint-Jean-de-Côle — Château de Puyguilhem — Abbaye de Boschaud — La Chapelle-Faucher — Brantôme — Bourdeilles — Lisle — Château-l'Evêque — Chancelade — Périgueux.

W E follow the N. 20 which passes through Orléans as far as la Ferté-Saint-Aubin where we will stop, at the entrance to the town, before the *château*, which was rebuilt from 1635 to 1650 by the Maréchal de la Ferté from the plans of François Mansart.

An early fortress, which was built by Jean de Meung, had been acquired in the 15th century from the d'Estampes family by a Chamberlain to Louis XI. In 1522 Marguerite d'Estampes brought la Ferté as her dowry to the Count of Saint-Nectaire. In 1617 the land of la Ferté-Nabert, which had become la Ferté-Saint-Nectaire, was raised to a marquisate for Henri de Saint-Nectaire, whose son was the Maréchal de la Ferté, in whose favour the marquisate became a dukedom in 1665. After belonging to the La Carte family and to the Marquis de Boudeville, the *château* was sold in 1748 to the Maréchal de Lowendal. La Ferté-Lowendal became la Ferté-Cosson, from the name of a stream which fed the moats, during the Revolution, and finally became the present name, which was given by reason of the church of the town, dedicated to Saint Aubin.

The various buildings of the *château*, whose out-buildings were erected by the Duc de Lowendal, are designed around a large *cour d'honneur* which is shut in by a beautiful Louis XIV gate framed by fluted pilasters, surmounted by a pediment and flanked by two pavilions. We reach this gate by a stationary bridge which crosses the wide moats surrounding the entire quadrilateral and which is succeeded by a footbridge which replaces the ancient drawbridge. To right and left are buildings consisting of a ground floor and an attic storey, both erected by the Maréchal de Lowendal. The main buildings at the far end attributed to Mansart are built on to other buildings which are older and lower, but which are also constructed of brick and stone. If the *ensemble* is lacking in grandeur, it nevertheless has a great deal of charm. A Renaissance chapel which was about to collapse was demolished in 1874.

We will take the D. 61 and, on the right, after six kilometres, the road which leads to the picturesque Manoir du Lude, surrounded by moats, woods, meadows and marshes. It was rebuilt during the reign of Henri IV by the La Rable family and it also is a pleasant design of brick and stone.

By way of Ligny-le-Ribault and Courménin, we will reach the Château de la Morinière, which is also of brick and stone and likewise surrounded by water, woods and meadows.

This small 16th-century manor is supposed to have been built by Guillaume du Rocher who was supervisor of the work of Chambord during the reign of Henri II. It occupies a square flat piece of ground surrounded by water. The chapel and an isolated pavilion are placed at the angles on the front, while the principal building, flanked on one side by a lower wing, rises at the far end of the *cour d'honneur*. It is an elegant brick construction with stone tying, whose two storeys are surmounted by a high slate roof with Renaissance dormers and a central bell-turret. In the meadow beyond the moats, there is a very pretty Renaissance well with a lantern-turret which terminates in a statue of Truth.

We return to the D. 20 which passes through Mur-de-Sologne and before reaching Lassay we will take, on the right, the road leading to the Château du Moulin.

The CHATEAU DU MOULIN is the most attractive brick castle I have ever seen. It is surrounded on all sides by moats and its rose-coloured bricks, sometimes broken up by darker ones to form a diamond-shaped design are reflected in the pure, still water. Three of the four angle towers have been razed, but a heavy, round machicolated tower, whose consoles support a round gallery surmounted by a high conical roof, still exists, as also do the two high semi-cylindrical towers which defend the entrance gate which is reached by a stationary bridge, followed by a drawbridge. The carriage gateway and the postern are surmounted by machicolation and by a small square bell-tower. A low wing, which comprises a large guardroom covered by heavy ogival ribs, is connected to the angle tower and the *ensemble* is completed by a first main building.

The second building, on the right part of the flat ground, is formed of a square construction on to which, on one side, a high round tower has been built, while, on the other, there is a square staircase-tower with, behind it, a small low chapel. Mullioned dormers and high chimneys rise above the slate roofs, while the gables are decorated with crockets. This dwelling is also of brick with stone tying, and the gate is surmounted by an archivolt in counter-curved arch adorned with curled rosettes.

The man who built this charming edifice was Philippe du Moulin, Counsellor and Chamberlain to Charles VIII, Captain of Blaye and Governor of Langres, who took for master-workman a certain Jacques de Persigny. Work was begun in 1480 and a charter of 1490 authorised Philippe du Moulin to erect his manor as a fortress. It was a smiling fortress, which was already very pleasant. It was in a very bad state when M. de Marcheville had it carefully restored. In the interior, where he has collected furniture and *objets d'art*, there are some reconstructed fireplaces and a handsome Louis XIII ceiling.

By way of the D. 20 and the D. 59, we reach Billy where we can see a church whose 11th-century nave is built in small-sized stones and has retained its 15th-century mural paintings. The gable of the façade is decorated with three 11th-century bas-reliefs.

By way of the D. 119 and the N. 156 we reach SELLES-SUR-CHER. From the banks of the river, when we reach the 16th-century bridge with its ten stone arches, there is a beautiful view of the castle lying on the opposite bank. This was built by Philippe de Béthune, younger brother of the great Sully.

It is a curious, certainly a rather hybrid but charming structure with its juxtaposition of the remains of an ancient fortress, a Renaissance manor and a Henri IV design. The fortress, which Mahaud de Mehun-sur-Yèvre had built about 1217 for Robert de Courtenay and which later belonged to the Counts of Tonnerre of the Houses of Chalon and Husson, is represented by a part of the ancient *enceinte* with its moats, its curtain walls, several towers. There are those which flank the ancient entrance to the countryside behind the Renaissance dwellings; another with machicola-tion at the far end of a very pleasant perspective which we owe to the stationary bridge which leads to the castle of Philippe de Béthune. This castle consists of an entrance portico, connected by ancient remodelled curtain walls to two brick pavilions with stone tying. Somewhat farther on, a footbridge leads to a picturesque postern which is also in the Henri IV style. But why does the present owner who wants to attract visitors (since he has set aside an automobile park at their disposal) not allow pictures to be taken? The Renais-sance dwelling and the heavy pavilion on the right have preserved some fine rooms whose furnishings are also worth seeing.

In addition to its castle, Selles-sur-Cher has some ancient houses, including one with a turret, of the 16th century, and the remains of its ancient abbey which originally was the hermitage of the solitary Saint Eusice. Disciples grouped around him and Childebert came to him for help and prayer before going into battle against the Visigoths. When he had won victory, he showered the abbey with wealth and erected a basilica where Eusice was buried in 542.

Pillaged by the Normans, the abbey was rebuilt from its ruins in the early 12th century and regular canons were established there in 1145. About 1300 the nave and the side-aisles were rebuilt. Of the early church only the wall of the façade and the wall of the south aisle set against the cloister survive.

In 1562 Coligny pillaged the abbey and set fire to the choir, of which only the outer wall of the ambulatory and the radiating chapels remain. The choir was afterwards repaired rather better than worse and a drawing by Gaignières shows us the abbey as it was in 1707: to the south of the church there extends the square choir, which was rebuilt in the 16th century. It is bordered by single-storey buildings, and a large garden divided into eight squares and set out by an arboured path. Behind the cloister is the south side-aisle of the church whose windows are surmounted by the oculus of the nave. The square steeple rises above the transept crossing and the choir has a large roof.

The restoration which was undertaken in 1882 commanded attention but became excessive. The choir, the ambulatory and the arms of the transept were rebuilt "as they ought to have been in the 12th century", the nave was restored, the steeple consolidated and surmounted by a new tower and the façade itself was somewhat too rebuilt. Nevertheless, the church of Selles is worth a visit. In the interior, we can see the wall of the ambulatory and the chapels, the nave and the side-aisles, notably the south side-aisle, some handsome capitals with stylized foliage, here and there embellished with figures of men, monsters and animals and with abacus adorned with palmettes.

The outer façade is Romanesque, so also is the apse which is richly decorated with a double frieze of personages which extends between tall engaged columns above and beneath windows which are enclosed by a cordon of palmettes supported by two slender columns. The cornice, which is supported by modillions with borings, also rests on the capitals of the columns.

The lower frieze is rather archaic with its heavy and compact personages with round eyes who represent scenes from the Old and the New Testament: *The Annunciation, The Nativity, The Presentation in the Temple, The Temptation, The Resurrection of Lazarus, The Washing of Christ's Feet, The Last Supper* and others.

The frieze above, later in date, is by a more skilful hand. It is devoted to the life of Saint Eusice. Several fragments of sculpture, including some which are perhaps from the 11th century, have been reassembled by the 12th-century architect around one of the windows of the ambulatory. They represent Saint Michel, a juggler, fantastic animals, signs of the Zodiac, *The Visitation*.

Of the ancient buildings of the abbey, there remain a few 17th-century constructions which are now occupied by the post office and the *mairie*.

We will continue to follow the N. 156 as far as VALENCAY which is one of our most beautiful Renaissance *châteaux*. It still belongs to the Talleyrand family and, on payment of an entrance fee, we are allowed to visit the gardens and a small museum devoted to the Duc de Talleyrand which is installed in the out-buildings. But it is regrettable that we are not allowed, at least, access to the inner courtyard of the *château*.

It was in 1540 that Jacques d'Estampes decided to build a *château*, which is still feudal in its general plan, but which was already a pleasant dwelling in its entire structure. It was to consist of a huge rectangular courtyard with a tower at each angle. But only the entrance keep and the main buildings which flank it on each side, each terminating in a tower, were built.

The keep is merely a keep because of its square mass. It is flanked by two cylindrical turrets and surmounted by some very decorative machicolation with corbels sculptured with heads of satyrs, angels or lions and connected by blind arcades.

The names of Philibert de l'Orme and Jean de Lespine, an Angevin architect, have been suggested for this first period of building, although there is no proof to substantiate it. The large east façade facing the park was built in the middle of the 17th century by Dominique d'Estampes. It is a long building in the classic style but in harmony with the early buildings. Pilasters frame the windows, the cornice acts as machicolation and the dormers are either rectangular with gable or circular. A central flight of steps, which is interrupted by a drawbridge, spans the dry moats and leads to the gardens.

A *fermier général* (farmer of taxes), Legendre de Villemorien, after buying Valençay, beginning in 1770 built the heavy tower on the south-west which is a copy of the tower which flanks the other side of this façade.

Let us now see the façade facing the courtyard, which is merely closed on two sides and which is limited on the two others by balustrades. The 16th-century wing consists, on the ground floor, of a gallery of arcades of elliptical arches, resting on square pillars decorated with pilasters, as also does the storey above. The 18th-century wing, remodelled in the 19th century, is also decorated with pilasters, but this time of a colossal order. A gallery of semicircular arches is the motive of the ground floor. It is regrettable that the arcades have in modern times been filled up by window frames.

After being acquired by Talleyrand in 1805, the entire ancient decoration of Valençay disappeared to give way to an Empire-style decoration. From 1808 to 1814 Valençay was inhabited by the King of Spain, Ferdinand VII, then from 1840 to 1845 by the Pretender Don Carlos.

We will continue to follow the N. 156 as far as LEVROUX, an ancient Gallo-Roman town which was known as *Gabbatum* and whose magnificent temple was destroyed by Saint Martin. When one of the municipal heads was cured by him of leprosy, the town took the name of *Leprosum* from which we have Levroux.

Of the ancient fortifications, there remains a rather

beautiful gate which was built in 1435, flanked by two round towers and surmounted by machicolation. There is a splendid timbered house, with the coat-of-arms of France, which served as hospice for the pilgrims on their way to Spain, and notably the Church of Saint-Sylvain which is built on the ruins of the palace of the Roman governors, the foundations of which have been utilised.

This is a very pure and very elegant 13th-century edifice whose façade of great nobility and great simplicity is flanked by two high towers shouldered by buttresses. A third tower, Romanesque this time, rises over the right side of the choir. On the portal, which has a pointed arch, the archivolts are adorned with statuettes and *The Last Judgment* is sculptured on the tympanum. A large rose-window opens beneath the gable.

The nave, which has four bays, is in six-sectional vaulting, while the side-aisles are in transversal vaulting. In the apse the beautiful ribs rest on the statues of the four saints who are honoured at Levroux: Sylvain, Corusculus, Sylvestre and Sainte Rodène: and they are joined beneath a keystone representing *Christ Blessing*. The *ensemble*, with the pillars formed of bundles of slender columns, creates the effect of great lightness. Beneath the choir is a crypt which contains the head of Saint Sylvain.

We will still continue to follow the N. 156 for a distance of six kilometres, then we will take, on the right, the D. 27 and the D. 7 which lead us to VILLEGONGIS where we will find a charming little Renaissance *château* whose architecture has taken its inspiration from that of Chambord. It is formed of an important main building flanked by two heavy cylindrical towers crowned by machicolation, which have a watch-path whose crenels, as at Valençay, have become square apertures between which loopholes have been pierced. High slate roofs with their richly adorned chimney top complete the *ensemble*. The two façades of the main building are decorated, as are the towers, with pilasters which frame the bays and the dormers of the roofs, whose pediments are divided by pinnacles.

In the interior, a beautiful staircase with straight balustrades is covered by a coffin vaulting with basket-handle decoration.

This elegant construction surrounded by fresh meadows, which are watered by a small stream, is said to have been built by Pierre Nepveu, known as "Trinqueau", who from 1524 to 1538 was one of the principal master craftsmen of Chambord, for Avoye de Chabannes, grand-daughter of a Bastard de Bourbon and a Bastarde de France and one of the richest ladies in the kingdom. She was the widow of three husbands: Edmond de Prie, Seigneur de Busançais, Jacques de la Trémoille and Jacques de Brisay, the King's Lieutenant in Burgundy.

By way of the D. 63 we reach ARGY, from which we are but a dozen kilometres, where we will see another Renaissance *château* which is no less fascinating.

It was originally a fortress of which there remains notably a heavy square keep of the close of the 15th century, which is flanked at the angles by three corbelled turrets and on the fourth by a turret descending as far as the ground and enclosing a spiral staircase. It is crowned by machicolation and surmounted by a high slate roof, as also is a heavy round tower which is flanked by a polygonal turret. Two buildings at right angles, set on one side against the keep and on the other against a building without character remodelled in the 18th and 19th centuries, are connected to the round tower. They are decorated, facing the courtyard, with a very delightful gallery whose arcades, with vertical finials, are supported by slender columns adorned with rope-moulding and a diamond design and extended by pinnacles. The gallery is vaulted with ogival ribs with prismatic moulding, supported by brackets sculptured with foliage, personages, birds and animals. Above, there is on one side a gallery with elliptical arches, while on the other the expanse of wall is decorated in a checkerboard design and pierced by a pretty bay, surmounted by a triangular gable with crockets, finials and pinnacles.

These elegant façades of the early Renaissance were built

by Charles de Brillac, Seigneur d'Argy who was *Maître-d'Hôtel Ordinaire* to Louis XII. He died in 1509 and after his death they were completed by his widow, Louise de Balsac.

We will take the D. 11 which crosses the Indre at Buzançais in order to reach SAINT-GAULTIER on the banks of the Creuse. In addition to some remains of its 15th-century fortifications, this small town is interesting for its 11th-century Romanesque church. The façade, shouldered by buttresses, is very simple and very pure. The portal with its large arch-mouldings is framed by two slender columns on each side, as is also the window above. Another portal opens on to the north and the walls are flanked on the outside by arcades resting on rectangular buttresses. A massive steeple, which is surmounted by a pointed roof somewhat mis-shapen, rises above the transept crossing.

The nave, with vaulting on cross ribs resting on the consoles of the square pillars on to which columns with foliaged capitals have been added, is flanked by narrow side-aisles and followed by a transept with transversal vaulting on to which open two apsidioles and an oven-shaped apse. The apse has great elegance with its decoration of semicircular arches which rest on tall slender columns with very handsome capitals.

We will follow the D. 29 and at Luzeret we will find a charming small manor of the 15th and 16th centuries which has been transformed into a farm. It has preserved its fortified gate which was originally preceded by a drawbridge and its walls are flanked by round towers. Some mullioned windows, a few of them walled up, are pierced in the curtain walls. Of course, here as elsewhere, peasants have appropriated this old building but have not taken care of it. We then reach Chazelet by way of the D. 59.

The Château de Chazelet is not lacking in emphasis with its austere and slender keep which is reached by a bridge over the moats which are fed by the waters of the Bouzanne. It dates from the second half of the 15th century and its curtain walls are still flanked by many round towers. It has long belonged to the La Trémoille family. In the church, which is in the Gothic style, there is a 16th-century tombstone of Guillaume d'Aubusson, Seigneur of Chazelet.

By way of D. 54 we return to Saint-Civran where we will find the D. 46 which passes through Roussines where the church of the 12th and 15th centuries has vaulting decorated with 15th-century paintings which portray the Cardinal Sins.

We then reach the small town of SAINT-BENOÎT-DU-SAULT, an old mediaeval town which has been built in a semicircle above the Portefeuille. Fortunately many old dwellings have been respected and it is enjoyable to stroll in the streets which have preserved their character. The belfry with its round tower, which is topped by a strange lantern-turret and flanked by an ancient fortified gate, is quite picturesque with all its surrounding old dwellings. There can still be seen the Maison de l'Argentier, the House of the Governor and, near the church, an entire series of old dwellings with their round towers and their accoladed doors, their mossy roofs of brown tiles, their walls embellished with valerian or wild flowers. Altogether a *décor* which would fascinate a painter.

The church, which is that of an ancient priory once a dependency of Saint-Benoît-sur-Loire, is an interesting building of the 11th, 12th and 14th centuries. The 11th-century nave is separated from the side-aisles by heavy pillars. The vaulting was rebuilt in the 17th century. The apse is oven-shaped and the 14th-century façade presents, on the terrace, between two heavy buttresses, a pretty tierspoint portal flanked by slender columns and surmounted by a beautiful mullioned window. The portal is placed in a heavy square tower. The priory buildings date from the 15th and 17th centuries.

If we have the time, we can see, two kilometres south-east of Saint-Benoît-du-Sault, a very picturesque place, the Rocs-Martes, which is described by George Sand. It is a wild heap of rocks where the Portefeuille tumbles in waterfalls amongst a grandiose but sinister scene which has inspired some sombre legends. "The fairies of the Rocs-Martes, their hair flowing to their heels", wrote George Sand in her *Rustic Legends*, "their breasts hanging to the ground, pursue the workers who refuse to aid them in their mysterious needs. They beat them and torment them until they abandon in full daylight their plough and team of horses."

Near by we can see a dolmen and the Château de Montgarnaud with its small square keep.

By way of the D. 1 and D. 2 we reach Saint-Georges-des-Landes whose church has preserved a 13th-century reliquary which consists of a cylinder of crystal mounted on a copper foot adorned with turquoise; then Meilhac where the church has preserved a 14th-century eucharistic iron and an 18th-century reliquary in the shape of an arm of silver which came from the treasure chamber of the Abbey of Grandmont.

At Magnac-Laval, where the 12th-century church contains the relics of Saint Maximin, Bishop of Treves, a fact which is celebrated on Whit Monday by a procession 50 kilometres long, we find ourselves on the N. 142 which we will follow as far as Le Dorat.

We have left Berry and are now in Marche, in the ancient Basse-Marche, a transitional country which is less rough than Limousin, less pleasant than Berry, but which is not less fascinating with its rolling landscape broken by hedges and clumps of trees.

The small town of LE DORAT is the most attractive of all those of this province because of its magnificent collegiate church which was served by a chapter of canons. It was fortified about 1480. It was a mistake to remove the entire defensive system; only a round tower set on the apsidal chapel has been retained, and it adds to the impressive aspect of the building, which has a proud look when we discover it from the top of the hill which overlooks the town as we arrive from Magnac-Laval.

The Church of Le Dorat, which was built in the second half of the 12th century, proceeds at the same time from the Romanesque School of Limousin and that of Poitou. Its design resembles that of the church of Bénévent: an ambulatory with three chapels, which here are semicircular-horseshoe in shape, covered with barrel-vaulting, oven-shaped at the penetrations; a transept whose crossing supports an octagonal lantern, covered by a cupola on pendentives, and whose very projecting arms have transversal barrel-vaulting on to which a semicircular chapel has been added; finally, a nave of five bays, very high with pointed barrel-vaulting and flanked by side-aisles with groined vaulting, which is quite narrow and high in order to shoulder the nave.

But the greatest originality of the Church of Le Dorat is its façade which was built on the same model as those of la Souterraine and Saint-Junien. These are massive façades surmounted by a heavy steeple flanked by two small bell-towers. The large portal, with its many arch-mouldings, is placed between two high, narrow arcades, which are blind or with a small window at the top. At Saint-Junien, slender columns are placed in the jambs and between the arch-mouldings; at la Souterraine and Le Dorat there are real festoons which give a wonderful grace to this plain façade.

Another steeple rises above the transept crossing. It consists of three storeys crowned by an elegant stone spire which is surmounted by a 13th-century angel in gilded copper which gave the town its name, "*Lou Dorat*". Each storey is decorated with bays and blind arcades in a simple and noble design: on the first storey, there are large semicircular bays with many arch-mouldings, on the second trefoiled arcades, and on the third twin semicircular bays.

The façade of the transept is compact, but of beautiful proportions with its porch opening between two powerful buttresses and surmounted by a high window with deep mouldings.

The interior gives a similar impression of force and harmony. If we enter through the west portal, we discover, from a stairhead which surmounts the nave by a dozen steps, the entire *ensemble* of the building built of a handsome grey granite. First of all, there is the pleasant design of the choir with its columns with handsome capitals decorated with foliage and topped by raised arcades, some being quite narrow; they produce a vaguely Oriental effect. There is an ancient 11th-century baptismal vat decorated with sculptured lions and, beneath the choir, a very beautiful crypt.

Quite clear on both sides, the Church of Le Dorat is less so around the choir; it is regrettable that houses have been built which spoil the view. This is all the more so since the small town is very picturesque and has preserved many ancient houses, some from the 16th century, including one with a corbelled angle turret and a door framed by pilasters surmounted by cannon balls. The ancient *enceinte* of the town, which was built in 1429 by Abbot Guillaume Lhermite, still partially exists with the picturesque Porte Bergère, which is flanked by two round towers and surmounted by machicolation.

We will leave Le Dorat by the N. 675 which leads us to Bellac, the birthplace of Jean Giraudoux. It is a town which is not lacking in charm but it is deprived of any buildings of real interest. A small 16th-century *château* divided by watch-towers is occupied by the *mairie*. The church, built on a terrace which overlooks the Vincou, is a building with two naves, the one Romanesque of the 12th century, the other Gothic of the 14th century, to which chapels were added in the 15th century and which is flanked by a square 14th-century steeple. We can also see a shrine from the first half of the 12th century in chequered copper, scattered with precious stones, cameos, intaglios and discs of champlevé enamel, which is a handsome Limousin work.

We will continue to follow the N. 675 which traverses the Forest of les Bois-du-Roi and passes through Mortemart at the foot of the Mountains of Blond. There we can see the ruins of the ancient *château* which was the cradle of the celebrated Mortemart family; Françoise de Rochechouart Mortemart, famous as the Marquise de Montespan, was one of its members. We can also see the ruins of a *chartreuse* which was founded in the 14th century by the Cardinal Pierre

CHATEAU DU MOULIN.

18. CHATEAU DE SELLES-SUR-C

Gauvain who was born at Mortemart. The church, which dates from the 12th and 15th centuries, is the ancient chapel of the Convent of the Augustins. In the choir there are some curious carved misericords and on the *parvis* there is a 14th-century *Virgin and Child*.

After crossing the Mountains of Blond, the road descends into the valley of the Vienne, which it reaches at SAINT-JUNIEN, a small town whose prosperity is due to its leather and glove industries.

The town owes its origin to an oratory which had been built by the Bishop of Limoges, Rorice II, on the tomb of a hermit who was also known as Rorice and who died about 550. This bishop had built a church and installed a chapter of canons. Destroyed by the Normans in 866, it was shortly afterwards rebuilt. The one we see is a beautiful edifice in the Limousin Romanesque style which was built in three stages, if we are to believe the chronicle of the Canon Maleu, written in the early 14th century, which attributes to the close of the 11th century the transept with the octagonal lantern-turret over the crossing, the two bays contiguous to the nave, and the two bays contiguous to the choir. This early part of the church was probably consecrated in 1100. This was followed, that is, in the early 12th century, by the first bay of the nave and the façade which, as we have seen, is similar to the one of Le Dorat with its massive and truncated steeple with three storeys flanked by two lantern-turrets, its portal with two arcades with pointed arches separated by a column and placed beneath an arcade also with pointed arches with many slender columns. Finally, the choir was extended by three bays which terminate in a flat chevet with a beautiful rose-window; between 1225 and 1230 the arms of the transept were enlarged.

On entering, we immediately see that the central steeple has collapsed, crushing the central section of the church; this was in 1922. The columns which had been damaged were rebuilt of grey granite whose colour clashes with the brown granite of the other columns. If it were not possible to use the old stones, at least stones from the same source should have

K

been obtained. The impression is less profound than that of Le Dorat, although the church is beautiful and impressive. There are some remarkable sculptures. First of all, the capitals of the transept crossing, adorned with animals and personages, then the two huge 12th-century ribbed holy-water basins which are near the entrance, the high altar, one of the spoils of the Abbaye de Grandmont, which is adorned with a very beautiful bas-relief of white marble representing *The Disciples of Emmaus*, and, finally, the tomb of Saint Junien, one of the most beautiful pieces of sculpture of the early 12th century which have survived. Two of the faces represent, the one, *The Lamb of God*, the other, *Christ in Glory* together with symbols of the Evangelists. On the two other sides there are sculptured *The Twenty Four Old Men of the Apocalypse* framed on one side by *The Virgin and Child*, *Jesus in Glory Surrounded by Angels*, and on the other, *The Lamb of God*. The tomb contains a 6th-century sarcophagus in which the saint was buried.

In the lower chapel we can see the remains of a 15th-century *Entombment*, which is against a pillar, a 16th-century copper engraved funerary plaque and finally a 13th-century shrine in gilded and enamelled copper.

In addition to its church, Saint-Junien is interesting for a few old 14th-century houses, a local museum which has been installed in an ancient 15th-century convent and finally its old bridge over the Vienne. It is a 13th-century bridge whose six arches have front pieces upstream and which has preserved, at the entrance, the charming Chapel of Notre-Dame du Pont, whose origin is very ancient, but which was rebuilt in the second half of the 15th century thanks to the generosity of Louis XI. It is in the shape of a rectangular chamber divided into three naves of the same height by elegant octagonal pillars and it terminates in an apse which contains a *Miraculous Virgin* that was found on the very site of the chapel.

After crossing the bridge we will take the N. 675 which leads us to ROCHECHOUART, built on a steep hill which overlooks the junction of the Graine and the Vayres.

First of all, there rises from the promontory the castle, which is now used for various administrative purposes, but which was originally a fortress forming a quadrilateral flanked by round towers. The entrance which was placed in a heavy square tower, flanked by a round, uncrowned tower, was preceded by a drawbridge, which has been removed. At the Renaissance different rows of windows were pierced in the nearby curtain wall which has preserved its beautiful trefoiled machicolation in three ledges. The heavy round tower at the following angle is intact with its machicolation and its granite roof. The façade facing the valley was also remodelled during the reign of Louis XII, with its dormers opening on the roofs, above the machicolation, its windows pierced in the curtain wall and a double-landing balustraded stairway leading to the gardens.

The two main buildings facing the courtyard have, on the ground floor, some pretty galleries with elliptical arcades resting on twisted columns. In the interior, during the afternoon we can visit the offices of the *sous-préfecture* and see a suite with some pleasant 16th-century frescoes representing a Dinner, a Stag Hunt, *The Labours of Hercules* and *The Entry into Rochechouart in 1470 by the Count of Pontville*. The ancient woodwork of the buildings is also worth admiring.

From the walk around the castle there is a beautiful view over the ravine and the mountains of Limousin. The 11th-century church was very much remodelled. It is topped by a small 13th-century octagonal steeple.

We will leave Rochechouart by way of the N. 701 which takes us to CHALUS, an extremely picturesque little town with the ruins of two castles. The one in the centre of the town, the Tour du Fort, is a 12th-century cylindrical keep, having lost its upper section, with a Gothic one resting against it. The other castle on a hill rising on the opposite bank of the Tardoire, is more important. It has preserved its keep, which is also cylindrical, and the remains of a Romanesque chapel. While besieging this castle in 1199, Richard Coeur de Lion, who had just been liberated from prison after the payment of a ransom of 25,000 silver marks, was mortally wounded by an arrow while inspecting the ramparts from the top of the Maumont Stone, which can still be seen.

By way of the D. 6 and D. 64 we can visit the CHATEAU DE MONTBRUN which is very well preserved on the edge of its lagoon. This magnificent fortress, originally known as Trados, was built about the close of the 12th century by a man named Aymeric Brun. It was rebuilt in the middle of the 15th century by Pierre de Montbrun, Bishop of Limoges. The square keep was then enclosed in one of the four round towers crowned by crenels and machicolation which flank the four angles of the *château*. Watch turrets have been added. In the centre there was built a new square tower, very high, reinforced at each angle by a buttress and it also is sur-mounted by crenels and machicolation. The *château* was occupied by the Huguenots in 1562 and pillaged at the Revolution. Some openings were pierced in the curtain walls and at the Renaissance some of the walls of the towers were pierced also.

We next see Dournazac with its pretty 12th-century church and cupola. We will disregard the Château de Lambertye, which has been entirely rebuilt, and by way of the D. 64 we will reach the N. 21 which we will cross. Then we arrive at a level crossing and from the other side we will take the D. 67 which leads us to the Manoir de Vieillecour. It has been given a fresh look as the result of an inopportune remodelling, but it has preserved its general outline, with its watch-path, its machicolation and its round or square angle towers. Then, taking the same route, we reach Saint-Pierre-de-Frugie where we can see the CHATEAU DE FRUGIE, fief of the Arlot family, at least since the time of Guillaume Arlot, who founded the Church of Saint-Pierre-de-Frugie in 1347.

After the pillage of the manor by the Huguenots, Jacques Arlot, who had married Madeleine Chapelle de Jumilhac in 1589, built within the ancient *enceinte* a fortress consisting of four main buildings terminating in four large pavilions and enclosing a central courtyard. This once had a high round tower, built on to one wing, and known as the Tour Saint-Jacques; but it was burnt down in 1653.

The entrance façade and a pavilion have been converted into living quarters. The arched portal, with two gates alongside it, all three surmounted by pediments and with ornamentation, form a very pleasant *ensemble*. Entrance is across a drawbridge. The curtain wall is surmounted by machicolation.

We will return by way of the D. 67 and shortly after Saint-Marie de Frugie we will discover, at la Coquille, the Château de la Meynardie. It dates from the Renaissance but has preserved a crowning of false machicolation. A balustraded flight of steps is surmounted by an ornamental door and rounded dormers with pediments break the line of the roofs.

By way of the D. 79 to the left, we reach JUMILHAC-LE-GRAND, the first important *château* of Périgord which we will encounter on our route. Built on the banks of the Isle in a desolate and romantic site, it was worthy of inspiring the pencil of Gustave Doré.

Built at the close of the 14th century, it was occupied by the English who were driven out by du Guesclin. Restored in the 16th century, it was acquired by Antoine Chapelle, *Maître des Forges*, enobled in 1597 by Henri IV, to whom he had supplied cannon. The Chapelle family took the name of Jumilhac and during the reign of Louis XIV they erected new buildings. In 1657 the land was raised to a marquisate. After having remained for a long time in a regrettable state of abandonment, the *château* was repurchased in 1928 by the Count of Jumilhac, who with the help of the Historical Monuments Administration undertook the restoration work which is now almost complete with the exception of one wing. 14 kilometres away, along the national highway, there is already a plaque to recommend a visit to Jumilhac. But it is still not allowed and numerous tourists are furious. Why should they not be permitted, at least, to see the courtyard which has something of the quality of a fairy-tale castle, or why not erect a gate with lattice work which would enable the visitor to see the interior?

It is an impressive construction crowned by machicolation

above which rises a swelling of corbelled turrets, of pepper-pot roofs, which are surmounted by curious weather vanes embellished with lead statuettes, dormers and lantern-turrets. Modern apertures have been pierced in the ancient curtain walls in the south façade, which is more massive; but the façade facing the courtyard is full of poetry and very picturesque: it is the Castle of the Sleeping Beauty. In the interior we can see some very beautiful fireplaces and some painting in the taste of Oudry.

Taking the winding and uneven, but picturesque, D. 78, we can see, on the left, a charming little fortified manor; one of its buildings has almost entirely lost its roof. When I mentioned this to the owner, he replied, "I'm not going to work for something useless". Thus in France so many beautiful buildings are disappearing because they belong to those who do not need them and disdain them.

We will reach the N. 21 which immediately leads us to THIVIERS where we can see an interesting 12th-century Romanesque church, no doubt originally with cupolas but remodelled in the 16th century and badly restored in the 19th century. It has preserved some beautiful historiated capitals on the transept crossing in a somewhat archaic style, one of which represents *The Delivery of the Keys to Saint Peter*.

Behind, we can see an old fortified house with machicolation which is occupied by the presbytery and the Château de Vauvocour of the 15th and 16th centuries, remodelled in the 18th century, and, alas, utterly disfigured in the 19th century. It is said to have kept some beautiful sculptured fireplaces.

Five kilometres away, two kilometres before reaching Corgnac-sur l'Isle, we can see the feudal CHATEAU DE LAXION which dates from the middle of the 16th century and is remarkable for its unity; but it is in a deplorable state of preservation. It is still a fortress, but already a country house.

Four main buildings, which are covered by flat tiles, enclose a square courtyard and connect the four angle towers, round and compact, whose crowning of machicolation support a watch-path and conical slate roofs. Entrance to the castle is through a heavy square tower in the centre of one of the main buildings which is itself surmounted by machico-lation. If the large embossed gate was surmounted by two high mullioned windows, the defence was also assured by the loopholes and a drawbridge whose slots can be seen.

After having belonged to the Chapt de Rastignac family, Laxion was raised to a marquisate in 1633.

We will return to Thiviers where we will take the N. 707 which leads to SAINT-JEAN-DE-COLE, where we can see the Château de la Marthonie which in the 13th and 14th centuries was a powerful fortress which commanded the frontiers of Limousin. There are some important remains. But the castle, which in the 15th and 18th centuries belonged to the powerful la Marthonie family and which had been damaged during the Hundred Years' War; was remodelled and largely rebuilt first by one of its members, Mondot de la Marthonie, First President of the Parlement de Paris, designated by Francis I to run the affairs of the kingdom with Louise of Savoy during the Italian War; then during the 17th and 18th centuries. Its terrace which is decorated with balustrades and its stairway with arcades and heavy balus-trades date notably from the 17th century. Its 15th-century principal main building, flanked by two square towers sur-mounted by machicolation and topped by high roofs, is completed by a building with mansard-roofs; and a wing in the classic style, which is quite simple with its elliptical *ensemble*, is very pleasant, but here again the maintenance has left much to be desired and certain buildings are about to collapse.

We can also see at Saint-Jean-de-Côle the buildings of an ancient priory of Génovéfains which date from the 16th, 17th and 18th centuries. It belongs to two charming ladies who enjoy showing the visitor around. From the garden there is a beautiful view over the apse of the church and there remain two sides of a pretty 16th-century, two-storey cloister. Large pointed arcades penetrate between round columns, above a simple abacus on which there rises an engaged half-column. This colonnade takes the thrust of the first storey, whose light comes from four rectangular bays which are separated by twisted columns mounted on half-columns forming buttresses.

The church, which was probably founded by Renaud de Thiviers, Bishop of Périgueux, who died in 1102 and who installed a college of regular canons there, was finished in the 12th century. It consists of a choir with a single bay; it was surmounted by a cupola which had collapsed, and is flanked by three radiating chapels. This choir was probably fronted by a nave with cupolas which had been destroyed or alternatively whose plan was never carried out. Very large in size, the choir has preserved the four large arcades and the pendentives which support the cupolas. We can see some fine wood panelling and some 17th-century stalls, also a tomb of a bishop recessed in the wall and some paintings of the close of the 17th century representing the life of Sainte Marguerite, Sainte Geneviève and Saint Augustine, the patron saints of the Génovéfains.

Outside, we can see the blind arcades which decorate the five-sectional radiating chapels and which rest on columns set at each angle and whose somewhat crude capitals are historiated. There is a *Story of Noah*, *Daniel in the Lions' Den* and others. A lateral, rectangular steeple, which seems to date from the 13th century, is pierced by simple semicircular bays.

By way of the D. 98 and the D. 68 we will reach Villars where we can see the charming CHATEAU DE PUYGUIL-HEM which was built by the same Mondot de la Marthonie whom we have just encountered at Saint-Jean-de-Côle. Work was begun in 1509, but as he died in 1517, it was finished by his son Geoffroy about 1530. After successive marriages, the *château* passed into the hands of the Chapt de Rastignac family, then to that of La Rochefoucauld.

It is much more ornate and has greater unity than the preceding one. Still preserving a feudal aspect, with its heavy round towers crowned by machicolation, it constitutes a typical Renaissance dwelling of Périgord and is one of the most richly decorated. Its dormers, notably, are quite beautiful with their medallions, their pilasters, their foliage design and their crownings of extraordinary fantasy. The chimney shafts are sumptuously embellished, while balustrades run all along the façades and a band of foliage encircles the watch-paths above the machicolation. The *ensemble* has much grace and originality. Puyguilhem, which now belongs to the State, is worth knowing as much as Montal and Assier.

Taking a small road on the right, which runs from Villars, we can also see the ruins of the Cistercian ABBAYE DE BOSCHAUD whose single-nave church built between 1154 to 1159 terminates in a semicircular choir, while a square chapel opens on to each arm of the transept. The nave was covered with a row of cupolas on pendentives and half-cupolas covered the apse and the chapels. Only the arms of the transept had barrel-vaulting. The Fine Arts Administration is now restoring what remains of the church, the transept and the choir. A side building in ruins includes the chapter-house on to which open some beautiful Gothic arcades.

By way of the D. 3 we will reach LA CHAPELLE-FAUCHER where, on the banks of the Côle, we can see an elegant 15th-century *château* which was probably built by one of the de Farges. Brantôme relates that Coligny, after capturing the *château*, here ordered the massacre of 260 peasants who had sought refuge in a lower room. Later on, during the Wars of the Fronde, the Maréchal de Chabans forcibly recaptured his *château*, which was defended by his own mother who was of the opposing party.

It consists of a main building which terminates in two round towers surmounted by crenels and machicolation, including one which is flanked by an octagonal stairway turret projecting over the central main building. Some magnificent dormers with triangular gables rise on the pepper-pot roofs. The door of the stairway has been embellished in the classic taste of the 17th century at the same time as the out-buildings were constructed. The façade facing the river is adorned with machicolation and dormers: and its angles are flanked by two corbelled turrets. Twenty years

ago the interior was destroyed by a fire, and it is hoped that
the Fine Arts Administration will aid the owner in restoring
it. The church in the village is partly Romanesque and has
preserved a rather picturesque portal surmounted by niches
in one of which a 17th-century statue has been placed.

A very good luncheon may be had near by at *Chez
Thérèse*.

We will take the D. 78 which leads us to BRANTOME.
At the entrance to the town, on the right, we can see the
small Manoir de Puymarteau, consisting of a main building
terminating in inclining gables and flanked, on the side
facing the valley, by two elegant turrets. Several of the
dormers have been demolished to the level of the roofs, the
remaining one is surmounted by a pretty pediment with
shell design which is well in the style of the Renaissance in
Périgord.

The small town of Brantôme is utterly charming with its
running waters and the park of the abbey. It would be even
more so if the fortified *enceinte* had not been demolished and
if M. Abadie, whose mischief at Périgueux we are going to
see, had not acted severely here also, demolishing a part of
the 16th-century conventual buildings and rebuilding the
church in his own manner.

The Benedictine Abbey of Brantôme was founded by
Charlemagne in 769 and from that time on was enriched by
the relics of Saint Sicaire, one of the Innocents. Pillaged by
the Normans in the 10th century, it was affiliated with la
Chaise-Dieu about 1075 by the Abbot Guillaume to whom
we owe the church steeple, which is the most remarkable
building of Brantôme.

This steeple, which is considered the prototype of the
steeples with gabled bays of Uzerches, Saint-Martial de
Limoges, Saint-Léonard, Saint Junien in Limousin, as well
as Saint-Michel d'Aiguilhe at Le Puy, Saint-Rambert-sur-
Loire, the Cathedral of Chartres and the Abbey of Vendôme,
is built on a rock above a grotto and consists of four storeys
which form successive retreats and are surmounted by a four-
sectional stone pyramid. The room on the ground floor set

against the rock, perhaps much older, is surmounted by a
rather crude cupola. On the first floor we can see the beautiful twin, semicircular windows with their capitals decorated
with intertwining and fluting; on the second, the high gables
which are above the large semicircular bays; while on the
last two storeys are the small twin bays.

The church, which suffered during the English Wars, was
originally covered with cupolas which at the close of the
14th century were replaced by Angevin vaulting, while at
the same time a new bay of the nave was raised. Outside we
can see from the south side the beautiful lateral design with
some pretty arcades, as well as that of the flat chevet which is
pierced by three lancet windows and an arched bay.

Of the four Romanesque chapels, M. Abadie has preserved
merely one with oven-shaped vaulting: we should also see a
beautiful Romanesque capital with an interlacing design and
converted into a holy-water basin and two 13th-century
bas-reliefs representing *The Massacre of the Innocents* and *The
Baptism of Christ.*

Of the conventual buildings, there remain a part of the
Gothic cloister and the Chapel of Saint-Anthime of the close
of the 15th century, also a large 18th-century main building
which is disfigured by a central pediment, but whose angle
pavilions are in good architecture. The one on the right has
a handsome square staircase. There are also the curious
vaulting of the refectory and the grottoes which served as
out-buildings for the monks. One of them contains a curious
Triumph of Death, dating from the close of the 15th century,
and sculptured in a rather crude fashion.

Of interest also are the 16th-century Porte des Réformés,
whose rounded arch is pierced in the machicolated wall
which closes the passage between the cliff and the river; the
parish church which was built in 1504 by the Cardinal
Amanieu d'Albret and whose single nave with prismatic
ogival vaulting terminates in a flat chevet with chapels
between the buttresses; the 16th-century bridge with, added
to it, a charming little Renaissance pavilion built by the
Abbot Pierre de Mareuil, to whom we owe also three pretty

aedicules. The most handsome of these has a large basket-handle arcade which is flanked by two Corinthian columns. There is also the very much restored 17th-century Médici Fountain.

Finally, we should not miss seeing in the town two old houses. The one has preserved its large bays with pointed arches, its large windows in trefoiled filling; and the other, which dates from the 13th century, a chimney in the form of a frustrum of a cone surmounted by a foliated finial. Then, on a height, we can see the elegant Renaissance Manoir de la Hierce (or de la Guerche) which consists of a high central pavilion with, on one side, a turret; and connected, on the other, by a gallery with a tower encircled by a band of plain moulding. The mullioned windows are cross-shaped.

We will take the picturesque D. 78 which follows the valley of the Dronne along the foot of the chalky cliffs with their numerous grottoes. Some, like those of Rochebrune, are fortified. Then, on the right, we can see the Château de Beaufort which has preserved a 15th-century hall. We pass through the hamlet of Fontseigner with its picturesque old houses and cross the Dronne over an old Gothic bridge with projecting piers-heads.

We next reach BOURDEILLES which was the seat of one of the four great baronies of Périgord and where the 12th-century church, which is disfigured, has three cupolas; but where we see notably, in addition to the picturesque 15th-century dwelling of the seneschals of the barony, the castle which is one of the oldest and most important in the province.

The Château de Bourdeilles was first mentioned in 1183, its fortress in 1258. In 1281 the Abbot of Brantôme obtained from the Parlement a decree stipulating that the Château de Bourdeilles was a fief of the abbot and of the convent. It was a partial decree, for, on the other hand, there were some who wanted to dispossess Bernard de Bourdeilles who maintained that the castle was a fief of the King of England, and to give it to Geraud de Maumont, brother of the abbot, Counsellor to the King of France.

Geraud repaired and reinforced the defences of the castle and, after his death, Philip the Fair exchanged with his heirs the castellany of Bourdeilles and those of Châlus and Chalusset for fiefs in Auvergne and in the Pays de Sens. Afterwards Philippe VI of Valois, in exchange for Bergerac, gave Bourdeilles to Hélie Rudel.

During the Hundred Years' War, the castle was occupied by the English in 1369, then recaptured in August 1377 by the Duke of Anjou and the Constable du Guesclin. Then the captains named by the Counts of Périgord, Archambaud V and VI, devoted themselves over to pillage to the misfortune of the last of the Archambaud. In 1481 the castle returned to the descendant of its ancient owners, François de Bourdeilles; but its military role had come to an end.

An early castle, that of the barony, would have been razed at the Renaissance when the new castle was built. But the castle belonging to the Count is still standing at the far end of the promontory overlooking the Dronne, connected by an *enceinte* which follows the escarpment as far as the entrance gate at the other end of the terrace, which is a construction or an important remodelling of the close of the 15th century. It formerly had a drawbridge, and was flanked by two round towers with loopholes, the one on the north-west being three-quarters set into the wall. The adornment in large-sized stones has been carefully executed. It is crowned by a continuous parapet resting on different types of consoles and pierced by arquebusiers.

The Count's castle consists of a seigniorial dwelling flanked, on the south, by a keep and provided, in front, with an *enceinte* which is fortified on three sides. These additional defences, which we owe to Géraud de Maumont, seem to have been built between 1281 and 1300, while the castle, properly speaking, seems to date from 1250. The *enceinte* is set against one of the sides of the keep and acts, on that side, as an outer fortification. It next forms a right angle towards the north and, by a new angle towards the west, it joins the north side of the castle. The walls, which are about four feet wide, are faced and surmounted by a parapet on corbelled machicolation. The north façade has a projecting central rectangular tower, beneath which opens the entrance corridor which is defended by a portcullis. The gate itself passes beneath a pointed arch with two twisted mouldings resting on slender columns with foliated capitals. We enter a courtyard where, on three sides, some small cells for look-out men have been arranged in the curtain walls. A spiral stairway leads to the central tower and from there to a watch-path which circles the *enceinte*.

The castle consists of two chambers. The one on the ground floor was transformed into stables in the 16th century. The windows, which have been greatly splayed and provided with benches, have two types of twin bays, some of them being quite remarkable.

The keep is an eight-sectional tower reinforced by a batter at the base, 96 feet in circumference and 90 feet in height. It is surmounted by a crenellated terrace with corbelled machicolation. Some small semicircular arches connect the lines of corbels in four courses. We enter the keep by the first storey and a spiral staircase in the prismatic turret serves the three storeys and the platform. Each storey includes but one room; they are octagonal and have flattened ogival-ribbed vaulting, which is prismatic in profile and radiates from a plain keystone. In the first chamber there is a circular opening set in the flagstones leading to the cellars which are vaulted. Whereas the first storey has merely one archery window, the second has three, and the third a very beautiful window with twin trefoiled arches.

It was Jacquette de Montbron, Dame de Bourdeilles and of la Tourblanche, wife of the Sénéschal André de Bourdeilles, who undertook the completion of the Renaissance *château* which had been left unfinished. The main building is very restrained in design, with two storeys, pierced by straight windows or by Gothic casements; and with a projecting square pavilion decorated with Tuscan pilasters supporting triglyphs and metopes. It is surmounted first by an Ionic order, then by a Corinthian one. The doors on the ground storey are covered with a semicircular arch embellished with rosettes with flowers, fruit and branches in the corner pieces. The interior has a very pleasant decoration of paintings and wood panellings.

After this description, inevitably a technical and analytical one, we must mention the powerful general impression, which is one of restraint and elegance, of the Château de Bourdeilles lying on its rocky spur. We can also lean from the summit of its curtain walls which overlook the Dronne, with the old mill in the shape of a ship at the foot of the cliff, and admire the landscape which is so very pleasant and well-designed.

We will continue to follow the D. 78 as far as LISLE where we can see an interesting church whose façade and steeple are modern, but which comprises a choir surmounted by a cupola on pendentives terminating in an oven-shaped apse decorated with a semicircular arcade in which three windows have been opened and framed by slender columns. This choir is preceded by a nave which originally also had cupolas, but whose two 13th-century bays with ogival vaulting have liernes and tiercerons merely dating from the 16th century, as also do the chapels which have been arranged between the buttresses. A few capitals are interesting: one represents a woman between two personages. The chevet has a raised arch.

The ancient castle was rebuilt during the Renaissance. The façade, which has alongside it a corbelled angle-turret on a series of quarter-rounds, is pierced by mullioned windows. In the interior, we can see a beautiful stone staircase, with straight stairheads mounted on fluted columns in the shape of truncated cones and on brackets decorated with personages which still have a Gothic look. The ceiling of the landings is enriched by scrolls sculptured in the stone and the flight of steps is supported by handsome balustrades. The fireplace is in the shape of a lantern.

We reach the D. 2, then the N. 139, in order to see at CHATEAU-L'EVEQUE the castle which was built in the 14th century by Adhémar de Neuville, Bishop of Périgueux. It was besieged several times during the Wars of Religion by the Protestants who had the Bishop Pierre VIII Fournier strangled there. It was in its chapel that Saint Vincent de Paul was ordained priest in 1600. Pierre Tison was buried there in 1384.

This important construction consists of several main buildings which are flanked by towers and in general crowned with machicolation. The *ensemble* is somewhat confusing, but very picturesque.

On the N. 139 we come to CHANCELADE where we will visit the abbey which was founded in the 12th century by Foucauld, monk of the Augustinian Abbey of Cellefrouin in Charente. In 1128 or 1133 Gérard de Monlava was consecrated first abbot by Bishop Guillaume d'Auberoche. It was then merely a small house of brick and stone built near a fountain enclosed by a *cancellis* (iron grille) which will have given its name to the monastery. But it was never prosperous and moreover suffered from the English, then from the Calvinists, and it was not until 1623 that the Abbot Alain of Solminiac restored the buildings.

The church consists of a single nave with five bays, a transept without apsidioles and a choir with two bays terminating in a flat wall which date from the 12th century, but whose upper sections were repinned in the 16th century. It is not a building in the Périgord style, but rather in that of Angoulême, the monks who had founded the abbey having adopted the building methods of the country from which they came.

The first bay of the nave, which is occupied by the tribunes built in 1630, forms the narthex. A round cupola, which is resting on four tierspoint arcades with double scrolls, rises over the transept crossing, while the arms of the transept have pointed barrel-vaulting.

The façade is pierced by a single tierspoint door beneath a monumental archivolt which consists of four rows of flat arch stones bordered by a torus and separated by a series of stars or checkered designs. The archivolt is resting on fluted columns. Above the door there is a series of arcades which rest on ringed columns mounted on a string course on corbels. The arcades are blind with the exception of one which is

CHATEAU D'ARGY.

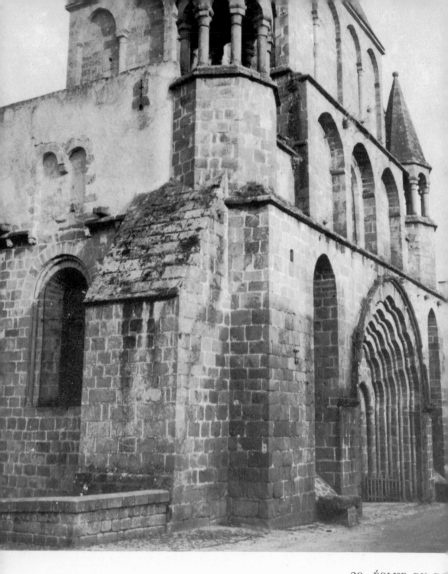

20. ÉGLISE DU DC

CHATEAU DE MONTBRUN.

CHATEAU DE LAXION.

pierced by a window. A cluster of three columns shoulders one of the angles of the façade, the other supporting a building at right angles.

The central steeple is a heavy square tower blunted at the angles by slender columns with a tierspoint ornamental arcade on the first storey, two large windows on the second and a small bay on the third. The summit was fortified during a later period.

The conventual buildings are not lacking in charm with the abbot's dwelling, which was rebuilt in the 16th century. It is flanked by two towers and an accoladed door with curled rosettes is embellished with the coat-of-arms of the Cardinal of Amboise.

Finally we can see, opposite the church, the Chapel of Saint-Jean, which is the ancient parish church. It was probably dedicated in 1147. Its single nave with two bays with pointed barrel-vaulting terminates in a semicircular chevet with the light coming from three windows whose semicircular archivolt is adorned with a checkered design and rests on slender columns with ringed shafts. The façade is the Saintonge type with its semicircular portal which is formed by three rows of arch-mouldings and its pretty window which lies beneath the gable. The chevet is decorated with a moulded string course, buttress columns and a cornice with modillions. All this forms an *ensemble* which is not lacking in taste.

The N. 139 leads us to PERIGUEUX which, with its Roman ruins, its two churches with cupolas, its Gothic and Renaissance houses, should have been one of our most famous art cities, if the harm caused by the Protestants in the 16th century and later on by the inhabitants themselves and the services of the Historical Monuments Administration had not reduced its artistic patrimony and diminished its interest.

Roman *Vesunna* had replaced a Celtic town of a certain importance, since the Petrocorii sent a detachment of 5,000 men to defend Alesia. It acquired great prosperity and had basilicas, temples and an amphitheatre whose ruins remain,

L

also those of a temple which had been erected to the tutelary goddess of the city.

The city was ruined by the Alamani invasion in 275. The following year the people of *Vesunna* erected on the north section of the ancient town, the highest part, an oval-shaped fortification which included the amphitheatre and for which they utilised the stones of their ruined monuments: shafts of columns, capitals, tombs and other things. This wall, which still partially exists, notably at the Château Barrière, must have been closely studied and we can see how carefully the stones had been utilised, the builders respecting as much as possible the engraved or sculptured surface. Of the three gates open in the wall of the *enceinte*, the Porte Romaine, on the south, enclosed by two towers, was destroyed in 1783. The Porte Normande, on the west, still partially exists. The Porte de Mars, which was the main gate, is more richly decorated. Unfortunately it is embedded in earth and débris and its owner refuses to clear it away. Some work was temporarily done in 1821 and 1858 and people realised that the Porte de Mars was an interesting piece of architecture. But the laws in France allow the first idiot who comes along to keep an important monument buried, if it so pleases him; he can even destroy it, if he wants to; and the State, which does not hesitate to expropriate for disputable reasons, does not take the trouble to interfere in order to save one of the most important Roman monuments in France.

During the entire Middle Ages, this *enceinte* continued to enclose this city of courts and bishops. Houses were built on to it, but the only one to remain is the Château Barrière, although it too was burnt by the Protestants in 1575. The keep dates from the 12th century; it is built on one of the towers of the Roman fortification and the entrance gate is decorated with an early 16th-century crocketed arch with rosettes and pinnacles.

We have seen that the amphitheatre had been utilised as an element of the *enceinte*. About 1150, the Count of Périgord, Boson III, constructed in its centre the Château de la Rolphie, which was demolished in 1420. An engraving of

1575 shows that the amphitheatre still existed almost in its entirely with two rows of seats. In 1644 the Visitandines utilised the near by section of the Roman wall and the amphitheatre in order to build their church. In 1688 they discovered, hidden in a secret place, several life-size statues of white marble which represented divinities. Since they were pagan, they were, alas, broken and we were deprived of an utterly unique *ensemble*.

Repurchased by the city in 1867, the amphitheatre was incomprehensibly destroyed in 1875 when it was transformed into public gardens; instead of clearing the amphitheatre, as should have been done, the authorities buried it beneath nine or twelve feet of earth planted with trees.

For centuries the *enceinte* has served as a quarry for the construction of *châteaux*, churches and private homes. However, the double composition of the wall, which has enabled its outer facing and the towers to be preserved, while entirely losing its thickness, still makes it possible for it to enclose the town. It is only in modern times that more and more openings have been made. Neither the city of Périgueux nor the Fine Arts Administration has sought to protect and enhance these remarkable remains. On his property, the Count of Lestrade has freed the lateral facings and constituted a kind of museum with the capitals, the columns and the sculptures which had been found in the interior.

A Roman monument was set up beyond the *enceinte* and it still exists; it is the *cella* of the huge temple dedicated to the goddess of the city. All the large-sized stones have been removed and utilised to construct the *enceinte* and only the shell of the *cella* has been left, built of rubble and covered with small-sized stones. In 1820 the Count of Tallefer acquired the Tour Vésone which was about to be destroyed and presented it to the town. In 1894 excavation work made it possible to draw up a design of the temple to which it belonged and to recover many plaques of marble which covered the *cella* in the interior as well as the exterior.

But Périgueux is even more interesting for its churches with cupolas than for its Roman remains. First of all, there is the Church of Saint-Front, which is one of the largest and most famous. The present building replaces a basilica which was consecrated in 1047, burnt down in 1120 and of which a part of the walls was utilised. But while the ancient church had a timbered roof, the new one, with its steeple forming the porch, was built on a Greek cross plan and covered with cupolas in imitation of St. Mark's at Venice, following the methods adopted at that time by the builders of Aquitaine. It is one of the most remarkable buildings of its kind in France. Unfortunately, its restoration was entrusted to M. Abadie who, beginning in 1853, completely rebuilt it, denuding its essential parts, crowning the cupolas with lantern-turrets of his own invention, resetting part of the large steeple and rebuilding its crowning. We thus have a stiff, soulless pastiche which is utterly lacking in interest. It is one of the most unpardonable crimes ever committed by the architects of the Historic Monuments Administration.

The ancient Cathedral of Saint-Etienne de la Cité was devastated by the Protestants who, in 1577, partly destroyed it. Saint-Front also suffered and the tomb of the saint especially had disappeared, but the building could still be repaired, while Saint-Etienne remains disfigured. The building consisted in the 16th century of a square steeple, fronted by a nave with three bays, the first two dating from the close of the 11th century and the last one dating from the 12th century, as also does the choir which follows; and all four are covered by cupolas on pendentives. The Protestants left standing only the third bay of the nave, which is more important than the two others, and that of the choir which was restored about 1640. This restoration was less barbarous than the one at Saint-Front in the 19th century, and that is why we are more touched by Saint-Etienne, although it has lost its two oldest naves and its steeple. Incidentally, I should like to mention that the two oldest churches in France with cupolas no longer exist: if the two 11th-century cupolas of Saint Etienne were destroyed by the Protestants, the Church of Leguillac de l'Ausch, the sole church in France with a cupola which dated from the second half of the 11th century, was recently demolished by our modern Vandals.

The Archbishop's Palace, which was built on the north side of Saint-Etienne, was also destroyed by the Protestants as well as the Franciscan, Dominican and Augustinian convents, but they spared the cloister, part of which still existed in 1850, and also the Chapel of Saint-Jean of the Palace, whose nave, which was Romanesque, was demolished in 1817 for the sole purpose of expelling the Brotherhood of the White Penitents. This explains why there remains only the choir which is of two storeys and finely decorated; it is one of the most remarkable examples of Renaissance art in Périgord.

Périgueux has preserved many old houses, although recently an entire row has been razed, and some of the most remarkable have been demolished in the past. In 1858 the Archaeological Congress visited the beautiful Hôtel de Saint-Aulaire, but two years later it was demolished for the opening out of the Rue Neuve. A magnificent fireplace in the Flamboyant style, now in the museum, makes us regret its disappearance all the more.

Two façades which are partially Romanesque can still be seen in the Rue des Farges and the Rue Saint-Roch. On the quay we can admire, at the corner of the Rue du Pont-Vieux, an elegant 15th-century construction, the Maison Cayla with its beautiful dormers in the Flamboyant style and on the back façade the turrets of its spiral staircase. Its neighbouring one, from the Renaissance, is characterised by its gallery in the Italian style and its staircase with its straight flight of steps, while somewhat farther on the Maison du Moulin Saint-Front has preserved its picturesque timbered façade.

In the Rue Limogeanne, we find at No. 12, a very pretty door in the Flamboyant style; at Nos. 5, 3 and 1 different Renaissance *hôtels*, the last with an elegant façade adorned with slender columns; and on the Place du Coderc a charming angle turret with brackets.

At No. 7, Rue de la Constitution, the beautiful Hôtel Gramanson which dates from the close of the 15th century, has an elegant turret staircase, windows with mouldings and a Renaissance well; the Maison Tenant at No. 17, Rue Eguillerie, is a Gothic dwelling with a large spiral staircase and windows with slender columns. We enter from another angle through a door with separated panels in a very original design.

Two houses which have a modest appearance have some very extraordinary staircases: at No. 1, Rue de la Sagesse, the Renaissance staircase which was built by a seneschal of Périgord and which is supported by twisted pillars or adorned with heavy arabesques, while the ceilings are decorated here with rosettes, diamond shapes and human figures, and there with coffers, while the pillars are in the form of bulbous pilasters of Spanish inspiration. The other staircase at No. 2, Rue de la Miséricorde, has a more restrained decoration, but one of great beauty with its round columns surmounted by classic capitals and its coffers adorned with rosettes and diamond points.

There are also two Renaissance doors at Nos. 3 and 11, Rue de la Sagesse; the 15th-century tower with machicolation in the Place de la Mairie; the 15th-century Hôtel d'Abzac de Ladouze with its watch-tower at No. 16, Rue Aubergerie; the 15th and 16th-century Hôtel de Sallegourde; a house with machicolation at No. 6, of the same street. On the opposite bank of the Isle, an ancient 12th-century leper-house is remarkable for its fireplaces.

Finally, Périgueux has preserved some 18th-century *hôtels*, like the Hôtel Belair, in one of the beautiful avenues planted in 1750 by the Intendant of Tournay, or that of Lagrange-Chancel, the author of *Les Philippiques*, which was transformed into the Hôtel de Ville.

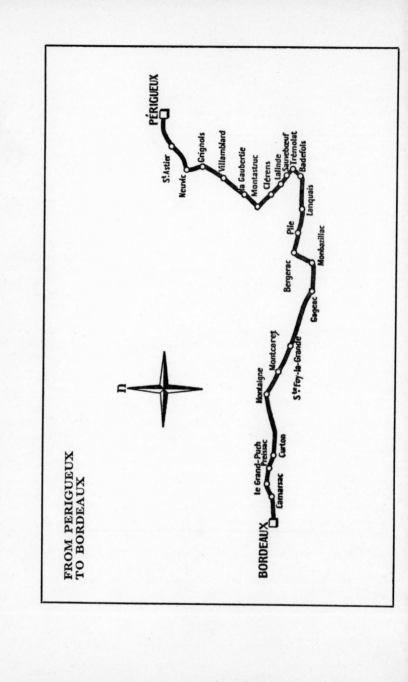

FROM PERIGUEUX
TO BORDEAUX

n

PÉRIGUEUX

St.Astier
Neuvic
Grignols
Villamblard
la Gauberdie
Montastruc
Clérens
Lalinde
Sauveboeuf
Trémolat
Badefols
Lanquais
Pile
Monbazillac
Bergerac
Gageac
Ste Foy-la-Grande
Montcaret
Montaigne
le Grand-Puch
Preissac
Curton
Camarsac

BORDEAUX

ITINERARY VIII

FROM PERIGUEUX TO BORDEAUX

*Saint-Astier — Neuvic — Grignols — Villamblard —
Château de la Gaubertie — Château de Montastruc —
Clérans — Trémolat — Lanquais — Château de Piles
— Bergerac — Monbazillac — Manoir de Gageac —
Sainte-Foy-la-Grande — Montcaret — Saint-Michel-de-
Montaigne — Château de Curton — Château de Preissac
— Camarsac — Manoir du Grand Puch.*

WE leave Périgueux by way of the N. 89 which
descends the valley of the Isle and passes through
Montanceix which is dominated by a rock on which
rise two castles, one dating from the 15th century. Three
kilometres further on we will take the road on the right and
cross the Isle in order to reach SAINT-ASTIER which took
the name of a hermit above whose tomb there was erected
in the 11th and 12th centuries a church with cupolas which
was remodelled in the 16th century. It was then fortified,
enclosed by machicolation and flanked by a defence tower.
On the façade there remains from the Romanesque period a
Christ surrounded by six figures of Apostles.

Two kilometres north-west, by way of the D. 3, we can see
the Château de Puy-Saint-Astier of the close of the 15th
century and, notably, two kilometres to the west, that of
Puy-Ferrat of the 15th century, one of whose façades is
flanked by two heavy round towers and the other by two
elegant turrets. A watch-path resting on some very decorative
consoles surmounts the façades draped with ivy. The
apertures have been rebuilt more recently, notably the

entrance portal whose triangular pediment rests on two Doric columns.

We will return to the N. 89 which leads us to NEUVIC where, on the banks of the Isle, we can see a more important castle which belonged to the Talleyrand family. It was acquired in 1520 and rebuilt by Amet de Fayolle whose initials and those of his wife, Charlotte de la Douze, can be seen near a gate. He bequeathed it to his nephew, Jean de Mellet and the Mellet family has owned Neuvic for more than three centuries. Its guests have included Henri IV and Sully.

It is a Renaissance building yet a very restrained one, built in a right angle with corbelled turrets at the angles: plain dormers with triangular pediments pierce the roofs above the mullioned windows, between which there runs a watch-path which is supported by consoles. The façade facing the Isle was remodelled in the 18th century; a central pavilion was added to it. During the same period, the far end of the right wing facing the courtyard was modified.

The decoration in the interior has been preserved. We can see a curious painted frieze and a large sculptured fireplace with the monograms of Henri II and Catherine de Médici. It is now occupied by a school for girls.

We will take the D. 44 eastwards which leads us to GRIGNOLS where we can see another castle which dates from the 12th and 15th centuries and which withstood several sieges: it was captured in 1377 by the Maréchal de Sancerre, later by the Count of Turenne, and by the Protestants in 1587, but it was notably during the War of the Fronde that it was greatly damaged. A section has remained in ruins and some beautiful fireplaces are standing in the open. The machicolation and the crenels of the central keep have been over-restored, but in spite of its state of decay the *ensemble* has retained much of its flavour.

We will next follow the D. 107 which leads us to VILLAMBLARD where another castle awaits us, the Château Barrière, which belonged to the same family as the castle of the same name which we have seen at Périgueux. It dates from the 12th century, but it was remodelled in the 14th and 16th centuries. It rises in ruins in the centre of the town, but a heavy round tower which is crowned with crenels and machicolation is still impressive.

By way of the D. 39 we will cross the N. 21 and reach the CHATEAU DE LA GAUBERTIE. It dates from the close of the 15th century and, starting in 1685, belonged to the du Pavillon family, when Pierre du Cheyron du Pavillon married Jeanne de Véra, daughter of Gabriel de Véra, Seigneur de la Gaubertie, and Barbe de Chaumont, heiress of the last seigneur of Clermont.

It is an elegant construction consisting of a main building, flanked on the angles by two round towers on one side and a square tower and a corbelled cylindrical turret on the other. The buildings are encircled by machicolation and a watch-path. Dormers with triangular pediments add to the charm of the very high roofs and the windows have mullions. The whole is graceful and restrained. A path, curiously enough, runs underneath the castle.

The D. 21 follows the charming little valley of the Caudau, and we descend to Lamonzie where we shall stop to see the CHATEAU DE MONTASTRUC which now has a very bourgeois appearance, but in the 15th century it was a powerful fortress. *Mons Abstructus* belonged to the ancient family of Abzac which became famous during the Crusades; they were attached to the English party and underwent several sieges in Montastruc. The *château* then passed in succession to the Ferrand de Mancerin, to the d'Escars and to the du Garrick d'Uzech families. It was entirely re-modelled in the 17th century, but it has preserved its narrow round pepper-pot towers and its ancient gable with crockets. The fortification wall has disappeared and has been replaced by a terrace from which there is a very beautiful view over the valley.

We will cross over to the D. 32 and follow it eastward as far as Liorac, from where we will turn southward to CLERANS where we can see the ruins of an important fortress. We can still distinguish an oval-shaped *enceinte* with a gate on the south and, on the east, a square 13th-century keep.

We will next descend to the N. 703 and reascend the Dordogne Valley as far as Lalinde, an old regular 13th-century bastion which has been built on the site of the Gallo-Roman town of *Diolindum*. Of its ancient fortifications, it has preserved the 13th-century Porte de Bergerac of stone and brick and the remains of the 14th-century House of the Governor.

We will continue to follow the N. 703 eastward and at Sauveboeuf, where we can see a Renaissance castle which has been very much remodelled, but which has preserved a beautiful monumental fountain, we will take the D. 31, twice crossing the Dordogne, which here makes a large loop, in order to visit the church with cupolas at TREMOLAT.

Saint Cybar was born at Trémolat in the 6th century. His birthplace stood near a church which was ruined at the close of the 6th century and replaced by another built by Charlemagne, who enriched its treasure chamber by a shirt of the Infant Jesus. In 982, the monastery to which the church was assigned, and which was a dependency of the Abbey of Saint-Cybar of Angoulême, was given by the Bishop Grimoard to his brother, Aymeric de Mussidan.

The church before us was built in two instalments in the early 12th century, beginning with the nave, but by utilising the walls of an earlier building. We have a single nave with three circular cupolas preceded by a heavy tower which looks like a keep and forms a steeple-porch. The transept crossing has an ovoidal cupola on pendentives, while the arms of the transept have pointed barrel-vaulting and the choir is formed of two bays which terminate in a flat wall.

The exterior has a massive aspect. In the 18th century, the tower was surmounted by a rounded pediment forming a steeple-arcade with twin bays with basket-handle decoration and the door was rebuilt beneath an entablature supporting a recess.

We will return as far as Traly by way of the D. 28 from where we have some beautiful views over the Dordogne, and we reach Badefos where we will find the remains of a castle which belonged to the House of Biron; it was partially destroyed by the People's Representative, Lakanal. We will now follow the left bank of the Dordogne and pass through Couze where we can see an 11th and 12th century church to which a chapel was added in the 13th and 14th centuries. By way of the D. 37 we will reach LANQUAIS, where one of the most important *châteaux* of Périgord awaits us.

It was originally, in the 15th century, an impressive fortress and a part of this remains: a rectangular main building equipped with machicolation and flanked, on one side, by an elegant hexagonal tower and, on the other, by a heavy round tower. Then in the second half of the 16th century, during the reign of Henri II or Charles IX, the main building was reconstructed on the same lines as the original one and to this was added a pavilion with a truly monumental aspect, its architecture being at the same time classic and full of originality. The lower storeys are decorated with tyings and ornamentation, while above the twin windows some large very ornamental dormers carry a touch of fantasy with the turrets which surmount them and which, likewise, adorn the chimney shafts. While the ancient buildings are of a very warm yellow stone, those of the Renaissance are of a colder grey. We must admire the door, inspired by Italian art, of the hexagonal tower and the beautiful fireplaces which we can see in the interior; for a visit can be authorised. Lanquais has been attributed to Nicholas Bachelier who worked at Bournazel, Montal and Assier.

Founded by the de Mons family, Lanquais belonged in 1577 to the Marquise de Lacropte. That same year her son, Galliot de la Tour, was beseiged there by his cousin the Vicomte de Turenne whose cannon fired more than 500 volleys on the castle and traces of this bombardment can still be seen. During the reign of Louis XIV, Lanquais was bought by the Marquis d'Antin and soon afterwards passed into the hands of the de Gourgue family.

We will continue to Varennes and then descend the

Dordogne Valley by, first of all, crossing to the right bank where the road is better. We pass through Mouleydier where we can see the Château de Tiregant which is nothing more than an orangery transformed into a dwelling place and which was a dependency of a great *château* begun by M. d'Augeard, President of the Parlement of Bordeaux, and whose construction was interrupted by the Revolution.

After Creyesse, we can return to the left bank in order to see the CHATEAU DE PILES which since the 15th century has belonged to the de Clermont family and since 1580 to the Durfort-Boissière family of the House of Duras. There remain a 15th-century round tower crowned by machicolation and a beautiful 16th-century pavilion to which, on the other façade, a building was added in the 18th century. The *ensemble* has grace and charm with the pillars surmounted by cannon balls and with the balustrades which adorn the courtyard entrance still limited by two small pavilions. The Château de Piles, which had long been left in a state of abandonment, has been very well restored.

We next reach BERGERAC which in the 16th century was one of the Protestant fortresses. In other words, it has preserved nothing of its past except a large 16th- or 17th-century building known as the Château de Henri IV. Thus we merely pass through it and take the D. 13 southward which leads us to MONBAZILLAC where we should not miss tasting the local wine as well as visiting the *château* which is an elegant 16th-century construction and very well preserved. The main building, flanked by four round towers, is not lacking in grace with its crown of machicolation, its stone dormers on two storeys, the picturesque silhouette of its pepper-pots and its high roofs. The entrance gate is surmounted by a decorative motif embedded in pilasters in Italian Renaissance taste. It lies on the top of a hill from which there is a pretty view over the vineyards of Monbazillac and the Dordogne Valley.

It was built by the d'Aydie family, several of whose members were Viscounts of Monbazillac. The Balacan family acquired it during the reign of Louis XIV.

Somewhat farther on, we will find the Château de Bridoire, between Ribagnac and Rouffignac, at the top of a steep promontory which overlooks a charming valley. Built in the second half of the 15th century and very much remodelled in the early 17th century, it was besieged and partially ruined by Montluc in 1638. It was again besieged and dismantled in 1649 by the Duke of Epernon. It belonged successively to the Houses of Aubeterre and Pardaillan de la Mothe-Gendrin. The Marquis of Souillac acquired it in exchange in 1753.

It consists of an *ensemble* of picturesque buildings flanked by several round towers with machicolation, watch-paths and pepper-pot roofs, the windows have mullions, and dormers with sharp pediments pierce the roofs. The courtyard is enclosed by a crenellated wall with entrance posterns which date from the restoration undertaken in the 19th century.

By way of the D. 17 and D. 15 we will go to see a final manor of Périgord, that of GAGEAC which dates, in so far as its main work is concerned, from the 14th century, with its two heavy square towers equipped with machicolation connected with a main building which was restored and remodelled in the 17th century. From this period date the large rectangular windows which pierce the walls of the building, also those of the towers. The crenellated wall, flanked by small watch-paths with a corbel course which encloses the forecourt, also dates from the same period.

By way of the D. 15 and the N. 136 we will proceed to SAINTE-FOY-LA-GRANDE, an ancient 13th-century bastion and a secure stronghold for the Protestants in the 16th century. Its fortifications have now been replaced by avenues, but we can see some old houses, including a 15th-century timbered one, in the Rue de la République, the ancient tower of a Commandery of the Templars and the covered ways which border the Place Gambetta on three sides.

We will continue to follow the N. 136 as far as MONT-CARET where, around the small Romanesque church, we will find the foundations of important Gallo-Roman thermals. The first Roman mosaic was disclosed in 1827 during the construction of a community wash-house along the edge of the cemetery. The *sous-préfet* of Bergerac then asked the *maire* to safeguard the mosaic and to extend the excavation. But the municipal council disregarded this suggestion and built its wash house on the mosaic, which illustrates what used to happen then to archaeological discoveries. This attitude is still, alas, very common.

Other archaeological discoveries were subsequently made and in 1921, since the cemetery was no longer in use, an inhabitant of Montcaret, M. Tauziac, transmitted a report of his excavations to the Historic Monuments Administration which decided to proceed with a systematic clearing of the ground.

An important *ensemble* of buildings has been disclosed, corresponding to a 4th-century establishment erected on the ruins of a 1st-century thermal baths, which had been destroyed about 275 by the Alamans. It was itself damaged by subsequent invasions from 406 onwards, but it was used as a place of worship and burial, as can be seen from the numerous 5th- to 12th-century tombs which have been found in three superimposed tiers.

Several chambers have preserved their large, beautiful 4th-century mosaics, decorated with a diamond motif, circles and octagonals. The most interesting is a large cross-shaped chamber with two rectangular arms and two semicircular ones, which was entirely paved with mosaics and heated by a hypocaust which has been protected by a glazed roof and around which there has been gathered all the objects found during the course of excavation.

Though its façade is modern, the transept and the choir of the Romanesque church are absolutely remarkable. We must admire the capitals and the arcades of the apse and, on the exterior, the sculptures of the north transept.

We will continue to follow the N. 136 as far as la Mothe-Montravel where we can see the remains of a manor which belonged to the Cardinal de Soudis and which was entirely razed by order of the Maréchal d'Elboeuf. There remains a

CHATEAU DE SAINT-JEAN-DE-COLE.

24. CHATEAU DE BOURDE

CHATEAU DE PILES.

26. CHATEAU DE MONBAZIL

circular tower which has kept its crenels and its watch-path, which is supported by consoles with attractive mouldings and surmounted by an elegant turret. Against this tower there has been built a small two-storey Renaissance construction which is limited by the gable of the ancient dwelling and whose pretty door with a pediment framed by pilasters is surmounted by two mullioned windows.

By way of the D. 9 we can visit the *château* where Montaigne was born and where he died, somewhat above SAINT-MICHEL-DE-MONTAIGNE. The *château* itself is of no interest, as it was burnt down at the close of the last century and has been rebuilt on a different plan and in an infinitely richer style with the stupidity which was too often characteristic of the wealthy people of that time, who transformed the beautiful dwellings which they possessed into pastiches.

Very fortunately, the tower in which the author of the *Essays* enjoyed writing and meditating, "*pour s'y soustraire à la communauté et conjugale et filiale, et civile*", was not touched by the fire and we see it as it existed in the time of Montaigne. The ground floor is occupied by a chapel, narrow and obscure, with the altar placed in a niche set into the wall. Montaigne's room was above and the top storey contained the philosopher's library. The books are, of course, no longer in their place, for there is no cult of great men in France, but his favourite sayings are still painted on the beams and the rafters of the ceiling. On the wall this inscription also can be seen: "In the year of Christ 1571, at the age of thirty-eight, on his birthday, Michel de Montaigne, long weary of the servitude of the Court and public employments, while still hale and healthy, retired to the bosom of the learned virgins where in calm and freedom from all cares he will spend what little remains of his life, now more than half run out. If the fates permit, he will complete it in this abode, this sweet ancestral retreat; and he has consecrated it to his freedom, tranquility and leisure".

We enjoy meditating on these wise words as we return to the N. 136 which we will leave at Tizac in order to visit the

M

CHATEAU DE CURTON which rises on the far end of a promontory overlooking the valley of a small river which somewhat farther on plunges into the Dordogne. In the 14th and 15th centuries, Curton was an important fortress which was defended by deep moats and a rectangular *enceinte*. The square keep is flanked by angle buttresses, two flat and the other two pointed, one of which contains a spiral staircase. It consists of six storeys with barrel-vaulting and surmounted by a platform.

Entrance to the castle, on the east, is by a tower forming a porch, to the right of which we can still see the ancient kitchen. Two stairway turrets were added in the 15th and 16th centuries in the east and west angles of the courtyard. The last named is very charming with its mullioned windows surmounted by heavy shell decoration. But the *ensemble* of the buildings has been left in a deplorable state.

As the family of the Sires de Curton was extinct in the last quarter of the 14th century, Henry IV of England gave the castle to Louis de Beaumont who, having joined the French party, was deprived of his new land for the benefit of the city of Bordeaux. After the conquest of Guienne by Dunois, Charles VII presented the barony of Curton in 1451 to Jacques de Chabannes-La Pallice who died in 1453 from wounds received during the Battle of Castillon. Curton belonged to the House of Chabannes until the Revolution.

Somewhat further on, near Espiet, we can see the **CHATEAU DE PREISSAC**, another very well preserved fortress, which also lies on the far end of a promontory. It is surrounded by an *enceinte* which is flanked by watch-towers and pierced by a pointed arch gate surmounted by machicolation. The *château* which is of an irregular design was rebuilt in the early 19th century, but it has preserved its entrance gate which is flanked on the outside by two beautiful round towers.

The first seigneurs called themselves "Soudans de Pireissac". They were succeeded by the de Montferrand, de Ségur, de Pierrebuffière and de la Chassagne families.

Passing a very pretty fortified farm whose gate is still

surmounted by its machicolation, we will return to the N. 136 which we will follow as far as CAMSARSAC, the very type of the ancient *castéras* of Dordogne. Built towards the close of the 13th or in the early 14th century, it was first restored in the early 16th century and again in the 19th century, but if windows have been pierced in the walls, it has retained its early silhouette, just as it appeared in the studies of Viollet-le-Duc. It was originally surrounded by moats and two round turrets and two watch-towers defended the angles. There was also some machicolation above the entrance gate and the *ensemble* was crowned with crenels and machicolation.

A kilometre away, in the midst of vineyards, we can visit another manor, that of le Grand Puch, built on the same model. It also is rectangular in plan with two corbelled turrets on the west and two high polygonal towers on the east. A watch-path is supported by brackets in four rows which are surmounted by steep roofs. Built in the 14th century by the Chevalier Gaillard du Puch, it came into possession of the House of Ségur in 1572. It was subsequently remodelled and rectangular bays caused it to lose its aspect of a fortress.

We will return to the N. 136 and this time follow it as far as Bordeaux.

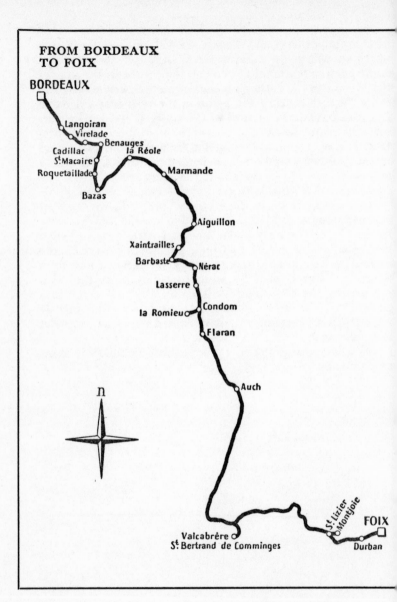

FROM BORDEAUX
TO FOIX

BORDEAUX

Langoiran
Virelade
Cadillac
St Macaire
Roquetaillade
Bazas

Benauges
la Réole

Marmande

Aiguillon

Xaintrailles
Barbaste
Nérac
Lasserre
la Romieu
Condom
Flaran

Auch

n

St Lizier
Montjoie
FOIX
Valcabrère
St Bertrand de Comminges
Durban

ITINERARY IX

FROM BORDEAUX TO FOIX

Latresne — Langoiran — Cadillac — Château de Benauges — Saint-Macaire — Château de la Roquetaillade — Bazas — La Réole — Aiguillon — Xaintrailles — Barbaste — Nérac — Condom — La Romieu — Laressingle — Abbaye de Flaran — Auch — Saint-Bertrand-de-Comminges — Saint-Gaudens — Saint-Martory — Saint-Lizier — Montjoie — Durban — Foix.

W E will leave Bordeaux by way of the D. 10 which follows the right bank of the Garonne which is especially pleasant with its *guinguettes* and its square steeple of 1628. LATRESNE has a 16th-century *château*. Camblanes has a noble dwelling and the fortified mill of la Rigaudière. Then, at Cambes, we see another fortified Romanesque church. But we will make a special stop at Langoiran.

The seigniory of LANGOIRAN, which in the 13th century belonged to the d'Escoussan family, passed in the middle of the following century into the hands of the House of Albret, then into those of the Montferrand family. In the 17th century, the Duke of Eperon undertook its demolition.

The ruins, which rise on the top of a hillock overlooking the Garonne, are extremely picturesque. Built in the 13th century on an irregular plan, the fortress was remodelled in the following century. The keep, a magnificent cylindrical tower which unfortunately has lost its crowning and whose walls were twelve feet thick, dates from the 14th century.

The ogival vaulting has collapsed, but we can still see the toothing stones of the three storeys of octagonal rooms. On the first one, there are the remains of paintings and the elements of a pavement of enamelled squares with coats-of-arms and other decorative motifs.

It is enclosed by a first *enceinte* which is flanked by towers and there are remains of the second *enceinte*. The building is absolutely in need of consolidation and clearance work.

At Rions we can see the beautiful Porte de Lhyan of 1304 and a high tower which has been restored. The church, very much remodelled, has lost all its interest, but a few old houses can be seen.

The D. 10 next passes through CADILLAC where we should not miss seeing the *château* which, thanks to M. D'Welles, is now being repaired.

It is an impressive construction of the close of the Renaissance and the period of Louis XIII, which was built from 1598 to 1615 by Pierre Souffron for Jean-Louis de Nogaret, Duke of Eperon. We are familiar with the role which the Duke of Eperon played at the Court of Henry III and that of Louis XIII. He himself held a real court in his own *château* at Cadillac.

It is a building which is already classic, but, still surrounded by moats, with its turreted bastions and watch-towers, it is a veritable fortress. The courtyard has a narrow central building which recalls the ancient keep; it is flanked by wings and the façade which faces the garden is separated from the narrow central building by a moat spanned by a small stone bridge, which has a narrow gate defended by openings for arquebusiers. The *ensemble* is a very impressive but simple design.

In the interior, the rooms for pomp and display on the ground and first floor still partly have their painted beamed ceilings and their monumental sculptured fireplaces by Jean Langlois. They are some of the most beautiful fireplaces of the Louis XIII period which we possess; some, like the one of Victory, are embellished with statues and bas-reliefs, the others offer merely a sumptuous decoration of marble and coloured stones. The sculptures have unfortunately been broken or disfigured.

We can also see at Cadillac the 15th-century church whose façade and steeple are modern, but which is flanked by the funerary chapel of the Dukes of Eperon built in 1606, containing a sumptuous mausoleum built by Pierre Biard; it was destroyed at the Revolution.

Finally, this ancient rectangular bastion which Pierre de Grailly, Captal (Seigneur) de Buch, had founded in 1280 to be the capital of the county of Benauge, has preserved the impressive remains of its ramparts which were built in 1316, notably the beautiful Porte de Mer, pierced in a square tower with machicolation. We can still see another gate along the road to Saint-Macaire, pierced in the Tour de l'Horloge, which is also square and topped by a slate roof.

By way of the D. 11, which we will follow for six kilometres, we will visit the CHATEAU DE BENAUGES which rises on a small isolated hillock. It consists of two extended *enceintes*, the second flanked by five round towers, the one on the east being the better preserved, although it has lost its crowning and was topped by a pepper-pot roof. The keep, which lies on the north-east, is in the shape of a trapezium. A dwelling, which is still in use, was built in the 18th century on the south-west side, while the crenels of the curtain walls were replaced by balustrades. The result is not always a pleasant one, but the feudal sections which have remained still have an impressive look. Likewise, no improper restoration has taken place here.

The Seigneurs of Benauges were known as early as the 11th century. Guillaume II Taillefer, Count of Augoulême, became one by his marriage and he was succeeded by his son-in-law, Guillaume Amanieu Gavarett. In 1253, Simon de Montfort, Count of Leicester, besieged Benauges in the name of the King of England and captured it. Thirteen years later it was given to Jean de Grailly; and Jean III de Grailly, the famous Captal de Buch, who died in the Tour du Temple in Paris where he had been held a prisoner by the French, held it. After him, Benauges passed to his uncle,

Archambaud de Grailly, who had married Isabelle de Foix. Their children took the name of Foix and Gaston de Foix was Seigneur of Benauges when the French captured it. He refused to submit to Charles VII and left to die in Aragon. His son, Jean, attached himself first to Henry VI of England who presented him with the county of Kendal or Candale, that is to say he became the head of the famous House of Foix-Candale. He returned to France and submitted to Louis XI. The military history of Benauges had come to an end. In the 17th century it was purchased by a President of the Parliament of Bordeaux, M. de Gombault.

We will return to Cadillac and by way of the D. 10 which continues to border the Garonne, we pass some hillocks which are famous for their vines. Loupiac with its white wines, Saint-Croix-du-Mont, Verdelais, where we can see the property of François Mauriac and, in the cemetery, the tomb of Toulouse-Lautrec who died in the 15th-century Château Bardot.

At the end of twelve kilometres, we reach SAINT-MACAIRE, a very picturesque little town which has preserved a part of its *enceinte* of the 13th and 15th centuries, with three of its fortified gates, the 13th-century Porte de Cadillac with its oblong tower, the Porte de Turon and the Porte Dumas; also several ancient houses, some of which are worth mentioning, like the 14th-century Maison Messidan, the house with the Gothic bay-windows in the Rue des Bans, the house with mullioned windows known as the "Poste de Relais" dating from the time of Henri IV. The Place du Marcadieu is enclosed by covered ways, the majority dating from the 15th century, but the houses fronting on them have been rebuilt or have collapsed. At Saint-Macaire, as with most of the small towns which have been fortunate enough to retain a certain picturesqueness, nothing is being done to safeguard them. This square which could be beautiful has become a commonplace; one of the ancient houses which has remained intact with its mullioned windows has recently been occupied by a garage for which purpose a large opening has been pierced, closed by a screen of sheet metal.

Saint-Macaire has at least its Church of Saint-Sauveur which is worthy of an attentive visit. The apse and the transept on a trefoiled plan offer an extremely remarkable design of the middle of the 12th century, with the blind arcades which decorate the three semicircles with their oven-shaped vaulting. The vaulting of the crossing presents a curious cupola resting on some heavy ogival ribs. It is adorned, as also is the apse, with some interesting 14th-century paintings which unfortunately were restored in a clumsy manner in 1859. The nave dates from a subsequent period and has ogival vaulting. After a bay, which dates from the close of the 12th century, there are three others dating from the 13th century, as well as the portal of the façade whose sculptures have been very much mutilated. An elegant 14th-century hexagonal steeple flanks the building at the angle of the nave and the north arm of the transept. The apse and the lateral façades are in an extremely pleasant design.

At Saint-Macaire we will cross the Garonne and on the opposite side we find Langon.

The municipal officers of this prosperous small town have not thought it worth while to show any interest in preserving the past of their mediaeval city which victoriously resisted du Guesclin in 1374 and Montgomery in 1566. The Church of Notre-Dame-du-Bourg, which was a dependency of the Monastery of the Grande-Sauve and which had been built about 1155, has been transformed into a dance hall. Its principal elements have been transported to the Cloisters Museum in New York, where you would be able to admire its very fine capitals.

By way of the D. 11 we will visit two buildings which are well worthy of this detour of some thirty kilometres: the CHATEAU DE LA ROQUETAILLADE and the Cathedral of Bazas.

At Roaillan we will take, on the left, the road which leads us to the Château de la Roquetaillade which in the 13th century belonged to the La Mothe-Langdon family. The new castle was built about 1306 by Cardinal de la Mothe, nephew of the Pope Clement V. In the 19th century it was restored under the guidance of Viollet-le-Duc, whose name unfortunately is no reference.

It consists of two castles included in the same *enceinte*, but distinct from each other: the old castle whose plan was semicircular and of which there remains a three-storey tower whose machicolation has been rebuilt, and the new castle. The latter rises on a rectangular plan with a round tower and is crenellated at each angle. Two other similar towers frame the entrance gate. The curtain walls, which have been pierced during the modern period with large windows, are crenellated and equipped with watch-towers. The huge square central keep is 105 feet in height. Only the façade with its fourth tower is still impressive. The three others are not at all interesting. A 14th-century chapel could not have been restored in a worse manner.

We will now follow the D. 125 which joins the N. 132 and leads us to BAZAS whose Gothic cathedral replaced a Romanesque one, which was destroyed by the English in 1198 and which itself replaced an early construction ruined by the Normans.

The first stone of the building we see was laid in 1233 by Arnaud de Tontolon, Seneschal of Agenais. It received considerable gifts from Clement V. However, work advanced slowly and it was not until 1537 that the façade was finished. But the Protestants managed to destroy it and only spared the façade and the portals after the inhabitants had paid them 10,000 *écus*. After their departure, the choir and the high vaulting had to be re-built.

It is a nave of ten bays, which is flanked by side-aisles followed by a shorter bay and a five-sectional chevet enclosed by an ambulatory on to which there open five radiating chapels. A steeple has been built on to the two first north bays.

The building is a beautiful design in the High Gothic style and its choir is especially impressive. Yet what most attracts us is the façade with its three 13th-century portals and numerous arch mouldings whose sculpture is extremely remarkable. The central portal is devoted to *The Last Judgment* with scenes above from *The Life of St. John the Baptist*, *The Resurrection of the Dead*, *The Weighing of Souls* and *Christ between the Virgin and Saint John*, while angels and numerous personages adorn the mouldings.

The portal on the right represents *The Death and The Crowning of the Virgin* with, on the moulding, *The Tree of Jesse*, *The Zodiac* and *The Labours of the Months*, while the portal on the left is devoted to *The Life of Saint Peter*.

On the ancient ramparts we can still see the 13th-century Porte du Gisquet between two beautiful towers with machicolation, then by way of the D. 12 we will do the 23 kilometres which separate us from la Réole.

The Church of Saint-Pierre at LA REOLE, an ancient abbatial church, is rather disappointing. It lies between the monastic buildings which were rebuilt in the 13th century and partially hide it. The interior is of a single nave and heavy; the nave is too large for its development, although it is true that it has lost two bays. We have a building, dating from the close of the 12th and beginning of the 13th century, of a single nave which terminates in a seven-sectional apse having an inner wall passage and endowed in the 14th century with a transept with lateral chapels.

The castle is even less interesting. There remain merely the supporting section of the walls of the fortress which was built by Richard Coeur de Lion and a few sculptured stones. Damaged during the sieges of 1224 and 1253, the castle was almost entirely rebuilt during the second half of the 13th century, while at the same time a third *enceinte* was built. In 1629 Louis XIII ordered the Duke of Eperon to demolish the fortress and one of the angle towers, also two of the curtain walls, were razed. All that remain along the edge of the promontory overlooking the Garonne are three uncrowned towers which are connected with dwelling houses and which have deserved a better fate than this kind of transformation.

But we must see above all the ancient Hôtel de Ville of la Réole which dates from the close of the 12th century and which is one of the rarest civil monuments we have of that period. It consists of a very curious ground floor which served as a market. Four arcades give access to a large hall resting on a row of five thick columns with enormous capitals. Above, an equally large chamber obtains its light from six small twin windows. In the 14th century the gables were rebuilt and the building was raised.

We will now follow the N. 113. After nineteen kilometres, at Marmande, we can visit the Church of Notre-Dame whose apse and choir date from the 13th century, while the façade and the nave are from the 14th century. But we should not miss seeing the two charming small galleries of a Renaissance cloister, which has great elegance with its delicate rectangular pillars decorated and surmounted by Corinthian capitals.

Still following the N. 113, which ascends the valley of the Garonne, as far as AIGUILLON, a distance of 28 kilometres, we can glance at the impressive castle of the Dukes of Aiguillon. It was rebuilt by Leroy, pupil of Soufflot, for the next-to-last Duke, Minister of Louis XV, in 1765; and one wing has remained unfinished. One can visualise, even in its present dilapidated state, the beautiful design of this building; and it deserves better treatment than the negligence it has suffered at the hands of the municipal authorities. Aiguillon was raised to a duchy in 1599 by Henri de Lorraine, Duke of Mayenne, who was killed in 1621 at the siege of Montauban. This again occurred in 1634 for Antoine Lauge, favourite of Gaston d'Orléans, then four years later for the mother of Richelieu.

We will cross the river and by way of the N. 642—and not the D. 108 which is very poor—we will reach XAINTRAIILES in order to see the 12th-century castle with its square keep which, about 1440, was almost entirely rebuilt by Pothon, the celebrated companion-in-arms of Joan of Arc, who was made Maréchal de France in 1454.

It is an extremely charming building with its handsome square 15th-century keep which is surmounted by crenels and machicolation, its two square towers, the one enclosing a spiral stairway, its dwelling with watch-towers, its inner courtyard, severe and serious, and a small 18th-century construction with a balustraded staircase added.

Returning along the D. 141 which passes the foot of the small town of Mongaillard, which is still enclosed by its *enceinte* on to which has been built a fortress, now in ruins, we reach the charming small village of Vianne which has preserved its beautiful 13th-century *enceinte* flanked by towers and pierced by four gates. The church is partially Romanesque and partially Gothic, and admirers of Marcel Prévost can evoke his memory at the Château de la Roche.

We will follow the N. 642 which passes through Lavardac in order to see the mill of BARBASTE, a fortified mill of the 14th and 15th centuries which was also a small manor which Henri IV often enjoyed visiting. In 1936 it was unfortunately damaged by a fire and it is now occupied by some sort of factory. It is regrettable that the Fine Arts Administration has not thought of clearing and restoring it. But its present state is worth seeing and from the old Gothic bridge which overlooks it we can see its impressive and severe silhouette, with its four crenellated towers above the yellow waters of the Gélise.

We will join the N. 130 which passes near the very much dilapidated remains of the old Château de Séguinot of the 15th and 16th centuries which belonged to the Calvinist captain, Lanoue-Bras-de-Fer, and is now occupied by a farm.

After six kilometres we reach NERAC where a great deal of wishful-thinking is needed to evoke the ardent youth of Henri IV. What a pleasure it would be if we could find within this small city the place where the princes of Béarn held their court throughout the 16th century, the *château* which was enlarged successively by Charles and Jean d'Albret, Alain le Grand and completed by Jeanne d'Albret, Queen of Navarre. It was one of the most graceful constructions of the Renaissance period. It was long inhabited by Marguerite of Valois, who received her brother, Francis I, there. His grandson, Henri of Béarn, the future Henri IV, installed his court there and it was especially gallant and gay. Here also in October 1578 he received his mother-in-law, Catherine de Médici, when she came to take part in the famous conference of Nérac which resulted in the peace of February 28, 1579.

It was from Nérac, during the war known as the "War of the Lovers", that Henri organised his successful attacks against the Catholic fortresses of Guienne and Gascony. It was from Nérac that he departed to seize Cahors. But all these victories were mingled with gallant enterprises for which the small town and its surroundings served as a setting—casual love affairs, tender idylls, like that of Fleurette, who made Nérac into a small Cythera.

At that time the town must have been very pleasant. Its situation is picturesque, lying astride the Baïse which it dominates with its *château* whose four wings enclosed an inner courtyard which also was decorated. Within its heavy walls there were a number of Renaissance dwellings and a charming old bridge which still exists, linked the Petit-Nérac and the Garenne with the city.

When the town was captured by Louis XIII, the fortifications were dismantled and the ancient Calvinist fortress gradually lost its importance. The Revocation of the Edict of Nantes completed its ruin.

At the Revolution the *château*, which the Dukes of Bouillon had inherited but had never inhabited, was partially demolished. Of the four wings only one was spared. After having remained more than a century in a state of semi-abandonment, a decision was finally taken by the town in 1928 to acquire it, restore it and install a museum.

As at Anet and at Assier, we therefore have merely a fragment whose interest we should not underestimate, but it cannot revive the heroic and gallant atmosphere we had sought at Nérac.

This inner courtyard façade is decorated with a charming gallery of elliptical arcades, with twisted columns and pretty historiated capitals. On the ground floor there is a guard-room whose elegant vaulting is adorned with liernes and tiercerons, and also the oratory and the council room with its triple fireplace.

But these stones have lost their souls, all the more since they have lost the noble *décor* which surrounded them, those beautiful gardens which descended as far as the Baïse. All that remains is the Promenade de la Garenne which extends along the other bank. Here and there beneath the elms and century-old oaks planted by Antoine de Bourbon, there is a reminder of the loves of the young king. After the Pavillon des Mariannes and that of les Bains we see the Fontaine de Fleurette, where according to an erroneous tradition a pretty gardener, who had been seduced by Henri IV, drowned herself after being abandoned by him. Another fountain farther on, known as the Fontaine de Saint-Jean, has been attributed to the Knights Hospitalers of Saint John of Jerusalem and, after the Fontaine des Marguerites and the Theatre of Nature, we can see still another fountain which dates from the 16th century and is known as the Fontaine du Dauphin.

Where Nérac does not disappoint us is near the ancient "ass's back" bridge with it view over the banks of the Baïse. There is nothing there but old houses, notably at the side of the Petit-Nérac, which, in other words, has not changed since the time of Henri IV with its ancient dwellings dating from the Middle Ages and the Renaissance, which line the steep, winding streets. The Hôtel de Sully still exists in the street which bears its name so, near the Vieux-Pont, does the house of Calvin. On ascending the Grand-Nérac we still find some old houses, notably the one which was inhabited by Théodore de Bèze in the Rue Pusogne.

The 18th century has left an unexpected building in Nérac: the church which was rebuilt in 1780 in the Greco-Roman style by Louis, the architect of the theatre at Bordeaux.

The rest of the town no longer recalls Henri IV, but rather President Faillières, the son of a magistrates' clerk of Mézin who began at Nérac as an advocate, became *maire*, deputy and senator. President Fallières admirably incarnated the honest mediocrity of our times. It is perfectly understandable that henceforth his memory will outshine that of Marguerite de Valois, Jeanne d'Albret and Henri IV.

We will leave Nérac by way of the N. 130 and after eight kilometres we will visit, two kilometres away on the left by way of the D. 112, the charming Château de Lasserre, which was built in 1595. It has a pretty façade with a gallery with large semicircular arcades on the ground floor, surmounted by a storey of mullioned windows and dormers which are already in a classic style.

After having belonged to the d'Albret and the Montagu families, the seigniory of Lasserre became about 1570, through marriage, the possession of Jean Paul d'Esparliès de Lussan who was Seneschal of the Condomois and the Agenais. It was he who had the *château* rebuilt by a Sieur de Lavallée, a Parisian architect, as we can see from an inscription: "*Lavallée, maitre masson m'a faitte. 1596.*"

We then return to the N. 130 which thirteen kilometres farther on leads us to CONDOM. Like Nérac, Condom is a small town which has fallen from its ancient glory, but it has preserved some fine 17th- and 18th-century *hôtels*, with their wrought-iron balconies and their beautiful yellow stones mellowed by time. An ancient priory, transformed into a school, in a countryside setting, resembles a dream palace with its *cour d'honneur* which is fronted by a portico with coupled columns. Who is the architect to have conceived this magnificent building in the Louis XIV style?

But Condom also has a very beautiful cathedral which dates from the close of the Gothic period. It is massive and powerful and was built from 1506 to 1531 by Bishop Jean Marre. When in 1569 the Protestant chief, Montgomery, threatened to destroy it, the inhabitants repurchased it for 30,000 *livres*. What a happy period when works of art could be saved by buying them! Today no such thing is possible, so long as bombs rain from the sky from thousands of feet.

The façade is severe and narrow, placed between two heavy buttresses and surmounted by a tower. The interior has a single nave without a transept; its beautiful vaulting

CHATEAU DU GRAND-PUCH.

28. CHATEAU DE CADI

has liernes and tiercerons; it is flanked by side chapels and
terminates in a five-sectional apse. In addition, there is a
pretty 16th-century chapel behind the apse and a sacristy
with two superimposed polygonal rooms.

Although of the 16th century, the cloister is still Gothic,
massive and powerful, with its high arcades placed between
strong buttresses and its two rows of pillars which expand out
into the vaulting and a network of ribs. The Hôtel de Ville
and the Palais de Justice occupy the ancient archbishop's
palace, which had Bossuet for its titular.

In front of the cathedral there is a square 13th-century
tower which was sold for a few thousand francs about 20
years ago when I was travelling near Condom. I have long
dreamt that I had bought it!

On the outskirts of Condom we will visit two interesting
small towns. The first, eleven kilometres to the east by way
of the N. 131, is LA ROMIEU, an old town which dates
from the 11th century but which owes its splendour to the
Cardinal Arnaud d'Aux, who was Bishop of Albano and
who in 1318 founded the collegiate chapel and the pretty
cloister whose four galleries have some elegant arcades in a
radiating style and capitals adorned with foliage and
figures. This is a serious and sad place which inclines us to
meditation. It is dominated by the towers of the church.
There is one at each extremity. The octagonal one of the
chevet contains the sacristy on the ground floor and the
chapter-house on the second floor. The square west tower is
astride the south gallery of the cloister.

The church has a single nave of four bays with a pentagonal apse. It is surmounted on the exterior by a watch-path.
Some tombs recessed in the walls contain the remains of the
d'Aux family.

The town, which is in the shape of a pentagon, has
preserved a part of its fortifications pierced by three gates
and a postern, some old houses and its central square with
semicircular arcades.

By way of the D. 15 we can also go westward to LARES-
SINGLE which is but six kilometres away. It is a typical
N

small fortified village of Gascony. Its walls date from the 13th century. The *enceinte*, surrounded by moats, is polygonal with a tower on each angle. A beautiful gate, placed in a high tower with machicolation, was formerly preceded by a drawbridge. All this is almost intact, but the village has been abandoned, the houses are falling into ruins, so also are the walls. The Committee for the Salvage of French Art has, however, acquired a part and is preserving it.

Let us enter the village. Most of the houses merely have sections of their walls covered with bramble and nettle. Yet several are still inhabited. Two old women can be seen knitting at the doorstep. A little boy and girl are playing in the corner. We next reach the impressive ruins of a 13th and 14th-century fortress which was a residence of the Bishops of Condom until the 16th century. An enormous keep in the shape of a trapezium, its interior having completely collapsed, has preserved its spiral staircase in an elegant 16th-century turret.

Behind, the church occupies the ground floor of the keep. It consists of a rectangular bay with semicircular vaulting, which terminates in an oven-shaped apse behind which two rectangular bays with barrel-vaulting have been added. The entrance is flanked by two columns surmounted by handsome historiated capitals, the door is semicircular and on the tympanum there is a lamb and a cross. A large room above served as a chapel for the bishops. Access is by means of *une vis de Saint-Gilles*.

We will return to Condom and definitely leave this time by way of the N. 130, but after eight kilometres we will stop in order to take a small road which immediately leads us to the ABBAYE DE FLARAN. Founded by l'Escale-Dieu about 1151, this Cistercian abbey is one of the best preserved in France, although it was burnt down and pillaged by the Protestants of Montgomery in 1569. Built in the second half of the 12th century, the church has three naves and five apses with pointed barrel-vaulting, divided into three bays by twin projecting cross ribs. While the south side-aisle has pointed barrel-vaulting on cross ribs, the north one has ogival vaulting, because of the storey above which communicates with the first bay of the nave by a straight staircase recessed in the thickness of the wall. The pillars are reinforced by twin columns beneath the cross ribs and the large arcades of the nave, as well as beneath the arches of the transept crossing.

The façade consists of a central door which is semicircular and without a tympanum and flanked by two narrow doors. The archivolt adorned with a chrisma between two crosses is surrounded by a checker design of billets. Above a heavy horizontal plain moulding are two narrow windows one above the other, whose archivolt is enclosed by a ribbon moulding, falling on each side of a slender column. They are surmounted by an oculus framed by a band of checker design with small round openings. The gable has a long archery window.

A small sacristy with four ogival ribs resting on a central pillar is followed by a chapter-house with three naves with four isolated columns of marble, the one red, the other black, and the two others white, and the capitals are adorned with long flat leaves. They give on to a charming cloister which dates from the early 14th century. Three galleries have merely simple chamferred pillars, but the west one has some pretty arcades with twin slender columns.

A criminal antique dealer had dismantled a beautiful 12th-century door with its carved *décor* which connected the cloister with the church. It has since been returned.

We will return to the N. 130 which soon passes by Valence-sur-Baïse, a bastion which was founded on the hill which rises on the junction of the Baïse and the Auloue, at the close of the 13th century by the monks of Flaran.

There are the remains of the *enceinte*, an ancient castle, and on a square place a 14th-century church with its Romanesque façade.

After 33 kilometres we reach AUCH, which cares little for our visit, since, after the Liberation, the inhabitants wanted to offer the Americans, for the Train of Friendship, the chapter-house of the ancient Cordelier convent. In other words, this ancient town has preserved little of its past. With the exception of a cathedral, there is merely an amusing 15th-century timbered and brick house on the Place Sainte-Marie, the ancient 14th-century keep, and the ancient Archbishop's Palace with its beautiful façade decorated with 18th-century pilasters.

The Cathedral of Sainte-Marie is a beautiful building in the Flamboyant Gothic style whose Renaissance façade is already in a noble, classic design. We must specially admire the stalls which were carved from 1515 to 1551. Together with those of Amiens and Saint-Bertrand-de-Comminges, which we will shortly see, they are the most beautiful Renaissance stalls in France. The Flamboyant ornamentation of the upper parts of the backs of the seats is mingled with the Italian–Burgundian character of the personages in half-relief which decorate the panels and the mythological figures which can be seen side-by-side with Christian symbols.

We must admire also the cloister of the choir of 1609 which we owe to Pierre Souffron; and the splendid stained-glass windows of the choir and the transept. We owe the most remarkable ones to Arnaud de Moles and they are some of the most beautiful of the Renaissance period.

By way of the N. 129 which is a straight road for almost 63 kilometres, we return to the N. 117 which we will take to the left and follow for 13 kilometres as far as Montréjeau. There we reach the N. 125 to the right and at Labroquere, after having crossed the Garonne, we take the D. 26, which after two kilometres leads us to the foot of SAINT-BERTRAND-DE-COMMINGES.

This is one of those cities where the past submerges you, wraps you in the folds of a dream, and conquers you. The present has no other existence except the one it draws from the past which it evokes and whose traces it seeks to rediscover.

Saint-Bertrand-de-Comminges was once an important Roman town where Herod Antipas, Tetarch of Galilee, was exiled with his wife Herodias in 37 A.D. by Caligula. In the Middle Ages it enjoyed a new splendour when Bertrand de l'Isle-Jourdain raised it from its ruins and became a pilgrimage stop on the way to Saint James of Compostela. Today it is nothing more than a small town timidly installed on its hill, in the shadow of its cathedral and in the midst of its fields of ruins.

Lugdunum Convenarum, settled by what remained of the bands raised by Sertorius and destroyed by Pompey in 72 B.C., was established on an ancient *oppidum* which was already known as *Lugdunum*, the Hill of the Rising Sun.

The town of the Convenae prospered not only because of its mines, its marble quarries and its thermal springs, which were frequented by the Romans who found themselves within the neighbourhood, but also because it was honoured by the favour of the Emperors. Magnificent monuments were erected there. In 408, the Gallo-Roman town was destroyed, but the upper town, which as early as the 3rd century had been enclosed by ramparts, was not captured and life continued there until the 6th century. It was then that Gondowald, who had sought to rule over the central part of Gaul, was tracked down by the armies of Leudégésile, general of Gontran, King of Burgundy. He took refuge in the town with the last of his partisans, but they betrayed him, pushed him from the summit of a rock which is still known as *Matacan* (dog-killer). But, instead of being rewarded, the betrayers were put to death and not a stone was left standing in *Lugdunum Convenarum*.

The town was abandoned and for six centuries it was merely a heap of ruins until the day when Bertrand de l'Isle-Jourdain, who subsequently became Saint Bertrand and was named bishop of the region, installed the seat of the bishopric there and undertook the construction of the cathedral which we are about to see. Once again, the town prospered and developed. It became a meeting place for the pilgrims from all parts of Europe on their way to Saint James of Compostela. This intense traffic resulted in a joyous and animated town. But the period of pilgrimages passed and Saint-Bertrand-de-Comminges lay more and more out of touch with economic life. At the Revolution its bishopric was suppressed. Like a balloon which deflates, life disappeared from the town which had become without purpose and today it is nothing more than a modest setting, yet one that is so rich in architectural treasures that it has become a kind of Pyrenean Mont-Saint-Michel.

How impressive it is from the height of its belvedere, with its ancient houses and their ogival doorways, mullioned windows and corbelled turrets, with their fresh and innocent aspect facing the valley and the green, sombre mountains! It has preserved a part of its fortifications, whose masonry adjoining the Porte Majou dates from the 4th century. It was here, where the coat-of-arms of the Cardinal de Foix are placed near an ancient funerary stone, that Gondewald was killed during the scene related by Gregory of Tours. The Porte Cabirole, which was the principal entrance to the town, has above its semicircular arch a mutilated Roman inscription which is a dedication of the *Civitas Convenarum* to an Emperor, while on the left gate-framing there is an inscription of 1661 which indicates the tax set by the chapter for the entrance of fish.

Opposite and overlooking the valley, a small square aedicule, which seems to date from the 12th century with its curious sculptured heads was either an oratory or is the remains of a barbican.

The two houses which flank the Porte Cabirole are old: the one on the left dates from the 16th century, the one on the right was inhabited by numerous bishops.

Farther on, the Maison Bridault, whose façade is flanked by a polygonal turret and whose door is surmounted by a curb bit, a coat-of-arms which tells us about the proprietor, has been carefully restored and is now occupied by the Post Office. Somewhat farther away, another 15th-century timbered house has also been intelligently restored. After a porch which is surmounted by a flying buttress, and which marks the remains of the original Bishop's Palace, we reach the Cathedral, which occupies the summit of the hill.

The façade of the Cathedral, with its steeple-porch surmounted by a plain wooden structure enclosing balconies, with its restrained tympanum which features *The Apostles* and *The Adoration of the Magi*, has the severe and tragic aspect of certain Romanesque buildings. It was intended to receive the pilgrims who had taken the vow of humility and poverty and who exploited their sins along the roads of Europe in their search for the sanctuary which would give them remission. Having crossed the porch, then two bays which are still Romanesque, we discover a huge Gothic nave which is extremely light and elegant and which must have seemed a marvellous celestial station to the pilgrims on their dolorous journey. It is a remodelling of an early building which we owe to Bertrand de Got, who had been Bishop of Comminges. Because of the affluence of the faithful who came to venerate the remains of Saint Bertrand, he decided in 1304 to enlarge the sanctuary.

Years later, during the Renaissance, some magnificent wood-panellings were erected in this precious Gothic casket: an organ chest which fills an angle rises as high as the vaulting and is of one piece with the pulpit, while a rood-screen and choir screen form a huge enclosure, a second church within the church, which houses the high altar and 66 extraordinarily executed stalls adorned with subjects profane as well as sacred.

This remarkable work was executed by Bishop Jean de Mauleon in 1535. The high backs decorated with figures of Prophets, Virtues and Sibyls in the shell-like niches, with the double framework crest which surmounts the canopies and which is adorned with railings and various ornaments, the misericords and the framing of the seats, present us with a world of utter fantasy.

But even more interesting than these stalls, than the mausoleum of Saint Bertrand, the tombs of Hugues de Châtillon and Bertrand de Miremont, or the treasure chamber with its ivory cross, is the cloister. It is the most ethereal, the best-lighted, and the one closest to Heaven I have ever seen. While one of the galleries is Gothic, being rebuilt in the 15th century, the three others are Romanesque and rest on twin slender columns of marble, reinforced by pillars. We must admire the historiated capitals, notably the one which represents the harnessed horses and, above all, the four statues of the Evangelists, stiff and hieratic, which are resting against one of the pillars. Some ancient sarcophagi, and the door of the chapter-house complete this *décor* of stone, enclosing a flower bed with a large opening facing the near-by wooded slopes. How light and pure we feel in this harmony of pink-coloured stones, of flowers and verdure, in this Paradise-like retreat lying alongside the cathedral, suspended between mountain and sky, a real resting place where the soul finds peace and faith! We feel that we are at the gates of Heaven and that already the angels are walking with us.

On leaving the cathedral, we can go to see the two museums which contain vestiges from the Gallo-Roman city which extended at the foot of the hill. In the ancient chapel of the Benedictine Olivetains are the discoveries which we owe to the zeal of a schoolteacher, M. Sapène; and in an old 18th-century *hôtel* are those from the excavations undertaken by the State.

We can see also the foundations of the different buildings which have been cleared, thermal baths, a temple, a Christian basilica.

If we still continue, we will find, near the ancient *Vallis Capraria*, by turning to the right on the square of the present church and by taking a small road which crosses the fields, the Church of Saint-Just, which was the early cathedral of the diocese of Comminges and which is enclosed by yew trees and cypresses which seem to be the symbol of the memory of Rome. A 12th-century Romanesque gate near a very old oak tree leads to the cemetery surrounding it. It has two sepulchral inscriptions, one of which is Roman. Built in the 8th century with material taken from Roman ruins, the church was rebuilt at the close of the 11th and beginning of the 12th century. It consists of a nave in barrel-vaulting, with side-aisles in quarter-circle vaulting; and terminates in an oven-shaped apse between two apsidioles. In the interior, the apse contains a very elegant colonnade. Two superimposed antique columns lie at the entrance to the choir; others are arranged at the entrance of the apsidioles, with inscriptions and fragments of Gallo-Roman sculptures appearing here and there in the walls. Finally, behind the altar, a 14th-century tomb on a dais shelters a sarcophagus which is reached on each side by stone steps.

We enter the church through a magnificent lateral portal which dates from the close of the 12th century, whose jambs are adorned with four marble statues personifying Saint Etienne, Saint Just, Saint Pasteur and Sainte Hélène, surmounted by capitals representing scenes from the lives of these several saints. It is one of the noblest and most interesting portals I know of this period, one which really helps us to feel the purity and innocence of the faith of the high Middle Ages. These statues have an extraordinary dignity and nobility and we feel that the man who created them had not entirely forgotten the lessons of antiquity whose models were before him. The tympanum, also of marble, represents *Christ between The Evangelists*. As in the cloister of Saint-Bertrand and on the tympanum of Saint-Aventin, they hold their own individual symbols in their hands.

Saint-Bertrand-de-Comminges, which is both a Gallo-Roman Pompeii and a Pyrenean Mont-Saint-Michel, is well worth our detour and a careful visit.

We will return to the N. 125 and three kilometres after Labroquère, we will take the road on the right which leads directly back to Saint-Gaudens where we will again find the N. 117.

We can ignore SAINT-GAUDENS and SAINT-MARTORY whose buildings have been either demolished, remodelled or disfigured. Though at Saint-Gaudens the ancient 11th and 12th-century collegiate church, which was inspired by the Church of Saint-Sernin of Toulouse and devastated by Montgomery, has none the less preserved a Romanesque cloister and a Flamboyant portal. In the interior, we can see some capitals, which are either historiated or of Corinthian derivation, and the ancient Gothic chapter-house of the close of the 12th century.

But this district has been responsible for another architectural tragedy. The ancient Cistercian Abbey of Bonnefont, which was founded in 1136 by six monks who had come from Morimont, lay six kilometres west of Saint-Martory. It was stupidly torn to pieces, like Saint-Michel-de-Cuxa, Saint-Génis-des-Fontaines and many other Pyrenean monasteries. The church dates from the second half of the 12th century. One section—there were 64 elegant arcades of the 13th-century cloister—was used to decorate some houses, while other sections were subsequently re-erected in Saint-Gaudens in a public garden. The arches are semicircular, but the capitals with their foliated decoration are already Gothic. Six other arcades, which belonged to the chapter-house, and a portal decorate the façade of the ancient gendarmerie of Saint-Martory, a house which we will immediately find, on the left, at the entrance to the town. The modern church has inherited a 12th-century Romanesque door and an 18th-century marble *Virgin* which came from the same abbey. The 26 other capitals resting on two coupled slender columns are now in the Cloisters Museum in New York.

It is difficult to understand the aberration of the public administration and the local authorities who dispersed such a monumental *ensemble* which, had it remained intact, would have been a source of touristic wealth, for these remains, which are now part of houses or are standing in a public garden, no longer evoke the past. Could not the Fine Arts Administration envisage their return to Bonnefont?

To console ourselves, let us glance at the beautiful 12th-century Romanesque church of Montsaunès, which is that of an ancient commandery of the Templars. It is of a single nave with barrel-vaulting, whose frieze and capitals have been imitated from the antique. On each side of the door, there are two tombs, recessed in the wall, dating from the 13th century.

Next, the road follows the valley of the Salat which at Salies-du-Salat, is dominated by the square keep of a castle of the Counts of Comminges.

At Prat, on the summit of the hill which overlooks the

junction of the Salat and the Gouarège, we can see the *château* of the Counts of Comminges which subsequently passed into the possession of the Maulein and the Montpezat families. The façade which faces the garden has some beautiful Renaissance windows. It is broken by a turret and a tower whose door is adorned with corbels and Corinthian columns. We probably owe this decoration to Jean de Mauleon, Bishop of Saint Bertrand-de-Comminges, to whom we owe also the stalls of the cathedral.

After 25 kilometres, we cross the Salat in order to see the picturesque little town of SAINT-LIZIER which is spread out on its hill.

The ancient capital of the Couserans, conquered by Pompey, it became under the name of *Austria* an important Roman town. It has preserved a large part of its oval *enceinte* which lies on the top of the rocky hill overlooking the Salat. This *enceinte*, which dates from the 3rd or early 4th century, extends for as much as 2,300 feet. It was built of irregular small-sized stones broken by three rows of bricks and it is flanked by 12 towers; the six on the north are square and the six on the south semicircular. In the 12th century, one of the square towers was remodelled to serve as a keep.

A second *enceinte* was probably built afterwards, but its traces are hardly visible. Furthermore, we are not so much interested in the military buildings of Saint-Lizier as we are in its religious ones, its cathedrals; for, like Forcalquier and Sisteron, Saint-Lizier had the privilege of possessing two cathedrals during a period that lasted for four centuries.

In 450 Saint Vallier established an archbishopric there. In the 7th century it had a bishop of Portuguese origin who was so successful in his prayers that the town withstood a Visigothic army and subsequently took the bishop's name. His body was buried in a small oratory built on the outskirts of the town. It was on this site that a church, which was to become the present cathedral, was built and dedicated in 1117. While the other cathedral, which lay within the ancient Roman *enceinte*, in what became the upper town, was founded a century later.

Saint-Lizier remained an episcopal town until the Revolution, but it had somewhat fallen from its ancient glory, for it never recovered from the sack of 1130, when Count Bernard III of Comminges put it to fire and sword. Another town, Saint-Girons, was created near by, replacing if from a commercial point of view and absorbing most of its activity.

The Cathedral of Saint-Lizier is the most remarkable building in the town. It is, as a whole, a 12th or late 11th-century Romanesque building, whose large nave with three bays was raised and given ogival vaulting in the 14th century. The transept crossing, which is narrower than the nave and also has 14th-century ogival-vaulting, supports an octagonal steeple of that period, but the crenellated crowning is modern. The arms of the transept have transversal vaulting, the choir, whose stones, as we can see, came from an earlier Romanesque church, has an oven-shaped apse; also oven-shaped are the two lateral apsidioles, which are the remains of a much older construction. On the exterior the chevet is polygonal. The portal on the north side is surmounted by a porch; it dates from the 15th century and is built of brick with multiple torus; the archivolt rests on slender columns with capitals of marble adorned with foliage on an almond-shaped astragal.

There are some interesting furnishings, including some 17th-century stalls, a 16th-century organ chest, a 14th-century fresco; but what interests us most is the cloister, for it is one of the most attractive Romanesque cloisters in France. Its construction dates from the close of the 12th century. According to a tradition, it was under these arcades that in 1216 Simon de Montfort signed an agreement with the Bishop of Saint-Lizier. It consists of 32 semicircular arcades resting alternately on single or twin columns of marble, whose very handsome capitals are adorned with an interlacing design like a basket-weave or with personages, masks or animals. The galleries have a wooden ceiling with a 15th-century timbered gallery, which has a simple roof of round tiles. There are some tombstones in the walls.

The Cathedral of Saint-Lizier is a modest *ensemble*, but one of great purity dominated by the elegant steeple which is in the Toulouse style of the cathedral.

The other Cathedral, that of Notre-Dame de la Sède, and the Bishop's Palace were built in the ancient *castrum*, as also were the three semicircular Romanesque towers which flank the long façade overlooking the town. Bishop Bernard de Marmiesse rebuilt the palace from 1655 to 1680; unfortunately both cathedral and palace have been incorporated in a large mental hospital which occupies the whole crown of the hill.

Although it is now only the hospital chapel, the Cathedral of Notre-Dame can still be seen, though, but for a portal which is partially Romanesque, it merely dates from the close of the 14th century. In the 15th century, Bishop Jean d'Aula built the side-chapels and a cloister which has been demolished. There remains a nave of three bays which is flanked on the north by three side-chapels and followed by a semicircular apse. We can see some tombstones and some fine wood panelling of the close of the 17th century. In addition, the 12th-century chapter-house, whose door and two façade windows are adorned with curious Romanesque capitals, was rebuilt in the 15th century. Two central slender columns support ogival vaulting. But it is now a surgical operating theatre and cannot be visited.

Most of the houses in the town have lost their character. There is little to notice except the curious vaulted passages which run along the ground floors of a few houses, a 15th-century house in the Place de l'Eglise and the 14th-century Tour de l'Horloge.

Instead of proceeding directly to Saint-Girons, we will take the road which leads to MONTJOIE which is but two kilometres away, and I am certain that, like myself, you will have much pleasure in discovering this precious little village with the valuable aid of the plan which is reproduced in Pierre Lavendan's *Histoire de l'Urbanisme*.

It is a typical example of those villages of refuge built by the peasants during the troublesome period of the Hundred

Years' War. They did not resort to famous technicians; but their own skilful masons built the walls in the form of a rectangle with the houses against them and, in the centre, the fortified church to act as the keep. All this has come down to us almost intact, without having been touched by what is known as "progress", just as the people in the 14th century built it.

This modest *enceinte* was not built to resist a regular army but merely pillaging bands. It is flanked on the west by two small towers and pierced by two gates. The façade of the church is a real fortress façade, massive, fearful and strange, with its two huge buttresses crowned by sectional turrets which frame two rows of crenels with a three-storey gable-steeple in the centre.

When we approach Montjoie and see above its modest ramparts, which are partially in ruins, the fine silhouette of this façade, we are overcome by real enthusiasm: here are the purest joys which the French landscape has in store for us. The large towns have been destroyed; the architects of the Historic Monuments Administration, on the pretext of restoring them, have almost entirely rebuilt and often distorted the buildings which had not been destroyed: we admire their work, where we can, without emotion. Here, on the contrary, our sensibility has no bounds: all these stones affect and exalt us, they vibrate in the sunlight, they confide in us, they sing and talk, for they have much to tell us. This village is much older than it seems: a temple to Jupiter occupied the site of the church and this gave the name *Mons Jovis*. But this detail of its history is there, sensible and alive, in the stones of its walls, its church and its modest peasant houses. All this has a language and I pity those who fail to understand it.

Three kilometres away is Saint-Girons, which comprises the town, properly-speaking, called Bourg-Sous-Vic on the right bank of the Salat and Villefranche on the left bank, a bastion created in 1300. From an architectural point of view, there is merely the Church of Saint-Valier which has a fine Romanesque portal in an edifice which was rebuilt in the

14th and 15th centuries with a heavy crenellated steeple-wall of the Toulousian type.

We will continue on the N. 117, which first of all follows the valley of the Baup, then that of the Augolle. Then after 11 kilometres we pass through Rimont, an ancient bastion founded in 1272. It has preserved practically nothing of the Abbey of Combelongue, which was founded about 1175 by the Prémontrés, then after five kilometres we pass through Castelnau which is dominated by the ruins of a castle which dates from the 13th and 15th centuries.

Somewhat farther on, at the hamlet of Segalas, we will take, on the left, the D. 15 in order to see at Durban the impressive ruins of the Château de Saint Barthélemy which dates from the 12th, 13th and 15th centuries. Three *enceintes* in the form of a parallelogram can be seen.

We will return to the N. 117 and follow it as far as FOIX where on arrival we have fine views over the valley of the Ariège and the castle of the Counts of Foix.

FROM BORDEAUX
TO JACA

BORDEAUX

Labrède

Budos
Villandrault   Uzeste
Préchac

Roquefort
Villeneuve-
de Marsan
Grenade
s/Adour   Lau
St Sever   Aire-sur-
St Jean   l'Adour
Hagetmau
Amou
Orthez

Nayarrenx

L'Hôpital-
St Blaise   Oloron Ste
-Marie

Sarrance

Somport

Canfranc

JACA

n

ITINERARY X

FROM BORDEAUX TO JACA

Labrède — Landiras — Budos — Villandrault — Uzeste
— Préchac — Circuit des anciens châteaux de Ciron —
Roquefort — Sarbazan — Aire-sur-l'Adour — Le Lau
— Abbaye de Saint-Jean-de-la-Capelle — Saint-Sever —
Hagetmau — Amou — Orthez — L'Hôpital Saint-
Blaise — Oloron — Sarrance.

WE will leave Bordeaux by way of the N. 113. After 26 kilometres we will take, on the right, the road which leads, after 3 kilometres, to LABREDE where we will visit a Château de Montesquieu. Montesquieu was born there in 1689 and spent the great part of his youth and many later years there; for it was in this *château* that he wrote his *Esprit des lois* and his *Grandeur et décadences des Romains*. We can visit his room, which has been preserved intact with his furniture and other personal things, also his library which includes 7,000 books and several of his manuscripts.

But in addition to its memories of the famous writer, the Château de Labrède interests us for its architecture. It is an irregular polygon entirely surrounded by large moats with running water and consists of several buildings of different periods assembled in a picturesque manner. The rectangular keep is of the 13th century, the chapel of the 15th, a round tower with machicolation of the close of the 16th century, while certain other buildings were remodelled in the 17th century. Before the entrance gate are two bridges, each with its own gate bearing a Latin inscription.

The *ensemble* is very graceful. In fact, it is a typical example
of these small fortresses which had been adapted to seigniorial
life during the classic period, yet still retained their defensive
character.

We will return to the N. 113 and at Virelade we will see a
pretty 18th-century *château* which replaced a stronghold of
which there are some remains and which belonged in the 15th
and 16th centuries to the Segin and the d'Aulède families.

At Cérons we will descend in the direction of the picturesque valley of the Ciron which is rich in *châteaux*. Though
many are unfortunately in ruins.

We will take the D. 117 which passes through Illats where
we will find some old 14th-century houses; we will stop to see
the beautiful Romanesque portal of the church which likewise is interesting for its curious capitals.

Next, by way of the D. 11, we will reach LANDIRAS
whose 12th-century church has some fine Romanesque
baptismal fonts. Here, two kilometres farther on, taking the
D. 116, we will see the picturesque ruins, surrounded by
stagnant water, of the fortress of Landiras, which dates from
the 13th and 14th centuries.

By way of the D. 116, then the D. 118, we will reach
BUDOS and, before arriving at the village, we can glimpse,
rising amidst the vineyards, the five towers of the Château de
Budos which was built in 1306 by a nephew of Pope Clement
V on the model of Villandrault. It is famous for the siege it
withstood against the troops of Henry V, King of England.
Of the four angle towers, three are round and the last
polygonal. Each façade is flanked by a tower. The square
entrance tower is still crowned by machicolation and from
the *château* the view extends over the valley of the Ciron to the
famous vineyards of Bommes and Sauternes.

At Budos we can take a glance at the church whose apse
and the capitals of whose porch are Romanesque.

The D. 114 leads us to VILLANDRAULT where I
recommend the *Hôtel de Goth* for its accommodation and its
excellent food.

The Château de Villandrault was built by Bertrand de

Goth when, from being Archbishop of Bordeaux, he became Pope, thanks to his designation by Philip the Fair and his agreeing to leave the English Party for the French one. He was the first Pope to install himself at Avignon.

The Château de Villandrault is one of the most perfect examples of the *châteaux* of the plain with its rectangular plan embellished by a heavy cylindrical tower, projecting at each angle. The entrance, in the centre of the south side, is flanked by two cylindrical towers of the same dimensions. They lead us to a square courtyard which is bordered on the three other sides by dwellings.

The fortress is surrounded by a moat with stone flagging 18 feet deep and 45 feet wide, which was fed by a spring. To reach the entrance gate we cross a bridge which has a wooden superstructure and a swing drawbridge protected by a keep. The entrance gate was also defended by a fall-trap, while a portcullis and two other fall-traps constituted the corridor defences.

The towers contain four superimposed rooms and the defence was ensured by archery windows in the form of *croix pattée*, which were subsequently enlarged for the use of firearms. Hoardings were provided not only for the top of the towers but also for the curtain walls.

Clement V had bequeathed all his possessions to his nephew, Bertrand de Goth, whose daughter married Jean I of Armagnac. Villandrault passed into the hands of one of his cousins, Aymeric de Durfort, and during the reign of Charles V the *château* was occupied by du Guesclin. In 1572 the Huguenots underwent a formal siege and did not surrender until the number of 1,260 cannon balls had been fired. A decision was then taken to dismantle the stronghold, but only the south-east tower was demolished.

At the Revolution the municipality decided to use the stones of the *château* for the repair of the local roads. The dwellings disappeared, but fortunately the *enceinte* and the towers remained more or less intact. We can visit the *château* at our leisure after asking for the key from a near-by butcher shop.

The municipality had the fortunate idea of clearing the surroundings and cutting the bushes which hid the lines of the towers and the curtain walls. It is a mistake in France to think that castles are suitable for bramble and copse; in England they are surrounded by well-trimmed grass.

From the Château de Villandrault, we can see, four kilometres away, the spire of the collegiate church of UZESTE which, if not built by Clement V, was at least enlarged by him to contain his tomb. It is a very beautiful Gothic church whose nave of three double bays has six-sectional vaulting. It is flanked by side-aisles and terminates in a choir with ambulatory on to which three radiating chapels open. A very beautiful early 14th-century *Coronation of the Virgin* adorns the tympanum of the south portal. A steeple with a stone octagonal spire was added to the north side in the early 16th century. We can see the tomb of Clement V which was mutilated by the Protestants in 1577, the 14th-century funerary statue of the Maréchal Jean de Grailly, and a beautiful *Virgin and Child* of the same period.

From Uzeste we will take the D. 11E in order to tour the CHATEAUX DU CIRON. They rise above the gorges through which the river has cleared its way. The walls, ranging in height from 90 to 180 feet, have been invaded by a luxurious vegetation. At Labardin a path enables us to reach the ruins of the Château d'Illon. But we must retrace our steps, for there is no road available to follow the gorges. From the bridge over the Trave, we can see, on the left, the Châteaux of de la Trave and de la Füe, which are both in ruins, the first dating from the 14th century. Unfortunately, a factory immediately opposite the ruins has destroyed this fine site. We will continue as far as PRECHAC, where we can see a very beautiful church which is remarkable notably for its Romanesque apse which has been decorated in the interior by high columns surmounted by beautiful windows, the central one being especially elegant, in its framing of slender columns. In the interior, the ornamental arcades rest on some interesting capitals and many are historiated. Three other Gothic naves have been added to the Romanesque one which has preserved its heavy capitals. On the façade, the Gothic door with its arch mouldings is surmounted by a gable-steeple with apertures.

We will now take the D. 9. A lane, on the left, leads us to the Château de Cazeneuve, which dates from the 15th century; though it was remodelled in the 16th and 18th centuries. We again return to the gorges and can visit the Château de Caussarieu, a square 12th-century fortress which lies opposite a fortified mill. By way of le Libet, we continue to Beaulac by following the course of the Ciron.

At Beaulac, we will take the N. 132 which leads directly to ROQUEFORT which, before the foundation of Mont-de-Marsan in 1141, was the capital of the country of Marsan. Lying at the junction of the Estampon and the Douze, which emerges from a narrow and picturesque gorge, Roquefort has preserved a defence tower, a 13th-century church whose Romanesque apse is fortified and flanked by a square 13th-century tower. A lateral Gothic porch with a Flamboyant door leads to the Gothic nave. A near-by building has a pretty Gothic door.

A small road leads us to SARBAZAN which is but two kilometres from Roquefort and where we can see another fortified church. It is related to those fortified churches of the Landes which we will encounter in Itinerary XI. At Sarbazan the square tower has been built on to the Romanesque apse which, unfortunately, has for the most part been destroyed. There remains merely an apsidiole with some very handsome historiated capitals. The Gothic nave is preceded by an 18th-century façade, creating a curious combination.

Another small asphalt road leads us directly back to the N. 134 which passes through Villeneuve-de-Marsan in front of the Gothic church which has a large nave of brick. A handsome Gothic portal is hidden by a horrible modern porch surmounted by a modern steeple which is sufficient to ruin the building.

By way of the D. 1 we can make a short detour in order to see, at the hamlet of Perquie, the Renaissance Château de

Ravignan. It has been over restored and it is difficult to tell
which parts are ancient. But the general effect is a handsome
one and the *château* is preceded by a fine garden.

We will continue to follow the N. 134 as far as AIRE-
SUR-L'ADOUR where we will find a cathedral, for the
ancient *Atura* was a seat of a bishopric from 500 until 1933,
on which date it was transferred to Dax.

The cathedral, which in its *ensemble* dates from the 12th
century, presents a characteristic Benedictine plan: an apse
flanked by four apsidioles opening on to the arms of the
transept, and a nave which has 15th-century ogival-vaulting
between two side-aisles which have preserved their ancient
groined-vaulting. Unfortunately, the apse was rebuilt in the
18th century and the façade in the 17th century, but the
latter has preserved a 14th-century portal. The ancient
Bishop's Palace partially dates from the 12th century, but it
was modified and rebuilt in the 26th and 18th centuries.

The church of le Mas d'Aire, an outlying part of the town
perched high on a hill, is perhaps more interesting than the
cathedral. It was built of brick in the 13th and 14th centuries
and presents a fine but disfigured portal whose tympanum
is devoted to the *Last Judgment* and a remarkable 14th-
century brick steeple in the style of Toulouse.

The interior was rebuilt during the classic period, but in
the choir we can see six magnificent Romanesque ornamental
arcades, the remains of an earlier building and, in the crypt,
also Romanesque, different Gallo-Roman sarcophagi, the
Fountain of Saint-Quitterie and, above all, a splendid
5th-century Christian sarcophagus, which is probably that of
Sainte-Quitterie.

We will leave Aire by way of the D. 39 which first follows
the left bank of the Adour, then heads in the direction of
Duhort where, if Baron Raymond de Cardailhac is kind
enough to allow us, we can see the delightful CHATEAU
DU LAU whose appearance is quite unexpected in these
places. It is a Flemish manor lost in Gascony, its builder,
Antoine de Castelnau, having been Chamberlain to Louis

XI after accompanying his master to Flanders. The building is topped by some typically Flemish gables, and two high round towers of brick, which create a fine effect, have been built on to them.

A perpendicular main building, which was made into a dwelling in the 19th century, connects the ancient wall of the *enceinte*, of which there are some remains, and the entrance gate which has been rebuilt.

In the interior, we can see some beautiful Renaissance fireplaces, the ancient kitchen with some fresco remains and a collection of Romanesque or Gothic capitals from the ancient abbeys of the region. They were saved by Xavier de Cardailhac, who has left us three volumes of racy *Propos Gascons* and an interesting study on the *Eglises fortifiées Landaises*. I am certain that, if the Fine Arts Administration decided to rebuild on the spot the cloister of the Abbey of Bonnefont by utilising the arcades transported to a square in Saint-Girons and the chapter-house set against a house in Saint-Martory, M. Raymond de Cardailhac would not hesitate to present as a gift the capitals which his father had saved and which he has always refused to hand over to the antique dealers, who would have sold them to the Americans.

After having belonged to the Marsan, to the Castelnau-Tursan, to the Foix de Candale, to the Benquet and to the de Chauton families the barony of le Lau passed through marriage into the Cardailhac de Lomné family without ever having been sold.

We will take the D. 65 northward which enables us to join the N. 124 at Cazères-sur-Ardour and, in passing, we can see the remains of the ancient ABBAYE DE SAINT-JEAN-DE-LA-CHAPELLE which was founded by the Prémontrés in 1160. In the 19th century, the church, the cloister and the abbatial buildings were demolished and only the dwelling for the guests, an elegant 18th-century building, was preserved; it still has its fine central staircase, its wood-panellings, its surrounding out-buildings and the magnificent Baroque portal of the abbey.

The N. 124 passes through Grenade-sur-l'Adour, a 13th-century bastion. Its central square with arcades, which are in rather a poor state, has a Flamboyant style church which was merely built in 1770 and which has been dolled up with two modern towers. We reach SAINT-SEVER where we will find the Abbey of Saint-Sever. It lies on a line of hills which overlook the Adour and near where one of the roads passed leading to St. James of Compostela. The town was formerly known as "Cap-de-Gascogne", which well marked the importance of its situation which had been recognised by the Romans who erected a *castrum* there.

According to the legend, Saint Sever and his companions had converted the Gascon princes to Christianity. But during the Vandal invasions, Saint Sever was decapitated and, carrying his head in his hands, he designated where he was to be buried. And on that spot a sanctuary was built and devoted to him, while a monastery subsequently completed the development.

Ruined by the Frankish invaders in the 9th century, the monastery was rebuilt by the Count of Gascony, Guillaume Sanche, after certain of his prayers had been granted. The new church was consecrated in the 11th century. In 1028, Sanche, son of Guillaume, summoned a Cluniac monk, Grégoire de Montaner, to direct the abbey, and he remained in charge for more than 40 years, adding to his duties those of Bishop of Lescar and of Dax. He rebuilt the monastery after it had burnt down and was also responsible for the building we now see which was finished by his successors.

Unfortunately, the wars with the English caused great damage to the town and the church. In 1435, notably, the monastery was burnt down by the army of Charles VII and the nave had to be repaired, including three pillars and the side-aisles. After the Reformation, the disasters continued. In 1569 the town was captured by the Calvinist bands of the Count of Montgomery who occupied it for eleven months, ruining the monastery and killing several monks. It was not until 80 years later that the church was repaired. Two pillars of the choir, the apse and the vaulting of the choir had to be rebuilt. The façade was given a classic portal which in modern times has been replaced by a horrible pastiche.

In spite of all these misfortunes, the abbatial church of Saint-Sever, from an archaeological point of view, is an important building not only because of its age, but also because of its plan and the quality of its sculpture. The nave, flanked by side-aisles, is extended by a projecting transept on to which six apsidioles have been added, spread out on one side and the other of the choir, which terminates in a seventh apse, this time larger than the others. It is the chevet plan known as "Benedictine" which can be seen at Château-meillant in Berry and in an earlier version at La Charité-sur-Loire.

Another original feature of the church of Saint-Sever was the tribunes which occupied the far end of each arm of the transept. Also, with its seven apses of decreasing depths, with its systems of vaulting, with its arches and intermediary ribs resting on magnificent columns of antique marble sur-mounted by capitals with splayed basket decoration, with its tribunes and its galleries and its cruciform pillars divided by four engaged columns, the choir has a wonderful design which is related to the great lost buildings of Frankish architecture.

But the church of Saint-Sever offers another great interest, namely, the relationship of its capitals with those of the Muslim buildings of Spain and, notably, of the Mosque of Cordova. Concerning this, M. Etienne Fels has said, "The splayed form of the basket decoration, the downward projection of the foliage are found again at Cordova in the models which have taken their inspiration from the antique. Finally, the projecting abacus extended by two scrolls along the very body of the capital, serves in the Spanish mosque to receive the mainspring of the intercrossed arches which support the framework".

The capitals of Saint-Sever are proof of the close relation-ship which continued to exist between the art of the different Christian kingdoms of France and of Spain with Muslim art itself. Moreover, let us not forget that it was at Saint-Sever that the celebrated manuscript of the Apocalypse was illuminated for the Abbot Gregory. It is now in the Bibliothèque Nationale in Paris and, according to Emile Mâle, was the inspiration of the portal of Moissac.

The monastic buildings, rebuilt in the 17th century, are now occupied by a presbytery, the Hôtel de Ville and various private parties. A Gothic cloister has been left in a state of abandonment. Some 18th-century houses with arcades and some fine wrought-iron balconies enclose the façade of the church in the Place du Tour-du-Sol.

Finally, we can see the ancient church of the Jacobins which is now a grain market. It is surmounted by an elegant octagonal turret and flanked by an 18th-century cloister.

We will continue by the N. 133 southward and, after 12 kilometres, we will reach HAGETMAU where, on the outskirts of the town, on the road to Mugron we can see the crypt of Saint-Girons.

In the 4th century, Saint Girons preached the Gospel to the inhabitants of Chalosse and died there. Pilgrims on the way to St. James of Compostela did not fail to venerate his tomb which lay in the crypt of an abbatial church which had been founded in the time of Charlemagne and devastated by the Huguenots in 1569. At the close of the 19th century there were only a few remains, which have since been destroyed.

Therefore, there exists merely the crypt which is protected by a low construction, without character, formed of the ancient choir, but having lost its crowning. Two staircases lead to the crypt, whose vaulting has been rebuilt. It rests on four central columns and, on each side, on two columns engaged in the walls and supported by a high base with mouldings. The central columns, which enclose the tomb of Saint Girons, have been taken from ancient monuments. They are surmounted by handsome capitals. One seems to represent a scene of martyrdom with lions devouring the limbs of the condemned, while the tormentors tear their ears and dogs eat them: a standing figure is holding two martyrs by the hair. A second represents men disputing with large birds the possession of the fruit the latter are holding in their beaks. A third illustrates the story of the wicked rich man at dinner with two guests, while Lazarus shares the crumbs with the dog. Alongside, Lazarus is welcomed in Paradise, while the wicked rich man sticks out his tongue in the flames of Hell. On the other sides, a dragon is advancing towards a man who defends himself by holding a globe before his eyes. The capitals engaged in the walls have either acanthus leaves, lions or birds and one has a history of Saint Peter. They all date from the 12th century and are treated in a rather clumsy fashion which, in spite of a certain number of subjects again found at Moissac and Toulouse, is far from the refinement of the great workshops of the Languedoc.

I should have been able to lead you now to see the Abbey of Pontaut which had preserved a very beautiful chapter-house of the transitional period, but it was purchased by Mr. Rockefeller and transported to the Cloisters Museum in New York, together with different sculptures of the ancient abbatial church. The Benedictine Abbey of Notre-Dame de Pontaut was founded about 1115 by Geraldus, Abbot of Dalon. In 1151 it adopted the Cistercian rule and was affiliated with Pontigny. The chapter-house, with its three magnificent arcades facing the cloister and the splendid capitals of its two central columns and the slender columns set against the wall, was one of the most remarkable in France. Let us therefore be satisfied to make a small detour in order to see at AMOU a 17th-century *château* with a central forward section surmounted by a triangular pediment which is said to have been built by Jules Hardouin-Mansart, but which still has its mullioned windows. The land of Amou was raised to a marquisate by Louis XIV for Leonard de Caupenne, Baron of Amou. The early castle had been burnt down by the Huguenots in the 16th century.

We will return to the N. 133 at Sault-de-Navailles whose picturesque site is dominated by the ruins of a 12th-century castle; we will leave, on the right, the Château de Sallespisse, also in ruins, and reach ORTHEZ where in the Rue Bourg-Vieux, we can see several ancient houses, including at No. 39, the dwelling of Jeanne d'Albret, a charming construction

which dates from about 1500. It is flanked by an elegant
turret draped with virgin vine and presents in the adjacent
street a long façade with mullioned windows and an archaic
décor of the courtyard of an inn. We can also see, at No. 15,
Rue de l'Horloge, at the far end of a corridor, a wing and a
staircase-turret of a 14th-century building. It is the ancient
Hôtel de la Lune where Froissart stayed in 1388.

Orthez is famous for its fortified bridge which recalls the
Pont Valentré at Cahors. Its bridge piers with the tower
rising on the central one were doubtless built during the time
of Gaston Phoebus. A defence chamber, which was reached
by a narrow staircase, was arranged in the tower whose
crenellation and roofing are modern. A parapet on the west
side protected the defenders. It was pierced by a large bay in
the axis of the central arch. From here, refuse was thrown
into the Gave. And it was from here also that numerous
priests were precipitately thrown into the river during the
massacre of the Catholics in 1569. In 1814 this parapet was
demolished by the troops of Soult on the approach of
Wellington's army.

The Church of Saint-Pierre which we next see, much too
modernised and dressed-up with a disgraceful steeple,
consists of a choir of the late 13th-century, two bays, the first
of a rectangular plan with side-aisles and lateral chapels, the
second terminating in a three-sectional apse. The 15th-
century nave is without side-aisles and has four bays with
ogival vaulting, the ribs resting on a cluster of slender
columns. A fifth bay was added in modern times. The south
side is pierced by elegant windows while the north side,
which was part of the ancient *enceinte* of the town, is
blind.

Now finally the castle. It should be the principal attraction
of Orthez but it has merely an uncrowned keep which was
built in 1242 by Gaston VII according to the plans of the
Château de Moncade in Catalonia whose seigneur he was.
Between 1368 and 1375 Gaston Phoebus had added two
storeys to the keep and his military engineer, Sicard de
Lordat, had also embellished the inhabited parts of the

building which was the scene of the brilliant fêtes described by Froissart.

In 1745 the castle being no longer in use and abandoned, the town put it up for sale and speculators despoiled it. The *enceinte* was demolished and the keep, which alone was spared, lost its last storey as the result of a stupid wager. In 1841 the town bought the ruins again.

The fortress of Gaston VII consisted of a lower courtyard surrounded by moats which are still visible, a barbican with a few remaining sections of the walls which protected the gate of the castle and a polygonal *enceinte* (each side being defended by three archery windows); also the living quarters and the keep.

Of the living quarters, there remain merely the foundation and the toothing stones of the staircases. The keep which was known as the Tour Moncade, is of a pentagonal design. The first storey, which was devoted to defence, communicated with the dwelling by means of a small door. A staircase, which was arranged in the thickness of the walls, led to the upper storeys, the last named being well lighted and heated thanks to the huge chimneys. The last storey had crenellation and machicolation. But what we now see is modern.

On the opposite bank of the Gave, we will take the D. 9 which leads us to Biron where we can see the charming Manoir de Brassalay, which dates from the 15th and 16th centuries, lying on a height above the village. During the Wars of Religion, the captains of Brassalay, who were the governors of the Château d'Orthez and Huguenots, fortified the manor and surrounded the ramparts (now in ruins) with moats and a drawbridge whose trace can still be seen.

The Château de Brassalay has a picturesque silhouette with its turreted staircase of hexagonal design, its mullioned windows, and its dormers with gables. In the interior, a large room, which now is used as the kitchen, has preserved a beautiful fireplace.

We will continue to follow the D. 275 in order to reach the N. 647 which leads us to the valley of the Gave d'Oloron where, on the right, we can see another manor, that of Audeux, which was built at the close of the 16th or beginning of the 17th century. Of the three main buildings which enclose the courtyard, only one is habitable; it was restored by Mme. d'Abbadie d'Arrast.

In one room there is a curious coffer ceiling. The *ensemble*, with the moats full of water, the sides of the wall covered with ivy and a handsome marble stairway, has a great deal of charm.

We will return to the N. 647 which leads us to Navarrenx, the site of an ancient fortress which has been pretty well abandoned, but which once played an important role. The town, which formerly lay on the other side of the Gave, was rebuilt and fortified on its present site by the King of Navarre, Henri d'Albret, in 1546. It was captured by Louis XIII in 1620. The fortifications were subsequently reinforced by Vauban. They are well preserved with their bastions and their watch-towers. We can still see the very bold 15th-century bridge and, in the open fields, the 15th-century Tour Herrère on the early site of the town.

After having crossed the Gave, we reach the N. 636 which we will take to the left and, after seven kilometres, we will follow the D. 25 for four kilometres in order to see a curious building known as L'HOPITAL SAINT-BLAISE. It was a hospital which had been founded for the pilgrims on their way to St. James of Compostela. There remains merely the church whose construction seems to date from the early years of the 13th century.

But its great interest stems from its relationship with the *Mudéjar* constructions of Spain (buildings erected by the Arabs during the period of Christian domination), not only on account of the stonework of the walls but also from certain peculiarities in the vaulting. Likewise, the windows have a lattice work in geometrical *décor* of Spanish inspiration.

The plan is somewhat that of a Greek cross, with a nave of a single bay, the arms of the transept slightly smaller, while on to each there opens a rectangular chapel. The choir, which is as large as the nave, terminates in a three-sectional apse. Above the transept crossing there rises a small octagonal tower which is topped by a modern, conical roof. Between the columns which soften the angles there open two small windows with cusped arches. The façade has been restored, but it has preserved its sculptured tympanum in a rather crude style representing a *Christ in Majesty* surrounded by symbols of the Evangelists.

In the interior, we can see the distinct *Mudéjar* character of the windows of the apse which are surmounted by multifoil arches. The vaulting itself has a Spanish character: that of the apse is a part of a sectional cupola, without ribs; the cupola of the transept crossing has an eight-sectional cloister-arch vaulting upheld by eight arches which rest two by two on stone consoles, and by their interlacing form an eight-branch star. It recalls the cupolas of the cathedrals of Téruel, Tarazona or Saragossa.

Those who are en route to Spain will therefore find, in this modest building of the Hôpital Saint-Blaise, a foretaste of Spanish architecture.

We will return to the N. 636 which follows the valley of the Gave d'Oleron and reach OLORON-SAINTE-MARIE on the junction of the Gave d'Aspe and the Gave d'Ossau. Ancient *Ilure* was a station on the Roman Way to Spain and its first known bishop, Saint Grat, was present at the Council of Agde in 506. The ancient feudal city of Sainte-Croix extends along a hill between the two Gaves; it is separated from the Notre-Dame quarter by the Gave d'Ossau and from the Sainte-Marie quarter, the old episcopal town, by the Gave d'Aspe. Of the castle of the Viscounts of Béarn, there remains merely a tower, but we can visit two churches: Sainte-Croix, in the centre of the old town and surrounded by old houses, and Sainte-Marie, the ancient cathedral.

Sainte-Croix is a Romanesque church of Benedictine plan, begun in 1070. Transferred in 1569 into a Protestant temple, it was returned to the Catholics in 1621. It was in a very bad state, and was enlarged and restored during the Second Empire in a rather regrettable manner.

If we overlook the modern porch, we have a nave of three

bays flanked by side-aisles, a transept whose crossing is surmounted by a cupola and whose north arm by a heavy steeple, and finally a choir with its apse decorated with ornamental arcades and in an oven-shaped style, like the apsidioles which frame it on each side. The cupola is perhaps closer to those of Aquitaine than to the Hispano-Moorish ones in spite of its arches decorated with stars. The blind nave has barrel-vaulting and is shouldered by the half barrel-vaulting which covers the side-aisles.

Sainte-Marie, built about 1102, has somewhat the same arrangements as Sainte-Croix. Burnt down in the early 13th century during an uprising, it was rebuilt, then after being partially burnt down by lightning in 1302 it received a new choir in the 14th century. The Protestants converted it into a stable. In 1602 it was enlarged and in 1880 it was as badly restored as Sainte-Croix.

It is, above all, its portal which interests us, for it is related to the façades of Poitou, like Notre-Dame-la-Grande and Saint-Nicholas-de-Civray and also the portals of Morlass, Avila and Saint-Pons-de-Thomières.

The tympanum is divided by two semicircles into two smaller tympanums. On the large one there is sculptured a *Descent from the Cross* and on the small ones *Solomon Seated on his Throne* and *Gilgamesh Strangling two Lions*. These three compositions are sculptured in very weak relief and in a rather dry manner. The pier, which has been rebuilt, rests on two chained captives which recall the pillar of the Apostles at Saint-Bertrand-de-Comminges and the caryatids of Beaulieu. The arch mouldings have as adornment *The Lamb*, *The Twenty-four Old Men of Apocalypse* and an entire series of small rustic scenes which represent The Preparation of a Wedding, The Slaughter of a Pig, The Fishing of Salmon and The Massacre of the Servants, while a monster devouring a human-being is the counterpart of a *Constantine* which seems to come from a church of the Angoulême country. The arcades of the porch are resting on columns whose capitals are decorated with grotesque figures.

We will take the N. 134 southward which ascends the

MOULIN DE BARBASTE.

30. CLOITRE DE SAINT-BERTRAND-D
COMMIN

valley of the Gave d'Aspe which narrows little by little. We will stop at SARRANCE where Marguerite de Valois wrote part of her *Heptameron*. We should not miss seeing the Convent of the Prémontrés which was rebuilt in the early 17th century. The church has a curious eight-sectional steeple, but we must admire especially the cloister which is one of the most charming of the period, with its two storeys of galleries with full arcades, each covered by a triangular roof and separated by heavy pillars flanked by a light, projecting buttress. The upper gallery is decorated with balustrades.

We will continue to ascend, passing below the Fort of Urdos or le Portalet, in which the accused at the Riom Trial were interned in 1941.

Urdos is the last French village. After making several windings, the road reaches the Col du Somport from which it descends into Spain by the valley of the Rio Aragon. We pass near the ruins of the Hospital of Sainte-Christine founded in 1108 for the pilgrims on their way to St. James of Compostela, and we will reach Jaca, from where my *Unknown Spain* will serve as your guide.

P

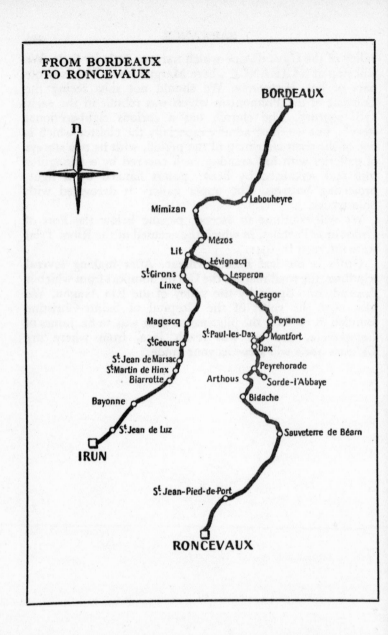

FROM BORDEAUX
TO RONCEVAUX

n

BORDEAUX

Labouheyre

Mimizan

Mézos

Lit

Lévignacq

St.Girons

Lesperon

Linxe

Lesgor

Magescq

Poyanne

St.Paul-les-Dax

Montfort

St.Geours

Dax

St.Jean de Marsac

Peyrehorade

St.Martin de Hinx

Arthous

Sorde-l'Abbaye

Biarrotte

Bidache

Bayonne

St.Jean de Luz

Sauveterre de Béarn

IRUN

St.Jean-Pied-de-Port

RONCEVAUX

FROM BORDEAUX TO RONCEVAUX
AND TO IRUN

*Mimizan — Mézos — (Lit, Magescq, Saint-Géours,
Bayonne, Saint-Jean-de-Luz) — Livignacq — Lesperon
— Lesgor — Pouyanne — Montfort-en-Chalosse —
Saint-Paul-les-Dax — Dax — Peyrehorade — Abbaye
de Sorde — Abbaye d'Arthous — Bidache — Sauveterre
de Béarn — Saint-Jean-Pied-de-Port.*

I WILL indicate an itinerary from Bordeaux to Roncevaux
and also an itinerary from Bordeaux to Irun which will
offer a few surprises. One usually traverses the Landes
without interruption by way of a straight and flat road which
is suitable for speed. The Basque coast is too well known for
anything fresh to be discovered. Art lovers stop at Bayonne
and Saint-Jean-de-Luz whose charm they appreciate.
Bayonne is famous for its Gothic cathedral, its cloister, one
side of which was unfortunately demolished during the last
century, its old houses—many of them are 18th century with
their handsome wrought-iron balconies—its streets with
arcades, its ramparts, its museums; one should not miss
visiting the Musée Bonat with its paintings by Goya, Rubens
and Rembrandt and its magnificent collection of drawings.
Saint-Jean-de-Luz is famous for its church with wooden
galleries, its picturesque houses and its port. The Basque
villages, such as Ascain, Saint-Pée, and Espellette, are well
known for their gaiety and their colourful character.

And yet, apart from their natural attractions, lakes, forests
of resinous pines and their coast bordered by dunes, are the

Landes entirely lacking in interest? It is true that they lack
any edifice of importance, but they possess a curiosity which
Brutails and one of his disciples, Xavier de Cardaillac, have
endeavoured to enhance: the fortified churches of the
Landes. Brutails and Xavier de Cardaillac have saved the
fortified nave and choir of the church of Magescq from
demolition. There were other fortified churches less fortunate. The steeple of Linxe was stupidly demolished;
successive restoration at Tarnos caused the disappearance of
the ancient defences; the steeple of Pomarez has been
replaced by a modern tower; and so on.

But many other fortified churches of the Landes still exist
and, for those who are interested, we are going to try and
group a certain number in an itinerary which will obviously
be less rapid than the N. 132, but an itinerary which
everyone can arrange as he pleases with the perspective of
the natural beauties of the Landes, like the Etang de
Biscarosse and Etang de Léon.

The majority of these fortified churches are characteristic
for having been fortified from the time of their construction,
while with those of Guienne and Gascony the fortification
was added during the period of the Hundred Years' War.
The most beautiful of all is that of LESGOR which one can
only see by leaving the N. 132 at Castets and heading in the
direction of Dax.

We will follow the N. 132 as far as Labouheyre where we
can see, beneath the steeple-porch, the pretty portal of the
15th-century church. The town was formerly surrounded by
ramparts of which a gate still exists.

By way of the N. 626 which, 13 kilometres farther on,
passes near the Etang de la Forge and where we can see the
Chapel of Saint-Jean and the miraculous fountain of
Bourrices, which was formerly a step on the way to St. James
of Compostela for the pilgrims coming from Soulac, we reach
MIMIZAN, not far from the picturesque Etang d'Augreil-
han.

Mimizan has become a small summer resort with its village
extending along the dunes or among the pines, but it was

once *Segosa* which figures in the Roman itineraries and during
the Middle Ages it was an important port. But the sands
covered the ancient town as well as its church and they have
both disappeared beneath the dunes which are now about
120 feet high. In 1770 an inhabitant of the country named
Teixoëres, succeeded in stopping their spread with the aid of
gourbets (sand rushes) and thus in saving the remains of the
ancient Benedictine abbatial church.

After having been utilised as a keep, the steeple, a square
and massive tower, was used as a lighthouse, and it contains
a handsome 12th-century Romanesque portal which has
unfortunately been very much disfigured. On the tympanum
there is an *Adoration of the Magi*, while the arch mouldings
have *The Twelve Signs of the Zodiac, The Twelve Prophets* and
The Wise and Foolish Virgins.

The abbey was a place of asylum and the limits of the
sauvetat were marked by pyramids. That of Cantegrouille
still exists on the south of the town.

By way of the N. 652 as far as Bias and the D. 38 we reach
MEZOS where we can see the first of our churches of the
Landes. A square, compact tower, pierced by loopholes,
supported by buttresses and surmounted by a small square
recessed construction, has been built on to a Gothic church
whose vaulting was rebuilt at the close of the 15th century.

By way of the D. 166 we continue to Saint-Julien-en-Born
and again follow the N. 652. The church at Saint-Julien-en-
Born dates from the close of the Gothic period, but some
thirty years ago an architect of the Historic Monuments
Administration, a good judge indeed, thought it worth while
to replace the ancient fortified tower by a modern Gothic
steeple. It is therefore useless to remain and let us hasten to
LIT where, at least, the lower section of the tower is ancient,
even if the nave is modern and its crowning has been rebuilt.
In the 15th century, the vaulting was reconstructed and
from that period also dates the inner door with its very
handsomely carved leaves.

We can also see the small Gothic Chapel of Mixe before
descending to Saint-Girons if we are heading in the direction

of Bayonne. There we can find another fortified tower which, with its two archery windows, seems to date from the 13th century, as does the Romanesque church whose apse is surmounted by a lookout post pierced with two loopholes. There also, 300 feet from Saint-Girons, near the road to Linxe, we can see one of the columns which limited the *sauvetat*.

The D. 44 leads us to Linxe where the square steeple, flanked by a round turret, was demolished in 1868. This was all the more regrettable, since the whole church was fortified. The apse is surmounted by crenels, and it dates, as also does the nave, from the 13th century, but they subsequently received new vaulting and a side-aisle was added during the Renaissance.

At Castets we find the N. 10 which passes through MAGESCQ which is the most interesting of all the fortified churches of this circuit. The small Gothic door which leads to the nave was surmounted by a bartizan and the nave was pierced by loopholes. Two lines of defence with square crenels and watch-path defended the nave, while a safety-bastion surmounted the apse. The vaulting of the choir, which had been arranged for defence, supported the position for retreat which was defended on the exterior by huge stone merlons split by loopholes and on the interior by a thick gable wall pierced by three openings and two oblique loopholes. The steeple is of a later date and in the 17th century it was surmounted by a square cap with rounded angles.

We can see the Romanesque capitals of the apse; one is decorated with winged griffons with serpents in their claws and *The Eternal Father Between Two Angels* decorates the triumphal arch.

We next pass through SAINT-GEOURS-DE-MAREN-NES, whose tower is the highest and best preserved of the Landes, with its three storeys above the ground floor, which is pierced by loopholes for muskets. A stone spiral turreted staircase has been built on to it. The nave and its side-aisles have been rebuilt, but the apse is surmounted by rectangular openings which function as crenels. Unfortunately, the *ensemble* has been given a rough coating of plaster, which is too often the case for rustic churches.

We can proceed directly to BAYONNE by the N. 10 or, if we want to see three other fortified churches, we can take the D. 12 which passes through Saint-Jean-de-Marsac. The 13th-century tower is without crowning, but in the 16th century loopholes were designed for the use of culverins, while at the same time a portal was added with a *Saint John Blessing* in a niche above. The tower is flanked by a 15th-century octagonal turret. The nave is pierced by loopholes and the polygonal apse, which received new vaulting in the 15th century, is supported by buttresses with drip-stones.

We next visit Saint-Martin-de-Hinx where the tower without crowning, forming a porch and flanked by a round turreted staircase is pierced by loopholes, as also are the walls of the 13th-century nave, which are flanked by elegant clusters of slender columns. The vaulting has been reconstructed. The walls of the choir, which are in five faces, have no trace of fortification. Their three, high twin windows with oculi date from the 14th century. The lateral door of a very pretty Flamboyant Gothic, the turret and the steeple with their wooden construction, make Saint-Martin-de-Hinx a very picturesque church.

Finally, the small late 12th-century Church of Biarotte presents a square steeple which also is without crowning, a turreted staircase, a Gothic nave and an interesting apse with its windowed arcades with stone beadings and its elegant Romanesque capitals. The vaulting of the apse was rebuilt during the Gothic period. The Romanesque windows are walled up, but in places where the coating of plaster has fallen we can see the pretty exterior design of the window.

We are now on the N. 117 by which we can reach Bayonne.

If, on the contrary, we had decided to head in the direction of Dax, back on the N. 652 we could have taken the D. 41 at St. Julien-en-Born and this passes through LIVIGNACQ where we will find a powerful square tower which is supported by buttresses and pierced by archery windows. The church is decorated with wood-panelling and a very curious painted ceiling of the 17th century. These paintings were made by a Bordeaux painter named Fautier.

At LESPERON we will find another fortress tower flanked by a rectangular turret which has a 15th-century octagonal swivel pin. It is pierced by narrow loopholes and two bartizans, one above the entrance gate, are added for defence. Like the tower of Livignacq it is crowned by a sharply-pointed polygonal pyramidal roof of the 15th century, which replaced the projecting wooden galleries whose corbels can still be seen.

We cross the N. 10 and by way of Rion we reach Lesgor. We should not linger at Rion; the church here formed a real fortress with a high surrounding wall flanked by a heavy tower, which was demolished in 1840. The restoration work, which was undertaken during the close of the last century, robbed it of all its interesting defensive characteristics, such as a high square steeple with loopholes and square crenels, and an apse also surmounted by crenels.

Let us, therefore, be content with LESGOR, a real small fortress which, during the Hundred Years' War, was equipped by the English with a perfect defensive system. The square tower, shouldered by six buttresses with drip-stones, including four in triple recess, is pierced by a door which dates from the 15th century and which is defended by two loopholes. A bartizan, of which three huge arch-stones remain, was added at the close of the 14th century.

The nave was defended by loopholes and the Romanesque oven-shaped apse, with its decoration of corbels, was surmounted at the close of the 14th century by a semicircular bastion pierced by four large crenels.

By way of Tartas, which was one of the principal fortresses of the Protestants of Gascony, but whose fortifications were dismantled by Louis XIII—only two towers remain—we reach POYANNE by way of the D. 7. The Château de Poyanne is an impressive *château* of the early 17th century with a narrow main building and two heavy out-buildings on each angle, a beautiful embossed gate and some elegant dormers. An early castle was built in 1315 by Bernard de Poyanne.

In the park there can be seen a bower of laurel which was planted by Henri IV, as is witnessed by this letter of the king to his companion-in-arms.

"Great rascal, I'll arrive to-morrow night at your place with Madam Corisandre to plant your alleys of laurel. Plenty of warmth, good wine and good cheer. Always yours, Henri".

After having been inhabited by King Joseph Bonaparte who had fled from Spain, the Château de Poyanne became the property of the Jesuits who had been expelled from the peninsular and it was occupied by a training college for the priesthood.

We next stop at MONTFORT-EN-CHALOSSE, whose church outside the town consisted of a 12th-century Romanesque nave, flanked by side-aisles in the 15th century and fronted by a heavy square tower forming a porch which, like the previous ones I have mentioned, was an ancient fortified tower. A turret has been built on to it and the *ensemble* is very picturesque with the roof extending from the nave and apse. We must admire, above all, the beautiful Romanesque arcading of the nave with its historiated capitals, but unfortunately it is all a dreadful splodge of colour.

Some 10 kilometres farther on, we can visit the Trappist Abbey of Divielle (*Dei Villa*) which was founded in the 12th century on the banks of the Adour at the foot of a hill. It was burnt down by Montgomery in 1560 and there is little more than the 15th-century chapter-house in the midst of the buildings which have been rebuilt by the Trappists who have once again installed themselves there. They make a kind of Port-Salut cheese.

We reach Dax by way of the D. 32. We will go first of all to SAINT-PAUL-LES-DAX, just to the north of the main town. The church consists of a modern nave which is of no interest, a 15th-century steeple, shouldered by powerful buttresses which originally were isolated and by a 12th-century choir which was connected with the nave by a large arch resting on high columns with capitals decorated by interlacing. The apse is decorated by semicircular niches of three windows framed by slender columns.

But it is the exterior decoration of the apse which especially interests us. It is shouldered by some square buttresses between which are semicircular arches resting on slender marble columns. The very delicately sculptured capitals represent birds, animals, personages, foliage; some were re-used at the close of the 11th century, while others are contemporary with the apse and date from about 1120. Above the ornamental arcading are three windows framed by slender columns and they are enclosed by a bas-relief which is rightly famous. We can see various subjects: fantastic animals which might be the grasshoppers of the Apocalypse, *The Holy Women at the Tomb*, three seated Apostles who are holding books, three animals who resemble hyenas, *The Last Supper*, *The Kiss of Judas*, *The Crucifixion*, *Samson Overcoming the Lion*, *Sainte Veronique*, a dragon, *The Resurrection*. These sculptures, which belong to different workshops and some of which are rather crude, seem to date from the first third of the 12th century.

DAX, where we next arrive is a very popular watering place and the hotels, whose architecture is peculiarly ugly, even uglier than elsewhere, have replaced the ancient castle and whatever this old town, which is beautifully situated on the left bank of the Adour, had preserved from former times. Its Gallo-Roman walls, flanked by round towers, were intact at the close of the last century when they were partly demolished, preserving only a few remains, in spite of the protests on the part of the archaeologists and some 1,500 inhabitants of the town. These walls are evidence of the importance of Dax in the past. They had withstood numerous sieges: that of Richard Coeur de Lion in 1176, that of John the Fearless in 1199, that of Philip the Fair in 1288, that of Charles VII in 1412. But the inhabitants of Dax have preferred those taking cures to those making tours, and their mud baths to their glorious memories, since the former are more profitable.

We can visit the Cathedral, although it was rebuilt in the

classic style from 1656 to 1719 on the ruins of a vast Gothic edifice which had collapsed and which itself had replaced a Romanesque edifice which had replaced a Merovingian church. Some churches are unlucky. The Gothic cloister was demolished in 1523 for military defence purposes. The steeple collapsed in 1623, then in 1646. Only the façade and the sacristy were retained and the present church was built. But the church was hardly completed when the steeple again collapsed. In 1894 the Gothic portal was dismantled, to be reset at the far end of the north arm of the transept. It dates from the second half of the 13th century. A *Christ* occupies the door mullion, *The Apostles* are lined in the splayings, while the arch mouldings, with a part of their sculptures lacking, represent angels, women who are holding books, *The Wise and Foolish Virgins*, and finally saints. Above the lintel, which represents *The Resurrection of the Dead*, the tympanum, which is very much disfigured, represents *The Last Judgment*. It is a very complete portal with a plastic quality not entirely exceptional, but in the tradition of the great cathedrals of northern France. The style is somewhat related to that of the cathedral of Rheims. Let us not forget that we are on the way to Spain where many French master craftsmen and sculptors went to work.

A modern church occupies the site of the edifice built near the tomb of Saint Vincent de Xaintes during the early beginnings of Christianity. Demolished by the Visigoths, then by the Normans, then by the Protestants, it was no more fortunate than the cathedral. But we can see a Gallo-Roman mosaic which had been discovered in the foundations of the ancient church, the remains of a temple erected by the Romans to Lucina. The Palais de Justice has replaced the cloister of the Barnabites, and the Arena the Cordelier convent. Dax has really been given a new face. As for the *hôtel* where Mazarin stayed in 1659 and Anne of Austria in 1660 at No. 25, Rue Cazade, it is so disfigured that it no longer offers any interest.

However, three kilometres farther on, we can see the Romanesque portal of the Church of Oereluy which is very curious. Two columns set against the jambs and surmounted by historiated capitals support a tympanum with an interlacing decoration surmounted by a chrisma.

We will now take the D. 29. It is useless to make a detour in order to see the Church of Pouillon and the Benedictine Priory of Caznotte. These two buildings have been wilfully disfigured in a stupid manner. We will go straight on to PEYREHORADE where, overlooking the hill above the town, there are the ruins of the Château d'Aspremont with its heavy polygonal keep. This fortress, which belonged to the Viscounts of Orthez, was built in 1010, devastated in 1247, then rebuilt and burnt down in 1567 during the Wars of Religion by the Count of Montgomery.

We can still see, near the large bridge over the Gave, the Château de Montréal of the close of the 16th century, consisting of a large main building flanked by four heavy round towers. It is a typical example of a castle of the transitional period, between the fortress and the pleasure *château*. Permission should be requested to visit the interior which is rich in furniture and works of art.

We will continue on the D. 29 in order to see the ABBAYE DE SORDE. Its origins are very old; it prospered during the 12th and 13th centuries, but the Wars of Religion were its downfall. In 1523 the Prince of Orange destroyed almost completely the town and the Abbey of Sorde; in 1569 it suffered from the Huguenots of Montgomery and in 1616 from the Duke of la Force, Governor of Béarn.

The abbey was rebuilt, but at the Revolution since no one wanted to buy the buildings they were abandoned. In 1866 the church was repaired with such little skill that it lost the greater part of its interest. It is a nave of five bays flanked by side-aisles, a projecting transept on which two apsidioles open, and a choir formed of a straight bay followed by a semicircular apse.

The chevet, which is the best-preserved part, dates from the first half of the 12th century. We can see the four capitals on which the entrance arches of the apsidioles of the transept are resting. They represent *Daniel in the Lions' Den*,

The Arrest of Christ in the Garden of Olives, *The Virgin in Majesty* and *The Presentation in the Temple* and are the work of local artists whose treatment recalls the sculptures we have seen at Saint-Sever or at the Cathedral of Lescar.

The transept is contemporary with the choir in its lower parts, but in the 13th century it was raised and decorated with blind arcades and the vaulting was subsequently rebuilt, no doubt after it had collapsed in the 16th century. The nave has been the object of successive remodellings. Several Romanesque columns are contemporary with the choir, but the nave was rebuilt at the close of the 13th or beginning of the 14th century, then again rebuilt after the destructions caused by the Huguenots before being restored in the 19th century.

On the exterior, we can see the portal of the second half of the 12th century, but very much disfigured. It presents on the tympanum a *Christ* between the symbols of the Evangelists and the arch mouldings are decorated with the months and the signs of the Zodiac. The rose-window of the façade is modern, having been opened at the site of an ancient Romanesque bay. In the choir, there is a beautiful Gallo-Roman mosaic from a villa which occupied the site of the abbey. It is completed by panels subsequently added, one of which is certainly Carolingian.

Of the conventual buildings, there remain the bays of a cloister, a large abbatial building of the 16th century with a polygonal turret which is in a pitiful state, and a large building in ruins of the 17th century erected on the mediaeval foundations. These ivy-covered ruins are very picturesque. We should go as far as the banks of the Gave where we can see a terrace of flowers and a vaulted gallery in ruins; it was rebuilt in the 17th century. The site is magnificent. It has moreover been classified, which none the less has not prevented some large millers from demolishing the old mill of the abbey in order to build in its place a horrible factory which gives out an infernal din.

We will, however, return to Peyrehorade and, taking a small road along the Gave which leads as far as the ancient bastion of Hastingues, we will go then by a road on the left to the ABBAYE D'ARTHOUS which was founded about 1160 by the Prémontrés who had come from La Case-Dieu in Gascony. The monastery, which enjoyed the favours of the Viscounts of Béarn and of the Kings of England, was very prosperous during the 13th and 14th centuries, but the 16th century was its downfall. As early as 1523 the Spaniards invaded the countryside. This was followed by the Wars of Religion and the abbey was devastated and burnt down several times, notably in 1571. Arthous was rebuilt from its ruins and in the early 18th century its abbots once again became rich and powerful. But this wealth was followed by a slackening of religious life. At the Revolution there were only three monks left to disperse and the buildings were converted into farms. If they are in a deplorable state of abandonment, at least no indiscreet restoration has come along to change their character.

The church, which is Romanesque and dates from the second half of the 12th century, consists of a long nave without side-aisles, five bays, a transept and a chevet with oven-shaped apsidioles. The central apse is preceded by a straight bay with barrel vaulting. All this is in a sad state of neglect with the vaulting collapsed, the principal apse torn up to allow carts to pass, the interior broken up and divided into storeys: this is what has happened to one of the most remarkable examples of Romanesque art in the south-west of France. Villesalem, Salagon, Arthous . . . the list of martyrs of our Romanesque abbeys!

Access to the nave is through two doors. The one of the façade has preserved of the past merely the jambs with, on each side, two columns on which the archivolts rest. The other door, which is smaller and better preserved, opens in the north wall and gives on to the cloister.

The apse and the apsidioles have preserved their beautiful cornices with sculptured modillions, their columns which are set against each other, their windows framed by slender columns, their capitals, all executed in a very careful manner.

Little remains of the cloister and the conventual buildings. The refectory, almost entirely destroyed in the 16th century, was rebuilt in the following one. It has preserved its small lavabo and its wood-panellings.

By continuing the road we have taken, we return to a small one which ends at the D. 19 which we are going to follow as far as BIDACHE where we will find the ruins of a castle which belonged to the family of the Seigneurs of Gramont which merged with that of Guiche. It was largely destroyed by the Spanish troops who in 1523 burnt down Guiche and Hastingues as well as the Abbeys of Sorde and Arthous. In 1530 the Countess Claire undertook the reconstruction which was completed by her son, Antoine I, who died in 1586 after having taken the title of Prince of Bidache, then by the daughter-in-law of the last-named, the beautiful Corisinde d'Andouins, who became a widow in 1580. We know the role she played in the epoch of Henri IV and she died in 1620. It was in this castle that the Countess Louise, daughter of the Maréchal de Roquelaure, was condemned and executed. It was here also that the Count Armand de Guiche, son of Maréchal de Gramont, was exiled by Louis XIV as the result of a famous intrigue. Closed during the Revolution, the castle was burnt down by the administrator of the domain in strange circumstances.

Of the mediaeval castle, there remains a heavy round tower of the 15th century, connected with the Renaissance castle by a main building and the ancient entrance gate, flanked by two rounded towers, which were subsequently very much modified. The inner façade was rehabilitated and pierced by two storeys of bays with triangular pediments at the close of the 16th century, while, on the exterior, there was erected at the close of the reign of Louis XV an entrance portico decorated with furrows and surmounted by a triangular pediment.

The Renaissance castle, opposite the entrance gate, consists of a two-storey building with rectangular doors and mullioned windows surmounted by dormers with scrolled pediments which rise into the void, the roof having disappeared. A building of the same style connects this main building with the mediaeval tower and a turret rises in the angle opposite the Henri IV Pavillon which terminates the main building. Another pavilion lies opposite, on the other side of the courtyard, on the alignment of the entrance gate. Another main building was to have been built at right angles on the side facing the terrace, but only the foundation was built, as well as the beginnings of a façade with a pillar of a colossal order. The two Henri IV Pavillons are quite impressive with their windows framed by ornamentation and surmounted by triangular or rounded pediments. Notice that the door is framed in what is clearly a Spanish Baroque style.

But the ruins of Bidache have been left in a tôtal state of abandonment. The stones are loose; a large number have already collapsed and others will follow. The crowning of the entrance gate itself is of an unstable equilibrium. The Fine Arts Administration should do something at once.

In the church of the village, which is of the 16th century, we can see the tombs of the Gramont family, notably that of Duke Antoine III, Marshal of France, who died in 1678 and for whom Bidache was raised to a duchy in 1648. It was he who received Mazarin at the Château de Bidache in 1658 at the time of the Treaty of the Pyrenees.

By way of the N. 637 eastward which passes through Labastide-Villefrance, an ancient 14th-century bastion which has preserved its keep, we find the Gave d'Oloron which we will ascend as far as SAUVETERRE-DE-BEARN.

This small but important fortress was besieged and captured twice during the 16th century, the first in 1523 by Philibert de Challon, Prince of Orange, and the second in 1569 by the Basques. In 1606 the town still had not risen from its ruins.

Of the *enceinte* which formed an irregular quadrilateral, there merely remain a rather well preserved 14th-century gate and the ancient fortified bridge with its defence tower which recalls that of Orthez. The keep, which rises opposite the river, dates from the 13th century; it is pierced by a twin bay and surmounted by an oculus.

ABSIDE DE SAINT-PAUL-LES-DAX.

32. CHATEAU DE BIDA

Except for the modern porch, the church is a very pure and archaic building by reason of its date of construction which is not earlier than the early 13th century. It consists of a nave of three bays, with side-aisles, a transept, a choir, a bay terminating in a semicircular apse and enclosed by two apsidioles of the same shape. The nave, whose lighting is ensured by oculi, has ogival vaulting on heavy rectangular cross ribs like the side-aisles, while the apse and the choir have only one ogival vault. The portal has been rebuilt. The steeple consists of a massive square, pierced on each side by three twin bays. The upper part was fortified and crenellated in the 15th century.

We will take the N. 133 which passes through Saint-Palais, an old town which has preserved very little of its past. We ascend the valley of the Bidouxe and reach SAINT-JEAN-PIED-DE-PORT which has preserved some very picturesque aspects with its old 15th-century walls pierced by a pointed-arch gate, its church largely rebuilt in the 17th century, with its south side bordering the Nive and forming part of the defensive system of the small town. A gate opens onto an old bridge alongside the church. We climb the picturesque Rue de la Citadelle which is lined with old 16th and 17th-century houses of red sandstone. We pass the old Prison of the Bishops and reach a gate in the ramparts from which there is a path leading to the citadel. It was built in 1668 by the Chevalier Deville after the town was annexed to France as the result of the Treaty of the Pyrenees. It, as well as the ramparts, was remodelled subsequently by Vauban.

We will continue to follow the N. 133 which climbs the valley of the Petite Nive. Arnéguy is the last French village. After Valcarlos, the first Spanish village, we traverse a narrow gorge which borders a high wall of rocks, *las Peñas de Francia*, then the winding road between the mountain ridges and some beautiful forests of beech trees. We reach the Col d'Ibaneta or de Roncevaux where we can seek the insignificant remains of the Chapel of Saint-Sauveur, which is said to be of the era of Charlemagne, but which merely dates from the 13th century. This is the place of legend, but

Q

the vanguard of Charlemagne's army led by Roland was annihilated, not on this site, but farther on where there stands the Abbey of Roncevaux.

In *Unknown Spain* I have described this convent which was founded to help the numerous pilgrims who passed near by on their way to St. James of Compostela. Together with Jaca it is one of the most beautiful gateways to Spain. The road is beautiful and easy and takes you at once into a part of Spain which is rich in architectural masterpieces.

GLOSSARY

ABACUS: Flat slab on top of a capital.

ABUTMENT: Solid masonry placed to resist the lateral pressure of a vault.

ACANTHUS: Plant with thick fleshy and scalloped leaves copied as part of decoration of a Corinthian capital and in some types of leaf-carving.

ACROTERION: Pedestal for a statue at the angle of the pediment.

AEDICULE: Small structure sheltering altar or image of household god; small pedimented structure over a niche.

ANTA: A pilaster terminating the side wall of a Greek temple with the base and capital differing from those of adjacent columns.

AMBULATORY: Open or covered arcade or cloister; an aisle around a choir.

ANTIPHONARY: Book of chants or anthems.

APSE: Eastern end of church containing Bishop's Throne.

APSIDIOLE: Secondary apse.

ARCADE: Range of arches supported on piers or columns, free-standing. BLIND ARCADE: Arcade set against a wall.

ARCHITRAVE: Lowest division of entablature resting on capitals of supporting column. Collective name for various parts surrounding a door or window.

ARCHIVOLT: Moulding curving round the under surface of an arch.

ARKOSE: Rock composed of quartz and felspar.

ARMARIUM: Cupboard or chest.

Artenesado: Wooden ceiling coffered in Moorish style.

ASTRAGAL: Small moulding round top or bottom of column.

Atalaya: Watchtower.

ATRIUM: Open central court in Greek and Roman churches; forecourt in early Christian churches.

Ayuniamento: Town hall.

Azulejos: Glazed tiles.

BALDACHIN: Canopy, supported on pillars or fastened to wall, over throne, pulpit, altar, etc.

BARBICAN: Outwork defending the entrance to a castle.

BAROQUE: Style with sinuous lines, scrolls and exuberant carved ornaments, named after the painter Federigo Barocci, from Urbino (1528–1612). Born in Rome as a reaction against severe classical Renaissance, it spread throughout Europe.

BARTIZAN: Turret projecting from mediaeval tower.

BASILICA: In mediaeval architecture an aisled church with a clerestory.

BAS-RELIEF: Figures not standing far out from ground on which they are formed.

BATTEN: Long, thin piece of squared timber used for flooring or hanging roof tiles.

BAYS: Internal compartments of a building; each divided from the other not by solid walls but by divisions only marked in the side walls. Also external divisions of a building by fenestration.

BELVEDERE: Raised turret from which to view scenery.

BILLET MOULDING: Ornamental moulding consisting of small cylindrical blocks arranged in a sunk moulding.

BUCRANE: Sculptured ornament representing ox skull.

BUTTRESS: Projecting support built on to outside of wall.

CABOCHONS: Precious stones polished but not cut into facets.

CADUCEUS: Mercury's wand.

Calderium: Hot room in Roman baths.

CALIFAL: Associated with the rule of the Caliph.

CALOTTE: Skull cap.

CAMPANILE: Isolated bell-tower.

CAPITAL: Moulded or carved top of column.

CARYATID: Whole figure supporting an entablature or other similar member.

CASEMATE: Vaulted chamber in thickness of fortress-wall, with embrasures for defence.

CENSER: A vessel in which incense is burned.

CENSE: The act of burning incense.

CHALICE: Cup used in Communion service or at Mass.

CHAMFER: Surface produced by bevelling square edge or corner equally on both sides—moulding.

CHAMPLEVÉ ENAMEL: Work in which the metal ground is hollowed out and spaces filled with enamel.

CHAPTER HOUSE: Meeting place of members of religious order.

CHASUBLE: The outer vestment of the celebrant at Mass.

CHEVET: Apsidal east end of mediaeval church.

CHRISMA: A monogram of Christ formed by the letters χ and ρ.

CHURRIGUERRESQUE: Style created by Joseph Churriguerra, architect and decorator of Salamanca (1658–1725); a late Spanish form of the Baroque style.

CIBORIUM: Vessel similar to chalice in which the Host is deposited. Canopy over high altar.

CINQUEFOIL: Arch or circular opening divided into five lobes or leaves by projecting carving.

CIPPUS: Roman term for monumental pillar.

CISTERCIAN: Order founded in 1098 in Burgundy, at Cîteaux (Latin *Cistercium*) near Dijon, and which received a great impulse under St. Bernard, founder of the Abbey of Clairvaux. The monasteries of this Order express by their architecture the severity of the rule (more austere form of Benedictine rule).

CLERESTORY: Upper storey with rows of windows.

COFFER: Deep panel in ceiling, vault or dome.

CONSOLE: Ornamental bracket used to support cornice on which to place busts, vases or figures.

COPE: Ecclesiastical vestment worn over surplice.

CORBEL: Block of stone projecting from a wall, supporting some horizontal feature.

CORNICE: Uppermost member of entablature, surmounting the frieze.

COUNTERSCARP: Outer wall or slope of ditch, supporting covered way.

CRENEL: Open space of a battlement.

CROCKET: Carved ornament on angles of spires and on canopies.

CROSSING: That part of a cruciform church where the transepts cross the nave.

CUFIC: Pertaining to Cufa, a town on the Euphrates, south of Babylon; applied especially to an Arabic alphabet earlier employed there.

CULVERIN: Small firearm; large cannon, very long in proportion to its bore, used especially in 16th and 17th centuries.

CUPOLA: Spherical vault or concave ceiling.

CYCLOPEAN: Style of masonry with walls of large, irregular stones, unhewn and uncemented, which in ancient Greece were fabled to be the work of Cyclops, or one-eyed giants.

DRIP-STONE: Projecting moulding to throw off rain.

DRUM OR TAMBOUR: Upright part of a cupola.

Enceinte: An enclosing wall of fortifications.

ENGAGED: Built into. ENGAGED COLUMN: Column built into wall.

ENTABLATURE: Arrangement of horizontal members above supporting columns.

ENTASIS: Convex tapering of a column.

ESPADRILLES: Barbs used in bull fighting.

EXEDRA: Apsidal end of a room.

FAÇADE: Face or front of building.

FAÏENCE: Decorated glazed earthenware.

FINIAL: Ornamental feature placed on top of pinnacle or at base and apex of gable.

FLAMBOYANT: Late form of the Gothic style, characteristic for its "florid" enrichments of carved ornament, and for the "flaming" arrangements of the window stone-filling.

FLUTING: Vertical channelling in the shaft of a column.

FOIL: Lobe formed by the cusping of a circle or an arch. Trefoil, quatrefoil, cinquefoil, multifoil, express number of leaf shapes to be seen.

FOLIATED: Carved with leaf shapes.

FRESCO: Painting on plastered wall before plaster has dried.

FRIEZE: Middle division of a classical entablature.

GALLERY: In church architecture, upper storey above an aisle, opened in arches to the nave.

GALLO-ROMAN: Belonging to the epoch when Gaul was a part of the Roman Empire (1st–4th century).

GLACIS: Bank sloping down from fort, on which attackers are without cover from gunfire.

GOTHIC: Style which appeared in France in the 12th century, and prevailed in Europe from the 13th to the 15th centuries. Its chief elements are the vault with diagonal ribs with pointed arches and flying buttresses.

GROIN: Sharp edge at the meeting of two cells of a cross-vault.

HELICOIDAL: Resembling a snail shell; spiral ornament.

HENNIN: A high, conical head-dress with a muslin veil worn by fashionable ladies in the 15th century.

HERRERAN: Severe Spanish style inaugurated by Juan de Herrera, the architect at the palace and monastery of the Escurial (1584).

HIERATISM: Priestly tradition that made Byzantine art too rigid.

HIGH GOTHIC: see Flamboyant.

HISTORIATED: Adorned with figures.

Hôtel: Large house or mansion, in addition to meaning as in English hotel.

IMBRICATED: Overlapping.

IMPOST: Brackets in walls, usually formed of mouldings, on which the ends of an arch rest.

In commendum: Ecclesiastical benefice temporarily held in care of clerk.

INTRADOS: Inner curve or underside of an arch.

INTAGLIO: Engraved design; incised carving in hard material.

ISABELLINE: Late Gothic style of the reign of Queen Isabella of Castile (1450–1504) and King Ferdinand of Aragon, the Catholic Monarchs. Rich surface decoration.

JAMB: Straight side of an archway, doorway, or window.

JUBE: Screen between nave and chancel (rood-screen).

LANCET: Tall, narrow window with acutely pointed head.

LANTERN: In architecture, a small circular or polygonal turret with windows all round crowning a roof or dome.

LIERNE: Short rib connecting two main ribs.

LINTEL: Horizontal beam or stone bridging an opening.

Lonja: Exchange building.

LOMBARD: Early form of the Romanesque style (9th and 10th centuries) born in Lombardy, Italy.

LOZENGE: Diamond shape.

MACHICOLATION: Projecting gallery or parapet with series of openings for pouring molten substances on attackers below.

MANSARD: Form of curb roof in which each face of the roof has two slopes, the lower being steeper than the other. Named after the French architect, François Mansard (1598–1666).

MARQUETRY: Inlaid work arranged to form decorative patterns.

MERLON: Part of wall of battlement lying between two openings.

Mezzo-rilievo: Degree of relief in figures halfway between high and low.

MINIATURE: Painting on a very small scale.

Mirador: Balcony.

MISERERE: Projection on underside of tilt-up seat in choirstall.

MISERICORD: Room set apart in monastery where monks might take special food as an indulgence: the indulgence or relaxation of monastic rule itself.

MODILLION: Projecting bracket under a cornice in Corinthian and other orders.

MOORISH: Islamic style peculiar to the Moors of Spain (8th–14th century).

MOZARABIC: Christians in Moorish Spain who were allowed the exercise of their own religion on condition of owning allegiance to Moorish king and conforming to certain Moorish customs.

MUDÉJAR: Vernacular style of Spanish architecture blending Muslim and Christian characteristics, for which Moorish builders who survived in Spain when it returned to Christian domination were responsible.

MULLION: Vertical bar of wood or stone dividing window into two or more "lights".

NARTHEX: In early Christian architecture, a vestibule forming an entrance to a basilica, originally for women penitents and catechumens.

NAVE: Body of church.

NEWEL: Central post in circular or winding staircase; also principal post when flight of stairs meets a landing.

NIMBUS: Bright cloud or halo investing deity or saint.

Nymphaeum: Roman temple of the nymphs.

OCULUS: Circular or "bull's-eye" window.

OGIVE: Pointed arch or window, with double curve.

Oppidum: Latin for town.

ORDER: In classic architecture, column with base, shaft, capital, and entablature according to one of the following styles: Greek Doric, Roman Doric, Tuscan Doric, Ionic, Corinthian, Composite. Alternatively an Order of monks.

OVEN-SHAPED: This description is applied to the structures which have the dome shape of the old French bread ovens, e.g. mainly in the case of apses at the eastern end of the church.

PARADOS: Elevation of earth behind fortified place to secure it from rear attack.

PARVIS: Enclosed area in front of church or cathedral.

PATERA: Small flat circular or oval ornament in classical architecture.

PATINA: Bowl or pan. Encrustation of age to works of art.

PATIO: Courtyard.

PAVILION: Used in the text of this book as translation of the French *pavillon* in the special sense of a projecting sub-division of a building or a separate out-building. Not as more customary use of pavilion in English. Indeed it is a feature of French architecture that *pavillons* are frequently as large as, if not larger than, the main building.

PEDIMENT: Low-pitched gable used in classical, Renaissance, and neo-classical architecture above a portico.

PENDENTIVE: Spherical triangle formed between each pair of supporting arches in dome resting on square base.

PERISTYLE: Row of columns round building or courtyard.

PHALANSTERY: The dwelling of the phalange in ideal social system of Fourier (1772–1837).

PILASTER: Flat column against face of wall.

PINNACLE: Ornamental form crowning a spire, tower, buttress.

PISCINA: Basin for washing the Communion or Mass vessels.

PLATERESQUE: Extremely florid and decorative style of architecture (from *plateria*—silverwork) with minuteness of detail.

POLYPTYCH: Picture or carving with many panels.

PORTAL: Gate or doorway.

PREDELLA: In an altar-piece the horizontal strip below the main representation, often used for a number of subsidiary representations in a row.

PRESBYTERY: Part of church reserved for clergy, also dwelling house for clergy.

PSALTER: Book of Psalms.

Putto (plural *putti*): Small naked boy.

PYXIS: Sacred box containing Host after consecration.

RAMPART: Defensive bank of earth, with or without stone parapet.

RELIQUARIES: Chests or caskets containing relics.

ROCOCO: Late Baroque style with a profusion of rock-like forms, scrolls, crimped shells (from French "rocaille" —"rock work").

ROMANESQUE: Architectural style prevalent in Western Europe towards the end of 12th century, characterised by use of massive stone vaulting and the round-headed arch. Usually known in reference to English buildings as Norman.

ROOD-SCREEN: Open screen across chancel entrance in church.

ROSE-WINDOW: Gothic circular window filled with tracery resembling a rose.

ROTUNDA: Circular building, usually with domed roof.

RUPESTRAL: Rock.

SACRISTY: Part of church where sacred vessels and vestments are kept.

SARCOPHAGUS: Stone receptacle for corpse.

SERPENTINE: Decorative stone.

SOFFIT: Underside of lintel, arch or cornice.

SPRINGER: Bottom stone of arch.

SQUINCH: Small stone arch across an interior angle of square tower to support octagonal spire.

STEREOTOMY: Art or science of cutting stones into regular forms.

STRINGCOURSE: Projecting horizontal moulding or projecting course of stone or brick running across face of building.

STUCCO: Plaster work.

TELAMONES: Carved male figures serving as pillars.

TIERCERON: Secondary rib, issuing from main springer or central boss and leading to a ridge rib.

TORUS: Moulding in base of columns with semi-circular profile.

TRANSEPT: Transverse portion of a cross-shaped church.

TRANSOM: Horizontal bar across the openings of a window.

TRIBUNAL: Confessional.

TRIBUNE: Gallery of church.

TRIFORIUM: Arcaded wall passage or blank arcading facing the nave at the height of the roof of the side-aisle and below the clerestory windows.

TRIPTYCH: Picture or carving on three panels.

TUFA: Rock of cellular texture of volcanic origin.

TYMPANUM: Triangular space between sloping and horizontal cornices above lintel of doorway.

VOLUTE: Spiral scroll.

WAGON-ROOF: Roof in which by closely set rafters with arched braces the appearance of the inside of a canvas tilt over a wagon is achieved.

INDEX OF TOWNS AND PLACES VISITED

SOUTH-EAST FRANCE

SOUTH-WEST FRANCE